INTUITIVE TAROT
A TOOL FOR CONSCIOUSNESS

A COMPLETE WORKBOOK
FOR THE ALEISTER CROWLEY TAROT

Mangala Billson

Copyright © Mangala Billson 2007

All rights reserved. No part of this publication may be reproduced, stored in a retrieval system or transmitted in any form or by any means, electronic, mechanical, audio, visual or otherwise, without prior written permission of the copyright owner. Nor can it be circulated in any form of binding or cover other than that in which it is published and without similar conditions including this condition being imposed on the subsequent purchaser.

Paperback: ISBN 978-1-905-399-30-7

Cover design: Bookcraft Ltd (www.bookcraft.co.uk)

Published by
PERFECT PUBLISHERS LTD
23 Maitland Avenue
Cambridge
CB4 1TA
www.perfectpublishers.co.uk

Dedication

With grateful thanks
to the many who have shed light on my path.

And particularly to my beloved spiritual master, Osho,
whose immense understanding of the human psyche
endlessly inspires me.

INDEX

INTRODUCTION 9
FOREWORD – HOW TO USE THIS MANUAL 13

PART ONE: THE BACKGROUND 15

CHAPTER ONE: TAROT – A TOOL FOR CONSCIOUSNESS 15
How it Works 15
Understanding Yourself and Others 17
Putting Aside Judgements 17
Fortune Telling 18

CHAPTER TWO: THE CARDS 19
Brief History 19
The Aleister Crowley Thoth Tarot 20

CHAPTER THREE: INTUITIVE TAROT 20
The Intuitive Mind 20
The Voice of the Superconscious 21
Training the Intuition with Tarot 22

PART TWO: KEYS FOR INTUITIVE LEARNING 23

CHAPTER ONE: BEGINNING THE RELATIONSHIP 23
A Relaxed Relationship 23
Right Approach 24
Preparing the Space 24
Learning to Connect 25
The Mirror of the Mind 25
Single Card Meditation 26
First Impressions 26

CHAPTER TWO: PICKING 27
The Technique of Picking 27
Clear Purpose 28
Extra Cards 28

CHAPTER THREE: PATIENCE AND INTEGRATION 29

PART THREE: LAYOUTS 31

CHAPTER ONE: THE CURRENT LIFE READING 31
Laying out the Cards 32
Explanation 33
How to Read 35
    EXAMPLE OF THE CURRENT LIFE READING 40

CHAPTER TWO: THE QUESTION LAYOUT ... 44
Two Versions ... 44
Preparing the Question ... 44
Simplified Form – The Three-Card Reading ... 46
   EXAMPLES OF THE THREE-CARD READING ... 47
Full Expanded Form ... 49
   EXAMPLE OF THE FULL QUESTION READING ... 51

CHAPTER THREE: RELATIONSHIP LAYOUT ... 55
The Format ... 55
   EXAMPLE OF THE RELATIONSHIP READING ... 57

CHAPTER FOUR: THE CHAKRA LAYOUT ... 62
The Function of the Seven Chakras ... 62
Picking the Cards ... 62
How to Read ... 64
   EXAMPLE OF THE CHAKRA READING ... 65

PART FOUR: THE MEANING OF THE CARDS ... 69
How this Reference Section Works ... 69

CHAPTER ONE: MAJOR ARCANA ... 71

The Spiritual Journey ... 72
   0. THE FOOL ... 73
   1. THE MAGUS ... 76
   2. THE PRIESTESS ... 79
   3. THE EMPRESS ... 82
   4. THE EMPEROR ... 85
   5. THE HIEROPHANT ... 88
   6. THE LOVERS ... 91
   7. THE CHARIOT ... 94
   8. ADJUSTMENT ... 97
   9. THE HERMIT ... 100
   10. FORTUNE ... 103
   11. LUST ... 106
   12. THE HANGED MAN ... 109
   13. DEATH ... 112
   14. ART ... 115
   15. THE DEVIL ... 118
   16. THE TOWER ... 121
   17. THE STAR ... 124
   18. THE MOON ... 127
   19. THE SUN ... 130
   20. THE AEON ... 133
   21. THE UNIVERSE ... 136

CHAPTER TWO: THE MINOR ARCANA	139
The Court Cards	140
WANDS	141
Knight of Wands	142
Queen of Wands	144
Prince of Wands	146
Princess of Wands	148
Ace of Wands	150
Two of Wands – Dominion	152
Three of Wands – Virtue	154
Four of Wands – Completion	156
Five of Wands – Strife	158
Six of Wands – Victory	160
Seven of Wands – Valour	162
Eight of Wands – Swiftness	164
Nine of Wands – Strength	166
Ten of Wands – Oppression	168
SWORDS	171
Knight of Swords	172
Queen of Swords	174
Prince of Swords	176
Princess of Swords	178
Ace of Swords	180
Two of Swords – Peace	182
Three of Swords – Sorrow	184
Four of Swords – Truce	186
Five of Swords – Defeat	188
Six of Swords – Science	190
Seven of Swords – Futility	192
Eight of Swords – Interference	194
Nine of Swords – Cruelty	196
Ten of Swords – Ruin	198
CUPS	201
Knight of Cups	202
Queen of Cups	204
Prince of Cups	206
Princess of Cups	208
Ace of Cups	210
Two of Cups – Love	212
Three of Cups – Abundance	214
Four of Cups – Luxury	216
Five of Cups – Disappointment	218

Six of Cups – Pleasure	220
Seven of Cups – Debauch	222
Eight of Cups – Indolence	224
Nine of Cups – Happiness	226
Ten of Cups – Satiety	228

DISKS 231

Knight of Disks	232
Queen of Disks	234
Prince of Disks	236
Princess of Disks	238
Ace of Disks	240
Two of Disks – Change	242
Three of Disks – Works	244
Four of Disks – Power	246
Five of Disks – Worry	248
Six of Disks – Success	250
Seven of Disks – Failure	252
Eight of Disks – Prudence	254
Nine of Disks – Gain	256
Ten of Disks – Wealth	258

Appendix: Summary of Essence 261

Introduction

It was when I was a teenager faced with the need to choose a university curriculum that I first consciously realised I was interested in the human mind. I took psychology and for some years sat through endlessly boring lectures on scientific theory. I endured hours of experimenting with white rats in laboratories before I finally gave up in disillusionment. What all this stuff had to do with understanding the way the human mind worked escaped me. It was too impersonal, too objective, too dry – nothing to do with me. I found myself far more engrossed by the life I was leading as a part time waitress than by anything that was happening in the university.

The only apparent use of all this schooling and resulting qualifications was to get me a job as a feature writer on a relatively intelligent woman's magazine. This gave me a wonderful excuse to investigate anything and anybody that interested me. It was an open license to follow my curious mind into everything from the lives of the rich and famous to sociological phenomena such as the plight of the aged and the mentally handicapped. I even looked into all kinds of, what seemed then to be, weird alternative phenomena. I interviewed university professors and other 'experts' about the truth behind Ouija boards and mind reading, as well as visiting hypnotists, astrologers, tea leaf readers, and any other real or fake psychic practitioners I could find at the time.

For a few years this fulfilled my need to explore the world I lived in, other lifestyles, and most important, other minds. But it wasn't long before my curiosity in the external ran out. I understood that looking outside wasn't going to give me the inner understanding I wanted. I then began to dabble in various conscious-altering substances, and was fascinated and excited by the inner world they opened up for me. For the first time I became aware of the enormous potential of the mind and the depth of the available inner experience. It was my first taste of the subjective experience I had been looking for but it came without real understanding and at a high price. I wanted it all the time and my always -sensitive body soon suffered and refused to respond.

But the door was open and led to a rapid and radical change in my life. The desire to recapture these inner glimpses became the burning priority of my life. Within a short time I found myself in India searching for something that turned out to be meditation. I didn't even know what it was till I sat for the first time in a Himalayan retreat, and instantly it felt like coming home. Substances were traded in immediately for the bliss of sitting for long hours with my eyes closed. I realised it wasn't really the mind I wanted to investigate – it was how to go beyond it.

After three months of spaced out bliss, my meditation teacher, a Buddhist monk, suggested it was time to move on. He could obviously see that there was a quality of avoidance in my addiction to meditation. I wandered down from the magic of the Himalayan Mountains, blissfully stoned but very ungrounded by this form of meditation. After a couple of months of Indian travel adventures, I found myself in the Osho (then known as Bhagwan Shree Rajneesh) ashram in Poona. I was almost twenty-eight when I got there, and hungry for something without really knowing what it was. I didn't know I was looking for a spiritual master, so it took me sometime and a major dose of hepatitis to realise I'd found one. Within a couple of months I had been initiated into sannyas (disciplehood, or commitment to the spiritual path), and was given the name Prem Mangala.

Love at Second Sight

Only days after taking sannyas, a hotel neighbour introduced me to tarot cards. I had seen them once before from the detached objectivity of my journalist's role, but this time we really met and it was love at first (or second) sight. These seemingly ordinary pictorial cards had the ability to tell what was happening inside of me. I couldn't begin to understand how this magic was working; I just knew it was, and I wanted it. I was hanging around outside my neighbour's door with a yearning and obsession to play with them that I hardly knew how to contain. I can't remember how I got my own pack, but I know it happened quite soon. This itself was a minor miracle in India in 1975 where tarot cards had not been heard of and relatively few westerners lived.

It was the beginning of a relationship that has continued for over thirty years, and one I can't imagine ever ending. And I don't use the word 'relationship' lightly. One of my tarot students described learning the tarot as having a good wise friend to talk with; and that is was what it was like. A day would rarely go by when I didn't open the cards for myself. It became as much a habit to look into this mirror of my psyche as it was to look into the bathroom mirror to brush my hair. Just as one might turn to a trusted friend to ask for an objective opinion, so I could turn to the cards knowing I would receive feedback from the deepest truth in myself. Sometimes it was just a reality check; sometimes it was to clear issues of doubt or deep uncertainty. It wasn't till later that I realised I was also learning to trust my own intuition, to recognise that part of me that knew – my own inner guide or master.

Those first few years in Osho's commune were extremely intense. I threw myself into the increasing variety of psychotherapy groups offered at the ashram as more and more of the leading names in the western psychotherapeutic movement found their way to Osho. At the same time there were long hours of meditation and a little later the dynamics of living and working in a community around an enlightened master. The result felt like a powerful light beam being turned inside to investigate the hidden levels of my mind, and beyond it. So many things revealed themselves, some of them beautiful, even ecstatic; many of them horrific and painful. Every morning Osho discoursed on what he called the psychology of the buddhas: the subjective understanding of the human mind that has been studied in the East for thousands of years. There was so much coming in from the outside and up the inside that I felt sometimes like I was drowning in a sea of consciousness. I was struggling to understand and my tool for doing that was the tarot.

My learning to use the tarot and to understand my own being were happening hand in hand. They were (and have continued to be) one and the same thing. With every inner insight came a corresponding connection with the symbols of the cards. I guess I must have read at least one tarot book at some time, but I don't remember doing so until many years later. It was rather a series of 'ah ha!'s as my own inner exploration was understood and then connected to these ancient pictorial symbols. Sometimes I'd be lost in an emotional or mental trip, and suddenly a tarot card would come to mind and I'd be forced to stop for a moment to see my current state mirrored in the symbols. Sometimes I'd be giving myself a reading, and the insight in my mind and the meaning of a card fused together. The understanding was far deeper than intellectual. It was as though these symbols became part of my own unconscious: or rather that deep part of my mind simply recognised the truth that had created the symbols originally. This was obviously not a new journey I was on. And this was one of its wonders: the recognition of connecting with a pictorial wisdom so ancient its originators are largely unknown.

Over the years the process continued through the various stages of my life. It took me through a number of love relationships, living in numerous different countries, and through most of the new psychotherapeutic groups designed in the last twenty years. It continued as I tasted different spiritual paths and went through a diverse variety of spiritual and psychological reading. As my understanding of the human psyche became deeper, that depth was translated into understanding in the cards and mirrored back to me.

Branching Out

It was still in the early years when I realised that the knack of looking into myself through the cards could also be used for looking into others. I also recognised that the more I understood the mechanics of my own mind, the more I could understand the minds of others. And at the same time understanding the minds of others helped me to understand myself. Although as beings we are all unique, the human mind in its wondrous complexity is made up of a limited number of programmes arranged in an endless variety of ways. Giving sessions for friends was something that happened naturally. It wasn't that I felt a strong pull to do it and it would never occur to me to offer, but, when asked, I seldom refused. At first I was tentative, not secure in what I was delivering, but slowly I came to trust myself more and more.

It was some years later that something happened which, in retrospect, felt like an essential learning step in reading for others. I had made a personal decision that was contrary to the beliefs of those I lived and worked with at the time. The decision came very much from my inner truth, and I had no doubt that it was right for me; but a number of my friends and workmates came to tell me why they thought I was wrong. I had never fully understood 'projection' before, but as I listened it was so clear they were talking about what was right for them and not about me. It made me see that so much of the advice we give to others is based on our own needs rather than those of the person we are addressing. I never forgot this, and from then on it seemed that I was able to distinguish clearly between those two voices in myself. Projection 'felt' different, it seemed to come from a different part of my brain. And when I gave readings I knew beyond doubt whether what I was saying was a clear intuition, or contained some of my own projection. It was a skill that was to serve me well over the years when called upon to give readings to intimate friends – especially in situations where I was involved.

Turning Professional

My debut as a professional reader happened quite organically. I was doing a lot of readings for friends, but it never entered my head to make this hobby a profession. I still considered myself a writer, but was doing various jobs depending on where I was living. I was on my way back to the USA where I was living at the time and called into Hawaii to visit a friend en route. She was working as a tarot reader in a Waikiki market and had taken it upon herself to arrange a test session with the organiser for me to do the same. My main thought, as I remember, was 'Why not!'

For the next few months I spent several days a week sitting under a bodhi tree in the market giving readings. I suspect I often shocked innocent tourists who came to have their 'fortunes told' by confronting them with more home truths than they'd bargained for. But they came back, and I realised most people love to hear the truth about themselves, even if it isn't always very nice.

From then on, doing readings was simply the easiest thing to do. I never organised anything ahead. My lifestyle involved a lot of moving, and wherever I was people always wanted readings. I worked in growth centres and new age fairs, department stores and markets, and more and more just set up shop at home. It happened quite naturally and effortlessly, and it seemed there was always as much demand as I was willing to provide. I wasn't very career orientated, and if I had been I wouldn't have considered psychic readings my career. This went on for some years until, by a series of apparent coincidences, my style of working started to change. People began to organise things, and I travelled to various countries just to do my work. Apart from the apparently endless demand for sessions, more and more people wanted to know how to read for themselves. And so the teaching groups began.

Teaching

Because I had never really learnt myself, I had to turn my mind around to look at how I did what I did. My own introduction to tarot had little to do with the logical mind and now, to pass it on, I needed to bring what I knew into the realm of the rational. Why this card meant what it did to me, why I laid the cards out in the way I did, how I came to the knowing that was so obvious for me. This was a whole new journey that necessitated looking into the relationship between the logical and intuitive sides of the mind. Most people, I found, moved from the logical to the intuitive when they learnt something new. A certain amount of mental learning is needed, and it is from the groundwork of this knowledge that the intuition can leap. I realised that for me, with the cards, it had happened the other way around, and now I was looking backwards to see how I'd done it. I felt I was looking for this same bridge between the logical and intuitive, but from the other side of the river as it were.

It was the results of this investigation that went into the tarot groups that I have been teaching now for almost twenty years. And it is a synthesis of this understanding that has gone into this tarot manual.

Foreword

How to Use this Manual

This manual is a complete guide to tarot reading aimed both at beginners and those who are experienced readers. Its emphasis is on learning and using the cards through the intuition to promote consciousness and awareness.

It is designed so that, from the very beginning, you can give accurate and insightful readings by looking up the reference section. To do this, turn straight to the Current Life Reading in Part Three, to learn how to lay out the cards. Then check the meaning of each card in its particular position in Part Four.

The manual is divided into four parts.

Part One is the background to the approach used in this book.

Part Two presents the essential keys needed for Intuitive Tarot reading.

Part Three is a detailed description of the unique layouts used exclusively in this book. It includes example readings to support and guide you with these methods.

Part Four gives the meanings of the cards. Each of the major arcana cards is described in four sections. The first section, Essence, gives a few key words that sum up the meaning of the card and is often all you will need to read to get a quick feeling of what it symbolises. It is certainly all you need to memorise. The **Descriptive Meaning** goes into more depth and understanding of the meaning of the card. **Symbols** describes the major symbols used in the picture to create its meaning. The final section, **Variations in the Current Life Reading**, is given as a way of experimenting and playing with the many nuances of meaning that each card can have. It also enables you to give instant and accurate readings with this spread.

The minor arcana cards are described in the same way, except that the sections on the Descriptive Meaning and Symbols are combined.

PART ONE

THE BACKGROUND

CHAPTER ONE   TAROT – A TOOL FOR CONSCIOUSNESS

Tarot is a tool and, like any tool, it performs a function. How you employ that function is up to you. You can use the same knife to peel a potato, build a house, stab someone, or create a beautiful carving. Its use can be mundane, helpful, destructive or supremely creative. The same is true with tarot. You can use the cards to make your decisions for you, to look into the future, to find out about other people or simply as a toy, an entertainment.

The concern of this book is with using tarot primarily as a tool for consciousness. You will be learning how to let it help you become more aware of who you are. It is essentially a path of self-exploration, a tool for investigating the workings of your own mind and emotions and, through that, the spiritual dimension of being that lies beyond. In the process of getting to know the depths of yourself, you automatically become more aware and understanding of the depths in others.

It is not abstract. Once you learn how to master the basics this is a practical, helpful tool, something you can use again and again in all areas of your life. Becoming more conscious one day may mean investigating your programming around relationship to find out why you're so pissed off with your partner, or why you're always feeling wrong and guilty. And the next day it may involve looking at the pros and cons of holidaying in Bali, or whether you should take a new job offer.

How It Works

The tarot is an ancient system of wisdom presented in pictures. Pictures are the language of the unconscious mind. Before we learn to talk, we think in pictures. When we are sleeping we dream in pictures. And these pictures contain symbols that make up a universal language that transcends the limitations of the verbal and cultural. Each tarot card contains a number of symbols, and the symbols contain an energy that represents some state or experience in the human psyche. This energy is reflected and transmitted to the reader through the non-rational or intuitive part of the mind. In other words, the symbols bypass the rational mind and speak directly to the inner awareness of that experience. It is not necessary to consciously know the meaning of the symbols, although while you are learning to tune into the language of the cards it is very helpful to have an intellectual knowledge.

Underneath everything we are conscious of in the mind at any given time, there is always more. This is the very nature of the mind. Most of its functioning is unconscious – which means we are not aware of it. One estimate is that approximately 90% of the functioning of the mind takes place without our conscious awareness. To become conscious means bringing the light of awareness into that unconsciousness. This is the function of tarot. The cards are a tool for seeing the hidden parts of the mind. They externalise or mirror what we would be otherwise incapable of seeing. Sometimes this could be seen as contacting, in waking consciousness, the information that dreams portray in sleep.

My own experience is that what is mirrored in the cards at any time is the layer of the unconscious that is closest to the surface; almost, but not quite, conscious. That is why recognition is possible; the sense that 'of course I knew that, but I didn't consciously know I knew.' The cards will never mirror back more than you (or the person you are reading for) are ready to hear. It may not be what you want to see, but it will be what you are ready to see.

Tarot, then, can be a tool for looking deeper into yourself than you would otherwise be capable of, and the positive consequences of this in life are enormous. It is like being able to turn a powerful searchlight inwards, so the dark areas of the unconscious are lit with awareness. Through this consciousness, understanding, and if necessary change, can happen. It is the very nature of truth that bringing the light of consciousness to expose and explore positive aspects of the psyche will make them more solid, whereas becoming conscious of destructive aspects dissolves them.

The process can act like a peeling. Let's look at a possible example. You find yourself angry about something that someone has done to you. The conscious mind is full of the reasons why they are wrong and that they shouldn't have done what they did. You want to go and tell them all this, to blame them. If you stop long enough to give yourself a reading, the first message you may get is to hold back and look inside. Then a little bell rings in your mind that says: 'Oh, so this is something to do with me.' A little later you look at the issue again from this perspective and you're able to go deeper. Now you get a message about needing to take responsibility for having got lost into righteousness and indignation, and you recognise one of your old trips; that part of your mind that so readily jumps into judgements about how someone else should behave. From this space you are ready to transcend your initial reaction and look at the situation in a clearer way. You may pull cards for the person to see where they were coming from and find it has little to do with your projection.

Not only have you managed to use this situation to become more aware of how you function, but you have avoided an unnecessary argument with a friend. So when you meet again you are able say what had happened for you without blame, and the result can be a harmonious sharing that brings you closer together.

I couldn't begin to count the innumerable times I personally have used the cards to short-circuit my own destructive mind trips. And every time I do it there is more light into these dark spots in my psyche, until one by one they disappear through exposure and understanding.

Understanding Yourself and Others

When the cards are used as a regular form of checking in or looking at yourself, they act like a reality check in your life. At first it can be quite shocking to see that what you thought was going on was only a superficial layer of who you are, and underneath that there is a whole different scenario. You start to become aware that there is always some process taking place. The inner world, like the outer, is never static, but exists through change and movement. And to some extent that change is, in the nature of things, a movement between the positive and the negative. When this is recognised simply as a fact, there is a relaxation that comes from allowing life to have its own flow, its own unfolding, without the interference of the conscious mind trying to work out if it should or should not be happening.

This gives the space for inner understanding to take place: the recognition of how your mind and emotions function. You come to recognise how the early life experiences that conditioned the mind control who you think you are and the life you are living as an adult. You start to become aware of ever deeper layers of how you function, and why you are the way you are. As this self-understanding grows, so does the understanding of other people. You get to see that we are all in the same boat, all doing the only thing we can do at that time.

I remember the time in my life when I personally realised just how powerful the effects of this conditioning process are. It came to me with the memory of the white rats I had watched for hours and hours in my psychology laboratories at university. At the time the behaviour of rats had felt so irrelevant to my understanding of myself or other people. It must have been ten or fifteen years later that the penny finally dropped and I realised that it was actually exactly the same. Just as Skinner's rats would continue to push a lever to get food long after the lever had stopped producing it, so we would continue a particular form of childhood-learnt behaviour long after it ceased to give us what we wanted. I realised that in fact almost everything that we thought we were was simply the result of the conditioning we call our experience. And if not our experience in this life, then in a previous one. The realisation was, and is, a very humbling one.

Putting Aside Judgements

One of the side-effects of using tarot in this way is the dropping of judgements. You will find it is impossible to read for yourself or for others while there are judgements and opinions in the way. A judgement by its very nature will cloud the ability to see and read the situation objectively. It is objective awareness alone that allows transformation.

Something people often voice when I am giving them a reading is the concern that what I am mirroring back to them is good or bad. I may be pointing out that there is a level of fear or anger happening inside, and they immediately look worried and ask if that is okay. In the higher reality of things there is no good and bad; things just are. It is only the conditioned programming of the mind that has these ideas. And one person's ideas of right and wrong, good and bad, may be very different from another's, depending on how and where they were raised.

As you become familiar with the style of reading used in this book you will find that every state imaginable can, and does, get reflected back at some time as being the condition that the higher part of your being is encouraging you to experience. Fear, anger, jealousy, frustration, doubt, insecurity – every so-called negative state – needs to be honoured, and in that way becomes a door to something else. There are no 'bad' cards, and there are no mental or emotional states that are intrinsically wrong.

This doesn't mean that we must always like what is happening inside. Nobody likes feeling pain or frustration for instance, but having an opinion about it is quite different from thinking it is bad or wrong. When something is judged as wrong we automatically try to get rid of it, which means we repress it in the unconscious. Then we may no longer consciously experience it, but from the unconscious it continues to rule our behaviour and our lives. When we allow ourselves to experience these states non-judgementally simply as part of being human, they are no longer able to control who we are. What this encourages is a deep level of self-acceptance where different states are seen simply for what they are: passing experiences that come and go. And as we begin to move beyond the addiction to the so-called 'positive' or pleasure states, and consequent fear, repression or denial of the 'negative' or pain states, we start to understand that it is basically our refusal to accept and experience certain states that is the cause of our suffering rather than the states themselves. This is the miracle of becoming conscious.

Fortune Telling

As discussed earlier, tarot is a tool, and it is up to the user to decide the function of that tool. Tarot cards can be used to tell fortunes, in other words to look into the future. It's a fact – it works, as many of you may have experienced. Or better to say, it works – sometimes. The reason for this lies not in some mysterious power, but simply in the nature of the mind. As we have already seen, most of us live most of our lives according to our early conditioning programmes, according to our past experiences. To the degree that we live this way we live a mechanical life, a life that is predictable. What tarot, or any so-called future telling art, does is to read or tune into these unconscious patterns that have been controlling our lives. In other words it reads the past. And because the future is created by the past, it can be predicted from these patterns. There is a level of this patterning that is so deep and inevitable it could be called fate or karma. But even with these 'karmic' events, to the degree that we become consciousness and aware in the situation we can change the outcome of what happens.

For instance, let's say a woman has a pattern of relating in which she believes that men are not really to be trusted. So she trusts them until they do something to break that trust, and then she feels reinforced in her belief and will never trust them again. Maybe it is a result of something that happened with her father when she was a child, maybe from even further back from events in a past life. The details of what created the pattern don't matter too much. While she is unconscious of this pattern she is bound to repeat it, so it could be said that her 'fate' is to be with a man who will be unfaithful. That is the kind of relationship she is bound to attract into her life. It could be predicted that when, inevitably, he breaks her trust, the relationship will break up. And then most likely she will end up in another relationship with another man who does the same thing, and the whole scenario will be repeated. However, if she becomes aware of this pattern, she can use the opportunity to break the cycle and learn to forgive and to trust in this situation. Then the relationship may continue with deeper loving, or she will be able to move into a future relationship without repeating the pattern.

If she happened to have been to a fortune teller who predicted that her relationship would break up when the man was unfaithful to her, then that, of course, is exactly what would happen. And possibly she would always have a slight doubt whether it happened because she was expecting it to. But if she had been to someone who had used the cards as a tool to make her conscious of the pattern, then she would have a choice in the situation.

So basically fortune telling is at best not helpful, and at worst destructive and confusing.

CHAPTER TWO – THE CARDS

Brief History

The source of tarot cards is unknown, although there are theories that have them originating in countries as far apart as China, Korea, India and Egypt. Examples have been found in some of these places dating back to at least the eleventh century. Certainly they first appeared in Europe in the fourteenth century, when the symbols were used as a secret code for transmitting the teachings of medieval mystery schools.

In the eighteenth century they gained respectability among occultists with the theory that they were the remains of an ancient Egyptian book of magical wisdom that the Romany (gypsy) people had brought with them when they left their native Egypt. And at the end of the nineteenth century there was another wave of interest that sparked the designing of the two most popular and respected tarot packs of today: the Aleister Crowley pack that is the subject of this book, and the Rider-Waite pack.

From the 1960s and 70s, as new age consciousness started to spread in the western world, tarot cards came out of the domains of fortune tellers and esoteric scholars into the communes of the flower power hippies. And from there they started slowly moving into the lives and homes of ordinary people.

Today the markets are flooded with literally hundreds of different tarot packs, and it is no longer considered weird or strange to use them. Probably never before in its long history has tarot been so popular. More and more it is starting to return to its original role as a consciousness-raising tool.

The Aleister Crowley Thoth Tarot

Aleister Crowley was a famous occultist who investigated and tried to combine many different types of traditional wisdom and spiritual paths. From the end of the nineteenth century he was a member of the Hermetic Order of the Golden Dawn, an English Rosicrucian society that aimed to influence western society by introducing into it some of the ancient mysteries and values. The Rider-Waite pack also originated in this society.

His original intention was to spend just a few months modifying the designs of the classic medieval tarot, which an associate, Lady Frieda Harris, would then paint. But the project took much longer to complete. It is probably through Lady Harris's influence that it became the revolutionary and in-depth integration of so many different disciplines and systems that it is. It contains Egyptian, Eastern, Grecian, Christian and medieval symbols as well as astrology, alchemy, numerology and the Cabala. Although Crowley was undoubtedly the genius and inspiration behind the pack, Harris, an Egyptologist herself, was responsible for presenting the symbols in a pure and uninterpreted way. It is this purity that enables the cards to connect directly with the collective unconscious mind and gives the Crowley pack its great depth and subtle magic. And it is because of this that these cards are such an amazing tool for the individual intuition, rather than a substitute for it, as are many packs.

The project took five years to complete, with many of the paintings being done repeatedly until Harris was satisfied. Neither Crowley, who died in 1947, nor Harris, who died in 1962, were able to get the deck published. It was finally produced and published in 1969 by a friend of Crowley's, and has since become probably the best-known and most respected deck on the market, particularly among serious professional readers.

CHAPTER THREE – INTUITIVE TAROT

The Intuitive Mind

Intuition is the ability to know without using the rational thinking process. It is knowing without knowing how we know, or illogical knowing. Sometimes we call this insight, and it is very similar to what we call a hunch, or gut feeling. To some degree it is a natural part of the human psyche, but many of us have almost completely lost contact with it.

To understand why, we need to look at the nature of both the mind and of society.

The physical brain is divided into two sides, the left and right hemispheres. The left hemisphere, which is connected with the right side of the body, is the logical, rational part of the mind. It can be seen as the male side, the part that calculates and works out the right and wrong of things. It works sequentially and reasonably. The right hemisphere, which is connected to the left side of the body, is the female, creative, emotive, non-rational part of the mind. This side of the mind is the door to both instinct and intuition. This is making it all a bit simplistic, but it serves our purpose right now.

When a child is born it functions purely from illogical instinct. It has no choice but to be real and authentic with what it is experiencing. 'Growing up' is basically a process of developing the left side of the mind, of becoming 'civilised' by discovering what is right and wrong. We learn what is expected of us and what behaviour works to fulfil our basic needs of physical and emotional nourishment; basically to get what we want. We are trained to fit into the norms of the family and society around us, and in this process we inevitably lose contact with much that was real and natural in us. By the time our 'education' is completed, the logical side of the mind has become largely dominant and controls our behaviour. We don't get much positive feedback for the gifts of the right hemisphere, and very often it is judged as being irrational, silly, unproductive. Much of what we feel and who we are is repressed into the basement of the unconscious mind in the necessary attempt to 'be sensible', do the right thing, and get ahead in the world.

One of the many prices we pay for this left-brain dominance is the loss of intuition.

The Voice of the Superconscious

If we were to imagine a diagram of the human mind, there would be only a thin slice in the middle that we could label 'conscious'. This is the only part of the mind we know about, so when we say we 'know' ourselves we are usually referring to our familiarity with this relatively small section of our minds. Below that is the vast unconscious mind, the part of the mind that runs on automatic. Instinct, we could say, is the voice of the unconscious. It is the basic drives that we share with the animal kingdom. When we are connected with our instincts, hunches or gut feelings are experienced. This is why simple, less sophisticated people, those who are closer to the land or nature, often have a basic wisdom that is not found in the more highly educated.

When these instincts are repressed by the rational part of the conscious mind, an enormous amount of energy is suppressed, and therefore physically unavailable to move naturally through the body. This can sometimes be seen as a stiffness or lack of connection with the body's energy and emotions. It can manifest as a lack of simple awareness that sometimes looks like a kind of stupidity in those who are overdeveloped in the mind. When this energy is freed through the process of becoming more conscious of what is being repressed, it is available to move upwards to the superconscious mind.

Just as the unconscious is the part of the mind that is below the conscious, so the superconscious is the part that is above or beyond it. It is the part of the mind that connects us with the whole, or what is greater than our individual selves. We could say that the voice of the superconscious mind is the intuition. In other words the intuition is the part of the individual mind that connects with cosmic mind, existence, god – whatever term you choose to use. When we tune into the intuition we tune into that part of the mind that knows things that have nothing to do with the memory or with reason; the part of the mind that has the potential to know everything. We could also call this part of the mind the higher consciousness.

Training the Intuition with Tarot

Getting familiar with the intuition and learning to develop it is something that we are all capable of doing. It is literally a matter of exercising it, just like we need to exercise any muscle that has atrophied through lack of use. The more we use the intuition, the stronger it gets. The stronger it gets, the more we learn to trust it. To start using it 'cold turkey', as it were, in our normal activities and relationships is very risky. We're afraid of making mistakes, of looking a fool by saying or acting on something that other people may think is stupid. Maybe we're wrong – there's no proof, so how can we be sure it really is intuition? So we usually ignore or repress such insights or flashes and resort to the logical way of perceiving and acting that we know from experience is secure. A tool like tarot is a safe way of getting familiar with and developing the intuition without taking unnecessary risks.

The symbols of the tarot are talking to, acting on, that part of the mind that is not logical. When we relate to a card it gives us a certain feeling or experience, and if we go to the source of this feeling in ourselves we have the meaning of the card. This is not something that will necessarily happen immediately, but it is something that naturally develops with the use of the cards. A combination of cards in a reading is doing the same thing: it contains an experiential meaning beyond what the logical mind can see. It is, of course, possible to use the rational mind to understand a reading to a great extent, and that is what most of us do to start with. But it will always be limited. Beyond that is the intuitive dimension of reading the cards.

As we start to trust what we experience or know illogically when we look at the cards, we are training our intuition. When we are unfamiliar with intuition we tend to experience it as something magical, but once we simply accept and don't try to understand it becomes a very ordinary clear way of seeing things. Much is obvious to intuition that is hidden or mysterious to the logical mind. Through the use of the cards we can literally exercise this part of our psyche until it becomes familiar. A simple analogy would be that when a primitive aboriginal looks into a car engine the whole thing seems a mystery; when a car mechanic looks it is simply obvious what is happening. But when the aboriginal learns how to look then it becomes obvious to him too. Learning to look at life with the intuition opens up a whole new dimension of seeing and being.

PART TWO

KEYS FOR INTUITIVE LEARNING

CHAPTER ONE – BEGINNING THE RELATIONSHIP

A Relaxed Relationship

Some people are inherently more right brain orientated than others, and for those few learning the cards may happen naturally and easily through the intuitive part of the brain. Whenever I do a training group, there are usually one or two who simply take to the cards like ducks to water. They can immediately 'see' what the cards are saying. Most people have to plod along with a bit of logical learning first. But learning the cards quicker or slower has nothing to do with one's eventual capacity to be a tarot reader. I can think of a number of students who seemed slow in their learning process who are now successful professional readers.

This manual emphasises and encourages learning the cards intuitively. What that means in practical terms is you don't have to work so hard to understand or to retain information. The intuitive mind is available when the rational mind is out of the way. And the more relaxed you are, the less you are trying to 'get' it, the more the rational mind lets go of its control. I would like to emphasise that giving yourself the opportunity to go through the information in this book in a relaxed enjoyable way will teach you far more than trying to grasp or logically understand what is written. This is particularly so when you are looking at the meanings of the cards.

What you are aiming to do is develop a relationship with each card. Not learn *about* it, but become familiar with it, feel it, identify with it, experience it. It is as though these 78 cards are like 78 individuals that you need to meet and get to know. Like any other kind of relationship, sometimes it happens instantaneously and sometimes it takes time. So with some cards you may have an immediate connection while others remain just mental concepts for a while. Over a period of time you will find that each card becomes familiar and you gain an intimate experiential understanding of what it means for you. Basically there are two ways of developing this relationship: one is through the mirroring of your own current state that happens with use, and the other is through the nightly meditation on a card. These techniques are the foundations of intuitive tarot, and will be discussed in detail later.

Right Approach

Your tarot cards will give you back whatever you give to them. If you treat them in a frivolous, superficial way, then that is the kind of response you will get from them.

But if you treat them with the respect due to tools for wisdom and consciousness, then this will be reflected and therefore developed in you. This doesn't mean you have to be serious; you can approach your cards in a light and playful way and still be respectful and open to receiving at depth. If you regard your tarot cards as you might a loved and esteemed, wise friend, then a very intimate and direct communication can develop.

As an outward display of this, some people like to keep their cards in a special box or bag, or wrap them in silk, which is reputed to contain the energy. This is a personal choice. What is important is to do something that for you shows a certain respect. It will not necessarily affect the cards, but it will affect how you approach them.

Preparing the Space

Before playing with the cards it is important to put yourself in the mood. In other words you need to prepare yourself so that you are open and available to receiving the messages that are coming through them. If you don't do this but just casually pick a couple before you rush off to do something else, it isn't going to work for you. You may pick the same cards, but you won't be in the space to let them in and understand them. What will probably happen then is after a while you will get discouraged because it seems like you aren't getting anything from them. So you start to feel it is not for you, you can't read them – and you give up.

Countless numbers of times I have gone to the cards to find a quick answer to something that is buzzing around in my mind. Rather than taking time to really be with the cards, I have hurriedly picked a few that I then don't understand, so I put them back in the pack. Some time later I start thinking of the issue again and realise that I have no idea what cards I picked for it, because I hadn't been conscious and present at the time.

It is a good idea to make sure you have a substantial period of time to devote to your reading, or at this point your learning, without interruption. If your attention is scattered you will find it is much harder to follow and absorb what is being given.

Keep in mind that you don't need to learn or understand something as you might learn a school lesson. Rather this is a process of absorbing and reflecting that happens through the intuitive side of the mind when you are totally present, available and relaxed, without trying to get anything. So take a little time to create an atmosphere that is conducive to this feeling. For some this means simply sitting quietly with the eyes closed for a few minutes to let the busyness of the mind settle. Or it could be you have your own form of meditation. Others may find it better to dance or do something physical to clear the mind by coming into the body. Or maybe your way is to create an external environment with some incense and candles or some soft music. Experiment with inside and outside spaces to find what works to help you feel relaxed, open and receptive. And make this a basic habit whenever you are about to play with the cards. You will find that even a few minutes of preparation can make the difference between blankly looking at pictures or gaining insight.

Learning to Connect

There is a knack of looking at cards from an open and receptive space that allows the meaning to enter you. Particularly while you are meeting a new card, rather than coming from a concentrated mental space keep your eyes soft and even slightly unfocused and see the painting as a whole, rather than detail by detail. It may help to consciously take deep breaths as you are looking, almost as though you are breathing in the feeling of the card. How do the colours, the shapes and the imagery make you feel? What comes to your mind when you look at this picture? Give yourself space – there's no hurry. Always spend some time looking at the card and feeling it inside yourself before you look it up in the reference manual. This gives you the opportunity to make your own intuitive connection with a card before the logical side of the mind comes in with the knowledge that you read.

Remember that the meaning given to the cards is not arbitrary. In fact, each card contains a meaning, just as a crystal contains its own energy. When you allow it, the symbols used in each picture can trigger deep areas in the collective unconscious mind, the part of the mind where dreaming comes from. It is this part of the mind that experiences the meaning of the card. When you have made this connection with a card it becomes a part of your personal experience, not a part of your rational knowing. A simple analogy would be learning to drive. Once you have some practice, you no longer have to think about changing gears, or when to push the pedals; it is something you do instinctively or automatically. This instinctive knowing is something you are developing with the cards. And to the degree that you have this connection with the cards, you become an intuitive reader.

The Mirror of the Mind

The main way of learning this is through using the layouts given in this manual. Most of the positions in the Current Life Reading and the first position in the Question and Relationship Readings, are direct mirrors of where you are in various aspects of your life at that particular time. You already know where you are – it is your current experience, so when you look at the card that is representing that space it enables a direct connection to happen between the picture and the experience. You are using the cards literally to mirror back to you a certain aspect of what is happening inside.

Sometimes there is an instant recognition because that is a process or a state you are familiar with or conscious of in yourself, so the card 'clicks'. Then that card has become part of your deeper memory system without any mental effort. It has literally entered the unconscious mind. It is not necessarily that you have understood it rationally, but rather that you have recognised through experience what it represents to you on the inside. From that moment on, you know that card in a way that has nothing to do with the logical mind.

Usually this process of identifying with the whole pack takes some time. You are getting to know yourself at the same time as you are recognising the cards. Some of the states or processes represented in the tarot are experiences we have never fully allowed or become conscious of in ourselves, which means they function more in the darkness of the unconscious. And some are less dominant in our beings than others so it is easier to recognise them in other people. But in some way, to some degree, all the cards represent things that are part of us all. They are simply the states that make up the process of being human. And when these states are recognised through this mirror of the cards, there can be a feeling of 'Ah ha!' as some kind of submerged experience becomes more fully conscious.

Single Card Meditation

The other technique for this connection process is the nightly (or daily) meditation on a card. It is suggested that you make this a habit for some time until you feel you have connected with most of the cards in the pack.

Take a moment to still your mind, and then pick one card to most represent where you are in your life right now. Sit with this card for a while and allow yourself to connect with it, understanding that you are looking into a pictorial mirror of your current inner state. Don't be in a hurry; take some time to really feel the card. Only then look it up in the manual and read everything that is written about it, including the symbols and the variations of meaning. Finally take a few minutes to look at how this state or process is manifesting in your life at this time.

Leave this card out and keep coming back to it or bringing it to mind whenever you remember until the following evening or whenever you next pick your meditation card. Until that time this will be the card that most represents your inner state. You may sometimes find that something of the images or symbols enters your dreams, or that suddenly, at some unexpected time in the day, the image pops into your mind in connection with something you are feeling or experiencing. This is the process of the cards taking root in the unconscious mind. If this doesn't happen for you in this way don't be discouraged; trust your own process and way of meeting and absorbing the cards.

It could be that you pick some cards over and over again and still they don't quite 'click'. They are probably reflecting some state in your being so ingrained that you can't even identify it. Trust that in your own time you will get it, and in doing so will have brought consciousness to a previously hidden part of your psyche.

First Impressions

Because the layouts used in this book promote an intuitive, flexible style of reading, you may sometimes find yourself doubting or questioning what you seem to be seeing in the cards. Every novice tarot reader faces a degree of uncertainty about whether what they are seeing is their projections or their intuition. Projections are the clouds that the mind creates from its hopes and fears. This is particularly so when you are reading for yourself or for someone with whom you have a close personal involvement. Taking a little time to quieten your mind and establish yourself in the right space will help a lot to put aside your ideas, opinions and projections, and open the door to the clarity of the intuition. When you are reading for yourself, it can also be helpful to feel consciously the sincere desire to see what is really is happening inside before you start to read.

Over a period of time you will find that the feeling that comes when you are in your intuition is quite distinct and different from when you are in your projecting mind. It is as distinct as the difference between smelling something and hearing it; it comes from a different part of the mind. While you are developing this capacity, it is a good idea to practice trusting your first impression or feeling from the cards. The intuition is usually what 'pops' into the mind; the rational mind is what comes along behind and questions whether that is right or not. Particularly when you are reading for others, practice just opening your mouth and expressing whatever that first impression is when you look at a card or sum up a reading. Sometimes you will be wrong, but if you always stop to think about it first you will miss out on the valuable learning that comes through taking the risk and putting it out.

CHAPTER TWO – PICKING

The Technique of Picking

Picking cards is a very individual thing, but there are a couple of basic principals that are good to follow. Spread the cards out in front of you face down so that a part of each card is visible. You can do this by making a nice neat line or a great big jumble – whatever feels right for you.

Always pick with the left hand. Anatomically, the left hand is connected to the right, intuitive side of the mind and it is from here that wisdom can come through, either from the unconscious or from the superconscious. Maybe using the left hand doesn't make any difference to the cards you will pick – there is no way of knowing – but it does stop your picking from being so automatic and naturally activates the intuitive side of the mind.

As you become familiar with reading for others you will discover that watching how people pick cards can sometimes tell you a lot about how they function. Some people pick with their eyes. They look at the cards until one catches their eye and then pick it up. Others follow their hand and don't look at all. Some people take ages to sense the whole pack energetically before they finally pick a particular card, and then ceremoniously shake the hand to clear away the energy before they move on to find the next. Others just grab a bunch of them simply because they happen to be together. Some people will pick a card, put it back and pick another, or hover undecided over a couple of cards before they can choose.

The most amazing thing is that it doesn't matter how you do it. My own experience is that in the thousands of readings I have done in the last thirty years, no one has ever picked the wrong card. It appears to be totally impossible.

Clear Purpose

What is very important is that you, or whoever is actually giving the reading, know why the cards are being picked. Cards picked for no purpose, or for an unclear purpose, have little value. Make sure that the precise purpose of the card has been formulated before it is picked. One of main reasons people have difficulty reading cards is that they are not clear exactly what is being reflected back to them.

For instance, you may want to find out something about your relationship with a particular friend, so you pick a card with him in mind. Let's say that you pick The Emperor, the card that represents the quality of responsibility. Unless the issue has been clearly formulated you may not know if this card is telling you that you are feeling responsible for him, or that you should feel responsible for him. Or maybe you should be taking responsibility for yourself within the relationship, or he is feeling responsible for you. This uncertainty will create confusion and stop you being able to receive the message. However, if you formulated the purpose of the card clearly – for instance, what you need to find within yourself in your relationship with him – then the card will give an instant clear message.

Another important thing to remember as you get into your readings is only pick one set of cards for a question or issue at any one time. If you don't understand or don't agree, or if you think the cards are 'wrong', leave the spread out and keep coming back to it over a period of time to see if the meaning becomes clear. Alternatively, pick another card to add further clarity to the existing one (see below). Be aware that repeated picking, till you get cards that tell you something you want to hear, will make nonsense of the reading.

If, on the odd occasion when you go to pick one card, two unavoidably come out together, it is fine to put them both down in that position. You can trust that your unconscious needs both the cards to mirror that situation back to you. You can then read them as a combined energy.

Extra Cards

The technique of deliberately picking extra cards to add to or clarify the existing card in any position of a layout is a valuable reading tool. The key with this is to be very clear that you are adding something to the existing card and in no way replacing it.

To give an example, you may have picked Dominion, which means new direction, for some advice position. You are left wondering what that change of direction entails. With that question very clearly in mind, you pick a second card to cover the first. The card you pick is Strength, which represents independence or wholeness. From this you can see that the new direction has to do with coming back to yourself, going your own way, and becoming more independent of what anyone else thinks or feels.

Another example for an advice position is The Empress, which represents compassion and nurturing. You are not sure whether this means you should be more compassionate and nurturing for someone else, or that you need to give more compassion and nourishment to yourself. With that issue clearly in mind, you pick a second card to explain the first and get Ace of Cups. The advice is obviously to be more compassionate of yourself.

When you are working with the cards like this you are asking your higher knowing directly for information. The knack is to be very clear and precise about what you are asking otherwise these extra cards will create confusion.

CHAPTER THREE – PATIENCE AND INTEGRATION

You now have all the tools you need to begin your mastery of the tarot. What you are developing with your cards is a relationship, and like all relationships it takes time to move into depth. But that depth is something that can keep growing and growing if there is enough love and commitment involved. If you are using tarot as a tool for consciousness, you are not only learning how to use the cards, you are, at the same time, learning how to explore your own being. Through doing that, you will automatically learn how to understand other people.

You could view your mastery of the tarot as a continuous journey with seemingly endless discovery – if you are open to it. Don't be impatient if you reach certain points where you feel stuck, or think that you're not getting anywhere and there's no point in continuing. It could be that you need to consciously take a break from the cards at this time. Put them aside for a while, but don't give up or get discouraged. Wait a few days, or even weeks, and, when you are feeling fresh and open, come back to them again. You may find that you have moved into a deeper level of relating with them.

It is strongly suggested that for some months you make a nightly (or daily) habit of taking time to always do the single card meditation described above. Every time a card clicks and you get the 'Ah ha!' that happens as the symbols take root in the deeper layers of the unconscious mind, you have not only deeply understood the card, you have deeply understood that process in yourself. It takes time and patience to keep moving with the journey. In this way the symbols of the cards gradually become aligned with the experiential awareness of those states within yourself. It is a very enlightening procedure.

While this process is going on, you will be aware that there are cards in the pack that are 'alive' and those that are 'dead'. When they are alive, you know through your experience what they mean – you have an energetic connection with them. When they are dead, you only know their meaning through your mind – you don't recognise them on an experiential level. Don't be impatient or in a hurry with this process. Just be aware that every new card that becomes alive for you is a part of your own being becoming conscious.

PART THREE

LAYOUTS

The layouts outlined in this chapter are unique spreads that won't be found in any other publication. They are designed specifically to promote consciousness and to allow a free open space for the intuition to function. As you get more familiar with them and with your cards, you will find that there are many layers of understanding possible in any reading using the cards in this way. If your readings feel a bit one dimensional to start with, be patient. You are learning to develop your intuition and your understanding of yourself at the same time as you learn to read the cards. In time you will find increasing depths of meaning become available to you through these spreads.

CHAPTER ONE – CURRENT LIFE READING

This is the best reading for looking into yourself, or another, and seeing what is happening from a broad perspective. It is also the best way of learning the cards from an experiential feeling space. It functions as a mirror of the different aspects of your life and shows, not only what's happening in specific areas, but how these interconnect to produce the process or situation you are now in. It is concerned primarily with making you aware and conscious, not with answering questions. By using this reading to look into yourself on a regular basis – daily, weekly, or however often you use the cards – you will automatically be bringing a deeper level of awareness and consciousness into your life. It is a pure form of using tarot as a tool for consciousness.

Even if you are new to the cards, you will find that you can give yourself accurate readings with the Current Life layout from your very first day of learning. Under the meanings of each card in Part Four you will find a section entitled 'Variations in the Current Life Reading'. Here you can find a possible interpretation of the card in each specific position of this 13-card spread. By following the layout instructions below and looking up each card you will find that you are learning through the practice of reading.

The timing that the layout covers will tend to vary according to how often it is done. When it is used regularly, it will cover the time period until the next reading. But when it is done only occasionally, to check out the state of the being, it will cover a much longer time span. This means that although most of the cards will continue to reflect your immediate state, the advice cards, and the overall flavour of the reading, will be reflecting processes that are more long term. If you use it regularly but occasionally want a more long-term reflection, you can consciously ask the cards to give you this.

LAYING OUT THE CARDS: CURRENT LIFE READING

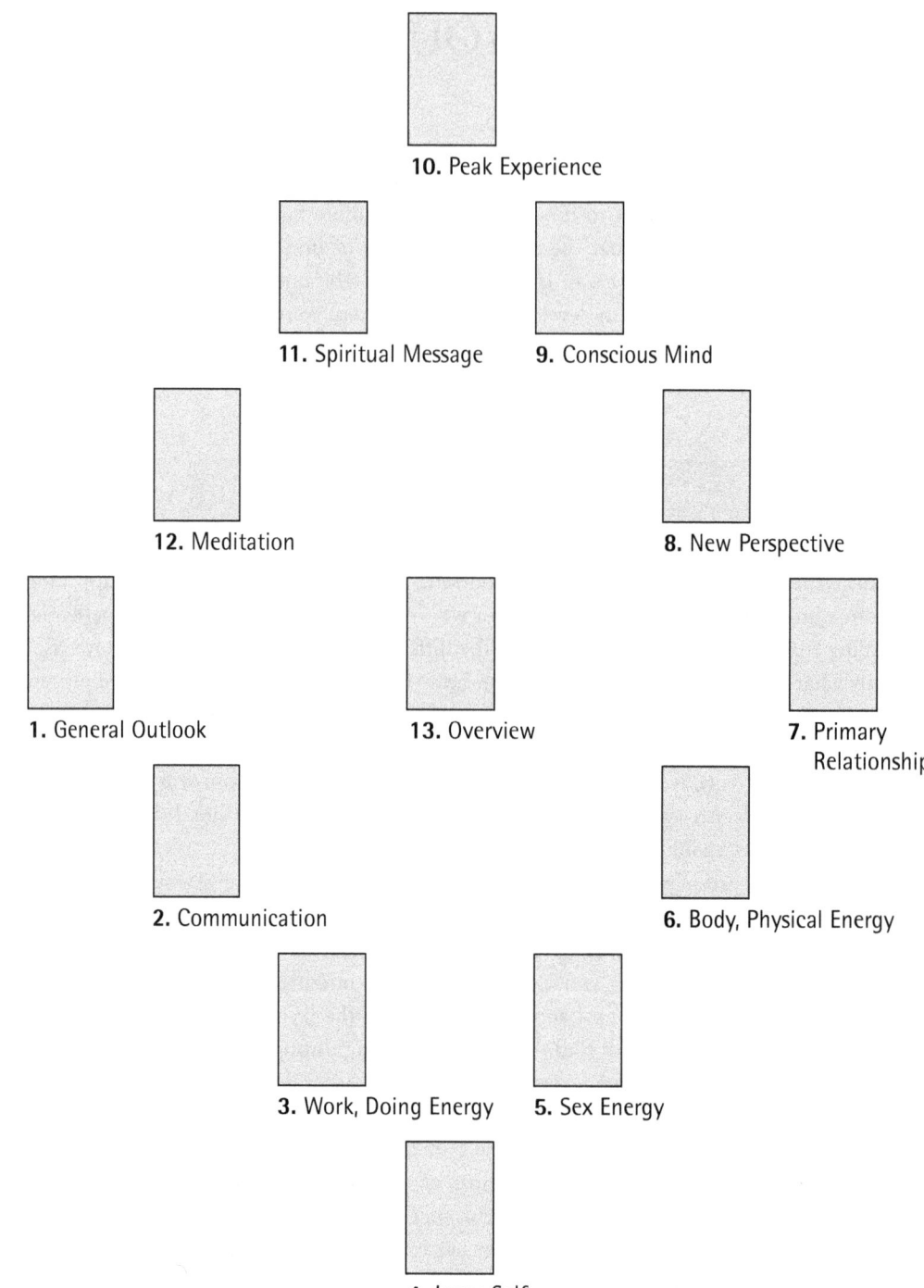

Explanation

1. **General Outlook.** This represents how you are looking at life right now. It can be seen as the glasses you place in front of your eyes to view the world when you wake up every morning. It's more the attitude to what is happening than the condition or reality.

2. **Communication.** This shows the way in which you express yourself with people, in other words how you talk or relate generally with those around. It could be seen as the personality level of relating.

3. **Work, Doing Energy.** If you have a specific job then this card will show what is happening for you there. If not, it will represent how you are using your energy in a practical sense, what you are doing, or how you are doing it. Or maybe where you are with getting work if that is relevant.

4. **Inner Self.** This is your connection with your inner being – what is happening inside of you independent of anything outside. It is your inner process. It can also show how you feel about or relate to yourself.

5. **Sexual Energy.** This shows the functioning of the basic sex energy, the sexual conditioning. If you are in a sexual relationship it will reflect the energetic dynamic of that situation. If you are not, it will show what is happening with this energy within yourself. It is not limited to physical sex but rather to your sense of yourself as a man/woman and how you relate with the opposite sex energetically. Sexual energy is our basic life force, so when it is stuck or blocked some of our life energy is stuck or held down. When we engage in sex this energy moves outwards; when it is flowing without the need for another it becomes an upwardly moving life force that energises the whole being.

6. **Body, Physical Energy.** This position reflects what is happening on a physical level. Health problems will come up here, not from a medically diagnostic point of view, but showing the mental, emotional or energetic reasons behind the condition. As body and mind are deeply connected, this position often reflects the physical side of whatever process you are going through.

7. **Primary Relationships.** This position reflects the dynamic that's happening in the main relationship in your life. If you have a husband or wife, a boyfriend or girlfriend then this will be represented here. If not, it will show your energy with those most intimate with you, or where you are with getting or being available for intimacy.

8. **New Perspective.** This card acts like a switch of gestalt, showing a new way of looking at what is happening. It is often making a comment on the card in Position 9, the Conscious Mind. You consciously see the situation in one way, and this card is suggesting you could look at it in a different and better way. It is recommending a new perspective, or something that could be happening if you allowed it to. It can be seen as an important key for understanding the reading.

9. **Conscious Mind.** This is showing the chief concern of the mind – what the mind is occupied with or what you're thinking about. As you will see, this may or may not have to do with what's actually happening.

10. **Peak Experience.** This is the best thing you can do or see in the current situation – the experience that is the peak of what is possible for you right now. It is usually referring specifically to the particular situation that is dominating your life rather than a general advice. You will see that this can sometimes be a card that might be judged as 'negative', showing that such states are just as valid and necessary as 'positive' ones.

11. **Spiritual Message.** This is the highest message that you can receive right now. If you have a spiritual master or teacher, you might like to experience this as what he or she would want to say to you at this time. If not, then you can see it as the message that existence wants to deliver to you. Whereas the advice in Position 10, Peak Experience, is usually referring to some specific situation, the Spiritual Message is giving a broader and more general direction.

12. **Meditation.** This position shows what your meditation is at this time. Meditation isn't necessarily about closing your eyes and sitting in the right position, and it doesn't mean something you need to think about, or contemplate. Rather, it is whatever is happening in your life that you need to keep bringing your awareness to and be willing to learn through. It will probably be something that you're not so good at or don't like, otherwise you wouldn't need to make it a meditation.

13. **Overview.** This position acts as though you are looking down on your life from a high hill and so can see the journey you are on from an extended perspective. From this height you can see where you have come from and where you are heading. The Overview could be seen as summing up the major issues or processes you are dealing with at this time or as showing the flavour or colour that is predominating the current direction of your life.

How to Read

Three Levels of the Being

As you become familiar with the reading, you may find your own way of entering it to reach the greatest depth. The guidelines below are just that – guidelines, not fixed rules – but they are the best way to start.

In a loose way, you could see the thirteen positions representing three levels of the being. The First Level is the **Apparent**, the most superficial view of the current life situation. If you were to meet an acquaintance who asked how you are doing, it is the information from these cards that you would naturally relate. The Second Level is the **Actual**, the direct mirroring of the reality of the different areas of your life at this time. The Third Level is the **Advice**. This is the part of the reading that comments on what is happening and tells you what to do. You could see this level as mirroring the knowing of the higher consciousness, or superconscious awareness of the being.

In reality we are not compartmentalised, so each segment of the being is connected with and affected by the others. One of the things that makes this layout such a powerful and insightful mirror is that it creates a space where you can see and get to understand these connections. If there is a major issue happening in your life, then obviously this is going to be the dominant thing that is mirrored here. The reading will show how this affects you as a whole, rather than just the isolated 'part' of you concerned with this issue. For example, it could be showing how a relationship issue is affecting your body, or your sense of yourself.

Remember that everything that you are looking at in this reading is you (or the subject if you are reading for someone else); it does not deal with the outside influences.

Preparing to Look

Shuffle the cards thoroughly with the feeling that you are putting your energy into them. Then spread them in front of you. Now close your eyes and see if you can find a space inside that is ready and wanting to really look at yourself.

This reading is about taking a good look at the reality of who you are and what you are doing in your life right now. You will not be able to read it unless you feel ready to drop your old ideas about what's happening and be open and available to looking at yourself in a fresh way. It is important to approach this and all tarot readings in a non-judgemental way. If you bring your ideas that some states are good and some are bad, into a reading, it will block your ability to see the reality that's there. We all have judgements and you are not expected to transcend them before you can read cards, but you are being asked to put them to one side. What is happening in your life, both inside yourself and out, is what it is. The ideas of good or bad, right or wrong are just the superficial concepts of the mind.

Checking out the Mirror, Step by Step

First get a general feeling of the overall colours and shapes. When you look at the whole spread as a cohesive picture, how do you feel, what's your first impression? Take a minute to let yourself experience this. Remember that you are looking into a clear mirror of your own being (or that of the subject) at this time.

Is there a predominance of one particular suit? Are there a lot of major arcana cards? Are there many 'problem' cards? Is your energy attracted to one particular area? Notice without analysing.

First Level – The Apparent: Cards 1, 8, 9 and 13

- Begin the reading by looking at No. 13 to get an overview of what's happening and the direction you are moving in right now. From here you will get a certain colour or flavour of the whole life situation and the major issues you are dealing with.

- Next bring your attention to No. 1, General Outlook, to see how you are looking at your life at this time; your attitude to what is happening generally. For instance, do you see what's happening playfully, negatively, through the filter of trying to make things work, to do the right thing?

- Next look at No. 9, Mind, to see what you think is going on, or what is occupying your conscious mind. As explained above, these three cards provide the same level of information as you would likely share with someone who simply asked you how you are doing. It is the most obvious or apparent level of what's happening.

- The last card on this level, No. 8, New Perspective, can be seen as that person's insight on what you had just shared. Put another way, you have already seen and related to how you think things are in No. 9 and your attitude to them in No. 1. No. 8 gives you another, clearer way of looking at it. It is basically saying, 'Well you could see it in this way.' It switches your gestalt, your way of perceiving what is happening, and often elicits a kind of, 'Oh, I see' response. It is effectively one of the advice positions, although possibly on a more mental or superficial level than the others, but reading it at this time can act as a key for the whole way you see what's happening.

Second Level – The Actual: Cards 2–7

Now you are ready to move into a deeper level of your current situation. These cards are mirroring the actual energetic reality of your situation in the different areas of your being. If you have a major arcana card in one of these positions, there is usually more energy in that area of your life. If there is a 'problem' card such as Worry, Cruelty, or Strife etcetera there is difficulty or processing in this area.

For convenience you can view this level roughly in three parts: **intimate relating**, the main partnership connection (Nos 5 and 7); **private self**, that part of you that has nothing to do with anyone else (Nos 4 and 6); and **public self**, the part of you that is involved with people generally (Nos 2 and 3).

First look for the major trouble spots – the areas where there are cards of difficulty or conflict, or cards indicating major change. If there is disturbance in your intimate relating, it is better to start here so you can identify and go beyond this layer. Many of us do much of our deep learning through the mirrors of our intimate relationships and it is here that we most easily lose touch with what is actually going on inside ourselves. This is particularly so when it is a man/woman relationship. This is where we will start now.

Intimate Relating: Cards 5 and 7

- No. 5 reflects the Sex Energy. If you are in a relationship, this position will show the basic male/female (or whatever sexual combination it is) dynamic that is the root of your energy connection with your partner. If you don't have a partner, this position will show what is happening with this energy inside yourself, or the kind of energy that is, often unconsciously, put out to the opposite sex. For example, are you open, dependent, in your mind, stuck, attached? It shows your sexual conditioning whether you are with a partner or not.

- No. 7 reveals more about the general situation that is happening between you and the other, what is more obviously going on. Are you in your head, your heart, concerned with security, vulnerable, giving or controlling? If you're not with someone, is your energy available, protected, confused, insecure, contentedly with yourself?

Private Self: Cards 4 and 6

- No. 4 shows what is happening within you, independent of anyone else. What is your inner being processing right now? Where are you at with yourself? Are you dealing with fear, enjoying yourself, feeling emotional? Does it tie in with your relationship situation, or your general outlook?

- No. 6 shows what is happening in your physical energy – your body. Is your body going through some process of its own or is it connected with what's happening in your relationship or your inner being? Is the energy blocked, influenced by the mind, intense, being in the moment, open, closed?

   This position may reveal some process that you are not consciously aware of. The energy of emotions or anxieties that we don't want to experience is repressed and then has to be processed through the body. This is the cause of many of our health problems. If there is a highly emotional or negative mental card in this place, it is a good idea that you consciously experience this energy, otherwise it can create real physical problems. If you are already experiencing a physical difficulty and you have picked one of the change or transformation cards, this indicates that whatever is happening physically is part of a deeper inner adjustment.

Public Self: Cards 2 and 3

- Now check out No. 3, the Work or Doing Energy. Are you bored, playing, looking into the future, having a problem? It could be that this is your major area of processing right now, and in that case could be strongly connected to No. 6, your Physical Energy, or No. 4, your inner process.

- The remaining card on this level is No. 2, Communication. This is how you are relating and expressing yourself with people generally. Are you talking too much, not expressing what you feel, being authentic, trying to be right?

So far, with the exception of No. 8, all the cards we have looked at (Nos 1 – 9 and 13) have been simply reflecting your reality, showing how it is. They are not telling you how you should be, whether it's right or wrong. There is no opinion, no judgement, just simple fact. Sometimes you may be able to relate easily to this mirror and sometimes it will be more difficult; it depends on how conscious you are in that situation. When you can't relate, often because you don't like what you see, you may be tempted to think you've picked a wrong card, or not be able to 'understand' it. There is no mistake and nothing to understand: just look into the mirror and experience. As you experience, on some level at least, the state that is happening in you in that area of your life, you are seeing it mirrored back to you in the symbols of a card. This helps to bring consciousness and give form and understanding to that state, while at the same time helping you to connect with the card on an experiential level beyond the explanations of the mind.

Third Level – The Advice: Cards 10–12

This part of the reading gives guidance and direction from the highest part of your consciousness. You may not be able to fully understand this advice until you are clear on the reality of your situation so, even though you may glance at it earlier, always leave this section till last.

- Position No. 10 tells you what is the best space you can be in or thing you can do or see in the situation that is most dominating your life. It might be telling you to be cautious, to feel your fear, to be playful, to face the problem. It's showing you the right direction in which to move right now; the peak experience you can have in this current situation.

- No. 11 is the spiritual message from existence or from your guru or teacher if you have one. This doesn't mean that this message is the only spiritual part of the reading. Spirituality is not something that is separate from your daily life: it is quite simply a deeper awareness *of* your daily life. But this card represents the highest or purest guidance you can receive right now; the most precious gift that you can allow yourself to experience or learn. It will tend to have a more far reaching message than the more specific advice of No. 10. It could be advising you to do something like recognise a process of completion, to go with the flow of things, or take responsibility. It is pointing you in the direction of your general spiritual path.

- Position No. 12 symbolises whatever is a meditation for you right now. This doesn't mean you have to sit down with your eyes closed and contemplate the state that is represented. It means that being in this state, experiencing it, is the greatest area of growth for you. It is the condition that you need to keep bringing your attention to again and again to learn from. It could be about letting things fall apart, waiting, needing to express, or understanding something. The doing of it will probably require effort, or constant awareness on your behalf – that is why you have picked it as your meditation.

Sometimes these three positions may operate independently, but usually they come together to give a cohesive message of advice. Because they represent positive guidance, they may well put you in touch with your judgements about states that you feel are definitely not positive, and are not experiences to be welcomed with gratefulness. For instance, when most of us see the card 'Interference' (confusion) or 'Failure' (fear), 'Defeat' or 'The Hanged Man' (transformation through suffering) we don't feel very happy about it. Acknowledging these states within ourselves, and seeing that it is okay to allow them, starts to create the possibility of accepting the whole spectrum of human experience simply as various realities, like the different colours of the rainbow (*see* 'Putting Aside Judgements', page 17).

EXAMPLE OF THE CURRENT LIFE READING

The best way to learn from the sample readings is to lay the cards out for yourself and compare your understanding of the reading with what is written.

When you are reading for someone else, it is helpful, although not necessary, to ask if they have any major issues at this time. This will save a lot of unnecessary guesswork even though what unfolds in the reading may not be what they thought was important. It is also a good idea to find out what his or her relationship situation is. In other words, are they married or in some kind of intimate relationship?

Sheila

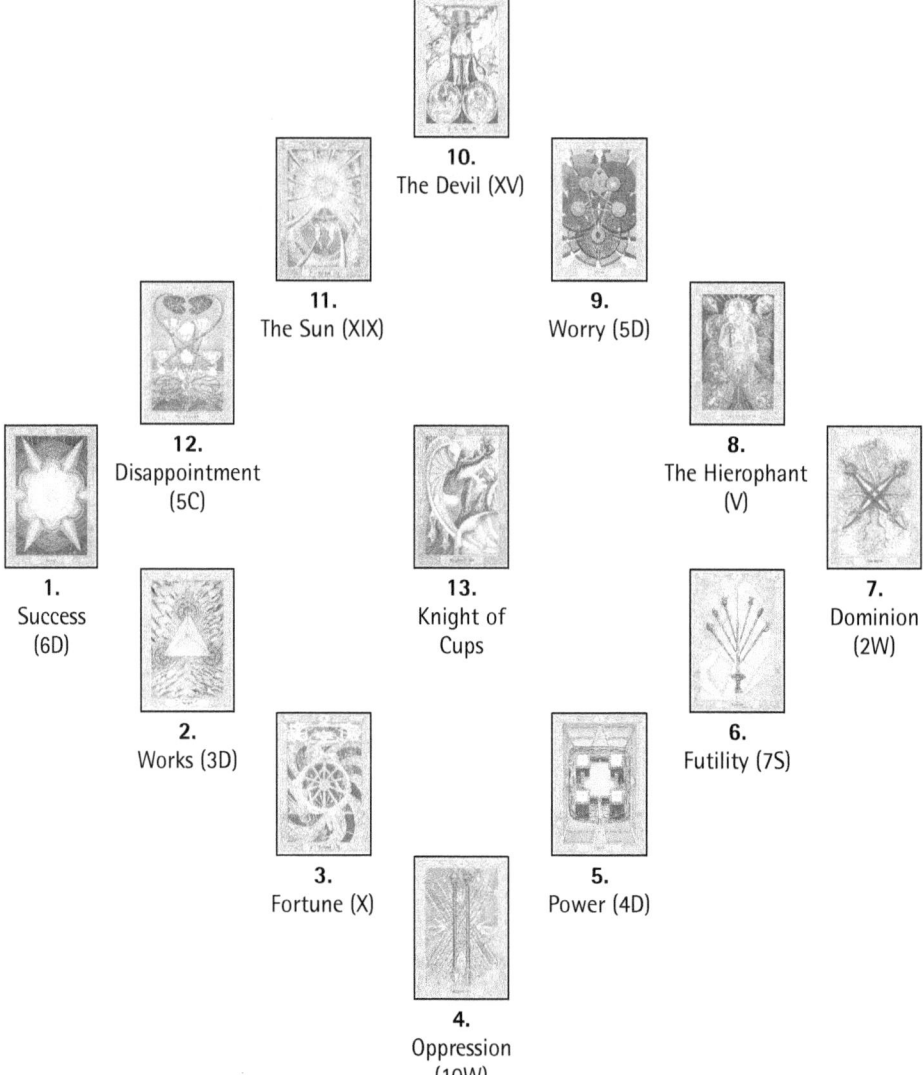

10. The Devil (XV)
11. The Sun (XIX)
9. Worry (5D)
12. Disappointment (5C)
8. The Hierophant (V)
1. Success (6D)
13. Knight of Cups
7. Dominion (2W)
2. Works (3D)
6. Futility (7S)
3. Fortune (X)
5. Power (4D)
4. Oppression (10W)

Sheila, the subject of this reading, is a 34-year-old woman who has recently finished a short but intense relationship. This has left her questioning what is happening in her relationships with men in general, as well as with this particular man. We will now go into this reading step by step as laid out in the 'How to Read' section above.

General feeling: At first glance the spread feels relatively positive. There are four major arcana cards, three of them in advice positions rather than reflecting where she already is. This suggests that there is something significant to be learned from the current situation that she has not yet seen. The most significant of these, looking from what we know of her background, is The Sun in position No. 11. This can be the symbol of learning in relationships, which confirms that this is relevant in her case. There are also four problem cards (Oppression, Worry, Futility and Disappointment) that bring attention to the areas of current difficulty. We notice that none of these are in the positions of relating, but one is her Inner Self and another Body, which suggests that the issue of relationship is being dealt with more inside herself than with another.

First Level – The Apparent

- **No. 13** (Knight of Cups) shows that the overview and main issue in her life right now is about the quality of how she shares herself or what she gives to others from a heart level. It is yang (male), outgoing emotional energy, which shows she comes from a putting out, giving space.

- **No. 1** (Success) shows that her general outlook or attitude on life is concerned with wanting to do the right thing, to make things work or succeed. **No. 9** (Worry) shows that she is consciously brooding or worrying about the situation. It makes sense that if she wants to share herself (Knight of Cups) in a way that is right or makes things work (No. 1), this will create worry or concern about how to be or what to do – because she cannot simply be herself. So already we have a good idea of where she is coming from.

- Now we move to **No. 8** and see that the new perspective Sheila could take on her current situation is that of learning or understanding (Hierophant). This means that, even though she is concerned (Worry in No. 9), she could get some understanding if she combined her intelligence with her experience. In other words, she is getting the message that, instead of trying to work it out with her head, she needs to see that there is something she hasn't understood or learnt from experiencing the situation we have just described.

Second Level – The Actual

- **Intimate Relating**: We know that Sheila has just finished a relationship, so we go first to Nos 5 and 7 to check out her sexual and energetic connections with her previous partner or men in general. Position **No. 5**, sexual energy, is Power (4D), which means attachment. This indicates that she is probably still holding on to her last boyfriend on a basic energetic level, or holding on to old ways of relating to men. This holding could mean her energy isn't really available for anyone else, even though she might like it to be. **No. 7**, the card of relationship connection, is Dominion (2W), new direction. We know that she hasn't just started a new relationship, so this is telling us that on this level her energy, either for her old partner or probably for partners in general, is moving in a new direction. This is reflecting her willingness to relate intimately in a different way, but we can see from No. 5 that something of the old is holding her back.

- **Private Self:** Now we look at **No. 4**, her inner process. Oppression (10W) tells us that there is something going on inside her that she doesn't want to look at. She is repressing or restricting some quality of her own being, and is not in connection with herself on some level. This indicates why her main issue is her concern with giving and sharing in relationships – because she doesn't want to look inside herself – and also why there is something she needs to understand (Hierophant in No. 8). It is reinforcing what we already suspected – that she needs to deal with this issue within herself rather than looking outwards to try and do it right.

- Now we move on to **No. 6** to see what's happening in her body. Futility (7S) suggests that there is a sense of pointlessness in her physical energy that is probably connected to an energetic pattern. Knowing that she is basically outward going in the sharing of her energy (No. 13) in an effort to make her relationships work the right way (No. 1), we can presume that this is the pattern that her energy is already experiencing as futile. This could mean that if she continues to force her energy outwards in this way she may experience some physical problems, or at least tiredness, as she is not listening to her body.

- **The Public Self: No. 2**, the card of communication, is Works (3D), indicating that she puts a lot of creative energy into her relating. This is not necessarily a bad thing, but it does indicate that she probably 'works' at relating; in other words she is not able to relax and just be herself with others. This ties in with what we have already seen in her connections with others.

- **No. 3**, the work/doing energy, is Fortune (X). This is a positive high energy card that indicates things are flowing along in an uneventful way in this part of her life right now. This doesn't appear to be an area of concern so we won't go into it in any more depth.

Now we have a mirror in front of us of where Sheila is in her life right now. Her relating energy is primarily outgoing and doing at the cost of being in contact with herself. She is so concerned with making her connections with others work that she is lost to herself. Naturally this creates an uncertainty and worry in her mind about what she should be doing or how she should be acting. Energetically she knows there is no point in continuing to do this, but she has not yet brought that awareness into her conscious mind and learnt from it. In her sexual energy she is probably holding on to her last boyfriend, although wanting to move into that, or maybe other connections with men, in a new way. There is something she is not understanding or learning from this situation that necessitates her looking inside herself and listening to her energy.

Third Level – The Advice

Now we are ready to look at the messages of advice that show the directions Sheila needs to move in or things she needs to bring attention to in her life right now. Even though we may have glanced in this direction before, it is only possible to really understand what is being shown here when we already know where she is.

- **No. 10**, the peak experience, is The Devil. This is telling Sheila that the best thing she can do in the current situation is see the reality of it as it is. This means she doesn't have to think or worry about what is the right thing to do to change it; she can stop trying to do anything and see things as they are. This will give her the space to feel what she is repressing inside and the sense of pointlessness that is already her physical experience. Then she will be able to learn and understand from this reality.

- The fact that all this is referring to her relationship patterns becomes unmistakable with **No. 11**, the spiritual message. The Sun (XIX) is a very clear directive that finding her inner unity or wholeness in relationships is the area that she most needs to be working on or doing something about. This means that to see the conditioning programmes around relating as restricting her authenticity or connection with herself is the highest growth for her right now. This is obviously referring to her intimate relating with men but also to any relationship where she tends to get caught in a giving pattern, trying to do the right thing at the cost of being with herself.

- **No. 12**, the meditation, is Disappointment (5C), telling her that she needs to bring her awareness to her inner feelings of disappointment, emptiness and unfulfilment. To pick this as her meditation means it is something she doesn't want to feel, so this is what she is repressing or avoiding inside of herself (No. 4). Until she allows herself to experience this, she will be caught in her current situation of trying to work out with her mind how to 'do' a relationship 'right' to make it work so that she doesn't have to face this emptiness within herself. While she is doing this, she cannot be in touch with her own inner needs and authenticity, which is the only way to make intimacy work. It is this understanding (No. 8) that she needs to look at, rather than repress, in her relating (No. 11).

CHAPTER TWO – THE QUESTION LAYOUT

The Question Layout is designed to bring light into specific questions or issues. It is suggested that you don't expect the tarot to take away your responsibility by telling you what to do or by giving you the answer. This will make you dependent on the cards, and in this way they become a crutch rather than a tool for consciousness and awareness. Instead, approach this reading with the desire to see more clearly what is actually going on in you with the situation, to open the doors of the unconscious so that you can become clear enough to make up your own mind and take responsibility for your own decisions. When you have this higher aim in mind, you may find that sometimes you don't get the kind of answers that you expect. You may think that you are asking a simple question, but your cards pick up on, and open out, a part of that issue that you weren't even aware of. Keep your mind wide open and you will find that you are always given what you need to see even if it is not the direct answer you were expecting.

Two Versions

The Question Layout is presented in two forms. The first, simplified form is the best way to start until you become more familiar with the cards and confident in your intuition. It is good for simple issues where you just need a quick look rather than going into the issue in depth.

The second, expanded version uses the same format but goes into much more depth and detail. It is a very fluid, flexible reading, designed to give your intuition plenty of space to function. For this reason the meanings of each position are not as precise as they are in the Current Life Reading. Rather the energy of the five cards flows into one another like colours in a painting to create a cohesive picture.

Both readings are based on the comparative awareness of three different states that are represented by three different cards or sets of cards. Basically it is showing you what you think is going on, what is really going on or what you need to see, and what will happen from this recognition.

Preparing the Question

It is very important that you form your question or present your issue in a way that enables the cards to reflect back your situation with clarity. You must know exactly what you are looking at or you will never be able to read it. Much of the confusion and uncertainty in reading cards comes simply from not knowing what you're looking at once you've picked. If you don't ask your question in a clear concise way, you'll never understand the answer.

Always take time before you pick to carefully formulate your question so that a precise answer can be mirrored directly back to you by the spread. After you have picked your cards is too late. You will be left wondering if that is what you really picked for.

When you are using the Question Layout, you need to compose your question or issue so that it can be reflected by this particular format. The first card must be able to reflect back where you are in your conscious mind, the second what you need to do or see, and the third the result or best place you can be. What you are really doing is looking at the issue that this question brings up, and in this way you will get your answer. A good approach is to fit your question into the format: Where am I at with…? What do I need to see about…? What are my issues with…?

You can't ask either/or questions. For example, if you are looking for clarity on a decision you have to make, it's no good asking, 'Should I do this or that?', because you won't know at which alternative you are looking. Your question must be, 'Where am I at with doing... (one specific thing)?'. Then the cards will tell you whether this is what is really happening for you. Maybe you need to do a second reading to check out the other option.

Also, don't ask compound questions. For example, 'What is my relationship with my business partner and should we expand our business together?' One part of the question may need a different answer to the other and you won't know what is being answered.

Remember that there are no cards for 'yes' and 'no', so it is no good expecting that kind of answer. For instance, 'Should I buy a new house?' Format your question so that it gives you space to look at the issue involved. In this example, you want to look at the issue of buying a new house. The first card will reflect where you are in your conscious mind with buying a new house and the second will tell you what you need to see or do about it. The third will tell you what is likely to result from following this advice or the best place you can be with this right now. In this way you will get your answer by becoming more conscious of the real issues involved, rather than expecting a simplistic answer from some mysterious power outside yourself that takes away your responsibility.

Keep in mind that you are directing your questions to the knowledge that exists hidden in your own unconscious mind, or your higher consciousness, the part of the mind that can tune into higher sources. You are using the cards to tap into the part of you that already knows.

Simplified Form
The Three-card Reading

1. Pick three cards and place them in a row.

   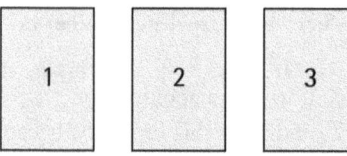

2. **First card – the Conscious Mind.** The first card shows your conscious understanding of the issue. It is something you will be able to relate to or recognise because it is what you think is happening. It is not giving you any advice or telling you what you should or shouldn't be doing. It does not contain any judgement or opinion. It is simply reflecting where you are with this issue in your conscious mind right now. By relating to this card first, you create a foundation or a context from which you can move into the next position to gain deeper insight or advice. Sometimes this first card will pick up on some particular aspect of the situation that you know but isn't necessarily what you would have expected or considered the most important.

   Note: For an insight on the possible interpretation of the meaning of a card in this position, you can refer to the 'Variations in Current Life Reading' section in Part Four under No. 9, Mind.

3. **Second card – the Advice.** The second card reflects what your unconscious or higher conscious mind has to say about the situation. It is showing you the deeper or higher level of your reality in this situation. Sometimes this position shows something inside yourself that you need to become aware of, and sometimes it can be seen more as guidance from a higher source. It is basically the message or advice for what you need to see or to do. It is not separate from what you picked in the first position; rather it is making a comment on that. The first card is in some way what is obvious, and the second is the deeper truth of that state, or what you need to do about it. Sometimes it might be saying something quite similar to the first card, and sometimes it will be saying something entirely different. It depends on how conscious you are in this situation.

   Note: For an insight on the possible interpretation of the meaning of a card in this position, you can refer to the 'Variations in Current Life Reading' section in Part Four under Nos 11 and 12, Spiritual Message and Meditation.

4. **Third card – the Result.** The third card is the outcome; it shows what can happen if you become aware of, recognise, or do what is indicated by the second card. It is the best place you can be, or move towards with this issue, and the second card is the method or understanding needed to get there. Even if you don't like what is reflected in this card, even if it is a space that you would not consider desirable, it is still the best place you can be with this issue right now. It may not be what your conscious

mind thinks you want to happen, but it is what needs to happen. Understanding and accepting this is to move to a deeper level of your own truth.

Note: For an insight on the possible interpretation of the meaning of a card in this position, you could refer to the 'Variations in Current Life Reading' section in Part Four under No. 10, Peak Experience.

5. Together, these three cards give you a complete message. Remember that they are all connected. It's not that the first card is reflecting some aspect of your life and the second one is picking on something completely different. The card in each position says something about the cards in the other two. Put briefly: **The first card is where you are, the third is the best place for you to be, and the second is the understanding or way needed to get there.**

EXAMPLES OF THE THREE-CARD READING

Example One

Manfred is thinking about applying for a new job. He is not sure about it so he picks three cards to look at the situation. The question is formatted: 'Show me what I need to see about applying for this new job?'

1 2 3

  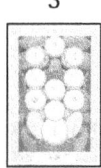

1. Interference, 8 Swords,
2. The Magus I
3. Wealth, 10 Disks

The **first card**, Interference, reflects what he is conscious of in this situation. He is confused; he doesn't know what to do. This he already knows, but it is important to have that mirrored back to him before he looks deeper.

The **second card**, The Magus, which means communicating or doing with intention, is the advice. Very clearly he is being told to go ahead with the application.

The **third card**, Wealth, is the result or the best place for him to be with this job application. The card means being present and letting things unfold one step at a time, so this is what will happen when he has applied, as advised in position 2.

In other words, he is being advised to apply for the job and then see what happens. There is no guarantee given here that he will get it or not, just that he needs to apply and let the situation unfold in its own way from there.

Example Two

Sarah wants to be in a long-term relationship, but somehow her connections with men never last for more than a few weeks. She has tried everything she can think of – being loving and compassionate, being independent and free, being forceful with what she wants, putting aside her own desires – nothing works. She is at the point where she doesn't know what else to do. She formats the question: 'What do I need to see about my relationships with men?'

1   2   3

1. Defeat, 5 swords
2. Virtue, 3 wands
3. Failure, 7 disks

The **first card**, Defeat, reflects what she is conscious of in her relating with men at this time. She is in a place of defeat, where she feels everything she tries doesn't work, so she has given up trying. She feels literally defeated in all her efforts.

The **second card**, Virtue, is advising her that all she can do is be real with wherever she is. In other words, now she has given up trying, she can be with what is authentic and genuine in her with men.

The **third card**, Failure, is the result that will happen out of being real and authentic. Failure means fear, so she is being told that the best place she can be right now is in her fear. She is being given the understanding that she is afraid of simply being real and herself with men, which is no doubt why her relationships haven't worked out.

Full Expanded Form

This expanded form of the Question Layout is a highly effective reading for giving large amounts of understanding and information about any particular question or issue. It opens up the bigger picture to bring a wider and broader perspective of the situation.

It is suggested that you don't try it until you are feeling relatively familiar and confident with your cards, otherwise you will get confused. It is designed specifically as a springboard for the intuition, so for the logical mind it may seem a little vague or complicated while you are still learning your cards.

The Format

1. Pick five cards three times, i.e. pick three piles of five cards, being careful to keep them in the same order.

2. Now place each pile down in this way.

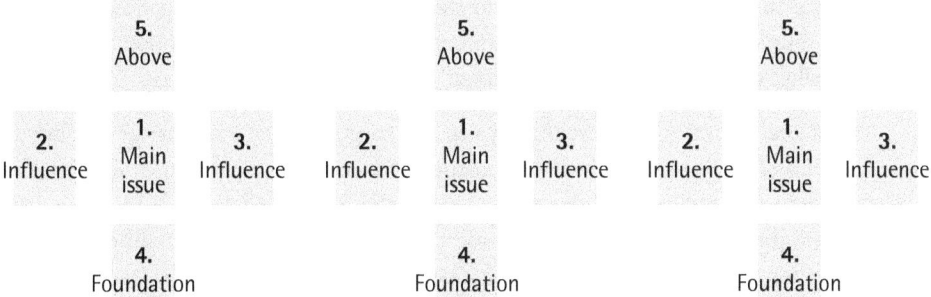

3. The three groups have the same meanings as the three single cards in the Simplified Form. The first group is a reflection of what is in the conscious mind. The second is the reality, the advice or the message from the unconscious or the higher conscious, and the third is the outcome or the best place you can be. (See above Simplified Form for more details.)

4. No. 1 in the group is the dominant energy, the central issue equivalent to the single card in the Simplified Form. The other four cards are adding detail, depth and background to this main card.

   Nos 2 and 3 are the energies or situations that are influencing and affecting the central symbol.

   No. 4 is what is underneath it; the foundation or place from which it arises.

   No. 5 is what is above it; what it develops into, what comes out of it, the place to where it goes, the direction to which the other cards are leading.

   These five positions are not rigid; they run into each other to form a cohesive whole.

As you are seeing the picture painted by these five cards, try to see it as though they are five different ingredients that connect with each other to create the whole. It may be helpful to see the first card as the dominant colour or shape in the painting, and the other four are supporting shades or patterns that compliment and complete the picture. See what happens when you keep your eyes in soft focus to receive the message that is being given. This is a way of looking with the intuitive side of the mind, rather than the logical, rational part.

5. The positions of the cards are usually equivalent and corresponding to each other in each of the three groups. This means, for instance, that influence No. 2 in the second group of cards is saying something about influence No. 2 in the first group; this position in the third group is giving the best outcome of the same influence. The foundation card, No. 4, in the second group is making a comment on No. 4 in the first group and pointing you towards seeing that No. 4 in the third group is the best foundation you can have in this issue. So it is with all of the five positions.

By reading the cards in this way you will see that there is great depth and flexibility possible in this reading. Not only do the five cards in each group flow into each other, but so do the three groups comment and mingle with each other to offer the possibility of profound understanding of your particular issue.

6. While you are learning to use this layout, it is suggested that you start by placing the first card in each position face up and the rest face down. In that way you will first be looking at and reading the equivalent of the Simplified Form. Once you have worked through and understood these three cards, you can start filling out and giving depth to the picture by turning over the others, one by one, in each position. If one of these doesn't make sense to you, don't worry about it. Just leave it alone and work with the cards that you can relate to. If you don't get one of the many ingredients or colours in the whole picture, you will not be missing very much.

EXAMPLE OF FULL QUESTION READING

To best way to follow the example is to pull the cards out of the pack and lay them out as shown below. As we move through the reading step by step, it is important to remember that it is geared mainly towards using intuition rather than the logical mind, so the positions don't have the same fixed meanings as in the Current Life Reading. We are following a logical form, but give your intuition plenty of space to function.

Margaret

The subject of this reading is a 40-year-old woman named Margaret. She has recently become involved in a psychotherapeutic growth group and wants to know more about how this group and its process is affecting her life. She formulates the question: 'What is happening for me with this psychotherapeutic group?'

1.

5. The Sun (XIX)

2. Ace of Disks   1. Lust (XI)   3. Knight of Cups

4. Princess of Disks

First Set – Conscious Mind

This is showing where Margaret is in her conscious mind with the group. In other words, what she is aware of and thinks is going on. The immediate impression of these five cards is extremely positive and strong. It contains two major arcana cards, two court cards and an ace; the colours are primarily bright and golden and the shapes very strong. Obviously the group is very important to Margaret on a conscious level.

Card **No. 1**, Lust, indicates immediately that she has a lot of lively, vibrant energy for this activity.

The first of the two influences that affect this exciting situation for her is Ace of Disks (**No. 2**), which indicates that she is present in the reality of herself and what's happening in this situation.

The other influence (**No. 3**), the Knight of Cups, shows that this is a space where she is putting out her energy and sharing herself emotionally; she is doing a lot of giving.

Underneath (**No. 4**) is the Princess of Disks, indicating that the base of where she is coming from, or the foundation of what is happening, is a patient, open, waiting for things to develop.

The card above, or where this is going (**No. 5**), is

The Sun. This shows that the direction this vibrant energy is moving in, the focus of the giving, is towards her relationships within the group.

To sum this up, her own perception is that in a positive exciting way she is putting a lot of energy, realistically and from her heart, into making relationships within the group, and waiting to see what will develop from this. We see that this is where her question is coming from.

It must be remembered that this is what she thinks is going on. It is a mirror of how she experiences the situation on a conscious level, so it is likely that she will be able to relate easily with this part of the reading.

Second Set – The Advice

Now we move to the second level of the reading, the deeper reality of the unconscious mind or the message from the higher part of her being. This is what she needs to bring to her awareness, the deeper reality of the situation she needs to become conscious of.

From first glance we can see that this is not as bright a picture as the first set of cards. The colours are mainly grey and blue, one of the two major arcana cards indicates difficulties, and two of the minor arcana cards (Defeat and Failure) are symbolic of negative or difficult states. This could come as a bit of a shock to Margaret, who thinks everything is great in this situation.

The **first card**, The Hanged Man, symbolises transformation through suffering or difficulties. Immediately we know that there is something uncomfortable or difficult in the situation that Margaret needs to be aware of and to experience. All the positive energy and enthusiasm (Lust) that she is putting into this group has another deeper dimension of difficulty and potential transformation that she needs to bring to her attention.

2.

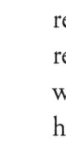

5. Ace of Cups / Failure (7D)

2. Luxury (4C)

1. The Hanged Man (XII)

3. Defeat (5S)

4. Art (XIV)

The first influence (**No. 2**), Luxury, tells us that there are issues of security, or keeping herself safe and comfortable, that she needs to own. The matching influence in the first set of cards is Ace of Disks, which could mean that she is consciously aware of this reality (she will know if that is so), or it could mean that even though she thinks she is grounded in what's happening in the group, there is a level deeper inside of herself where she is acting out of her need to stay safe.

The second influence (**No. 3**) is Defeat, which indicates that something in the situation is simply not working and that she needs to give up on it. When we refer back to No. 2 in the first set of cards, we find out that it is her way of giving and putting herself out that doesn't work.

Underneath (**No. 4**), Art shows that the foundation of what is needed for her right now is to allow the integration or subtle change of what is being described above to happen. This doesn't conflict with the waiting that is indicated in this influence in the first set.

In position **No. 5** there are two cards because, when Margaret was picking, two cards came out together, so she trusted that two were needed. Ace of Cups is the card for self-loving and saying 'yes' to yourself; Failure is the card for fear. Together they indicate fear of loving and saying 'yes' to who you are. This is what she needs to face in herself, what her higher consciousness is directing her towards, rather than concern with relationships (No. 5 in the first set).

What we see so far is that Margaret is being shown that the energy of putting out or giving to others in the group situation is coming out of a fear of really saying 'yes' to and loving herself. In other words, she is focusing outwards, giving her energy to others, to avoid facing the fear of really being herself. The real learning in this situation, and presumably her real purpose for being in the group, is to go through the insecurity of feeling uncomfortable or not fitting in that is needed to face this fear.

3.

5. The Chariot (VII)

2. The Fool (0)   1. Strength (9W)   3. Prince of Cups

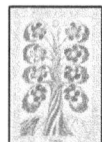

4. Prudence (8D)

Third Set – The Result

These cards show what develops from Margaret becoming aware of this situation in herself and facing it. It is the best place she can be with the group.

No. 1, Strength, shows that the main result for her is a sense of finding her own independence, a quality of wholeness and inner strength that has nothing to do with anyone else. She is in the group then for herself and to be herself, not for anyone else.

The first influence on this (**No. 2**) is The Fool, the symbol of having the courage to be open and spontaneous in the moment. In this independence she is able to feel more free to follow her own energy rather than having to keep things safe and secure, which this influence indicated she did in the second set of cards.

The other influence (**No. 3**) is the Prince of Cups, the card of emotional desire and wishes. When she gives up (second set) on trying to impress people by giving (first set), she is then free to listen to her own heart and look at what she really wants for herself.

The foundation of this situation (**No. 4**) is Prudence, which shows that this coming to independence, spontaneity and starting to look at what she wants is not something that can be hurried. It is something that will take time and she needs to be cautious and protective of herself and the process while this is going on. This fits in with this influence in the other two positions.

Out of this (**No. 5**) comes The Chariot, the ability to claim her own power and authority, which we can see from the equivalent cards she was not able to do.

To Summarise

Margaret is putting a lot of energy into her relationships with people in this group, which on a conscious level is creating a positive alive situation for her. But when she looks a little deeper she finds that she is compromising herself and her truth because she is afraid of being herself in the company of the others. Even though she was not conscious of this, on a deeper level she will have known it because something in her is ready to go through what is necessary to change this situation. (The middle set of cards will never tell you to do or be aware of something you are not ready to deal with. If you have picked it, you can trust that you are ready to see it.) Out of this change, she will gradually learn to become more independent and spontaneous, and not only find out what she wants for herself, but to recognise and claim her power to make it happen. This is the true potential of the psychotherapeutic group for her.

CHAPTER THREE – THE RELATIONSHIP LAYOUT

This layout is designed to give insight into our one-on-one relationships. This is an area that is difficult for most of us because it is here that we can most easily lose objectivity and get caught in our projections of what is happening. The layout works in the same format as the Question Layout but with an extra position to represent the other person. Only look at one specific person at a time with this reading, otherwise your answer will not be clear. You can use the reading in the Simplified Form, or the Full Expanded Form.

The Format

Shuffle and select your cards in the usual way and lay them out as described for the Question Reading but with one extra position: either four single cards in a row, or four groups of five cards.

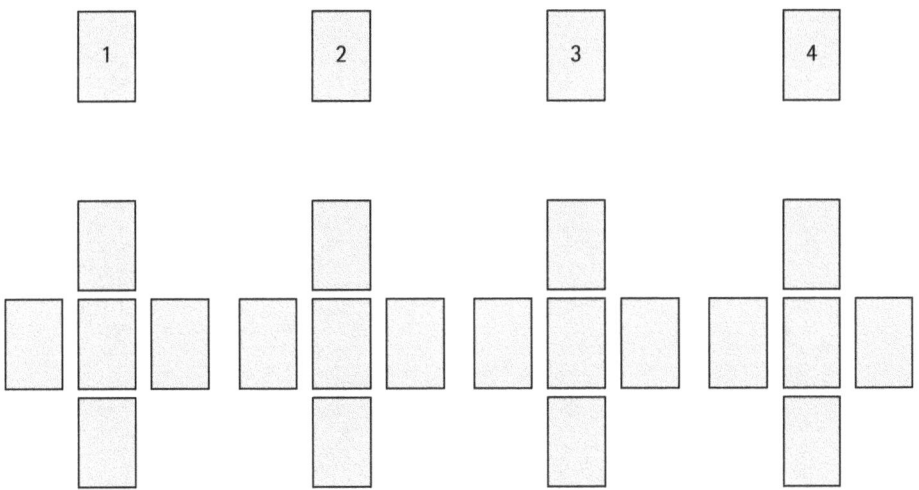

1. **The Conscious Mind.** The first card or first group of cards reflects where you are with the person concerned from your conscious being – what you think or where you feel you are with this person. Again, this is a reflection you will be able to relate to

because it is what you think is happening. It is important that you work with this position first until you feel and understand what aspect of your connection with the person it is mirroring, because this will form the context for the later cards and make them easier to understand.

2. **The Advice.** The second card, or group of cards, is the message from your unconscious or higher conscious mind. It is what is really happening for you in this relationship in a deeper part of your being, what you need to be aware of or do. Sometimes this will read like advice, telling you what you need to do in this situation. Sometimes it will simply be mirroring the deeper reality that you need to recognise and experience.

3. **The Result.** The third card or group of cards is the outcome or result of what will happen if you see or do what is revealed or suggested in the second position. It will show you the best space it is possible for you to be in this relationship right now.

4. **The Other.** The fourth card or group of cards represents where the other person is with you in this relationship. It is not advisable to delve too deeply into other people with the tarot. Not only is it a personal intrusion but also it can be dangerous to try to interpret another's deeper motives, especially someone with whom you are intimately connected and therefore invested. So when you are reading this position, see it mainly from the point of view of what you need to understand about their relationship with you. In this way it can give you very valuable objectivity and probably help you to understand why you are feeling the way you are feeling.

EXAMPLE OF RELATIONSHIP READING

Janet is a 42-year-old woman who is confused about her relationship with her brother. They had been very close, but a year back they had an argument and she felt they had never connected in the same way again. She formulates the question: 'What is happening in my relationship with my brother?'

We will look at this question first with the Simplified Form and then see how it can be expanded into the full version.

Simplified Form

 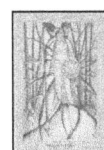  

1.
Completion (4W)

2.
Princess of Disks

3.
The Hermit (IX)

4.
Interference (8S)

1. **Conscious Mind.** This is where Janet is with her brother on a conscious level – in other words what she is aware of from her side. Completion shows that Janet wants to complete something. This is obviously whatever it was that happened in the relationship through their argument.

2. **The Advice.** This is what Janet's higher being wants her to do or see about this relationship. Princess of Disks indicates that she needs to be in an open and patient space with this situation right now. In other words, even though she wants to complete it (No. 1) she needs to wait patiently, let something grow in its own way and see what happens.

3. **The Result.** What results from this recognition is that she is thrown back into herself (Hermit). In other words, rather than trying to make something happen with the relationship, she needs to see that she is alone with this right now and find the answers inside herself.

4. **The Other.** Where Janet's brother is with her, is Interference, showing that he is in a state of confusion about his relationship with her. He really doesn't know where he is or what is going on with it. When we see this we understand why she has to be patient right now and work it out in herself.

Full Expanded Form

In this example we have used the technique of picking an extra card for clarity. If this feels too confusing, just ignore it; you will find you can get a lot out of the reading without this.

If you need more information about this technique, refer to Chapter Two in Part Two, 'Picking'.

1.

5. The Devil (XV)

  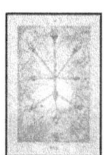

2. Gain (9D) 1. Completion (4W) 3. Ruin (10S)

4. Prince of Wands

First set. This is where Janet is with her brother on a conscious level – in other words, what she is aware of from her side. The **first card** here is Completion, showing that Janet wants to complete something, which is obviously whatever it was that happened through their argument.

The first influence on this (**No. 2**) is Gain, showing that she feels whatever happens out of this situation, completing the past is the right and positive thing to do.

The other influence (**No. 3**) is Ruin, showing that she wants to (or has) let go of whatever it was she was hanging on to. Underneath this (**No. 4**) is the Prince of Wands, showing that she has a lot of fresh enthusiasm for completing this old situation. From this she feels she is ready to really look at the reality between them as it actually is (**No. 5**, The Devil).

This is how she perceives the situation from her side: basically an attitude of wanting to complete and let go of the past to see what the reality is now.

2.

5. Princess of Swords

2. Queen of Disks 1. Princess of Disks 3. Indolence (8C)

4. Hierophant (V)

Second set. This is what Janet's higher being wants her to do or see about this relationship. The **first card**, Princess of Disks, indicates that she needs to be in an open and patient space with this situation right now. In other words, even though she wants to complete it (No. 1 in the first set) she needs to wait and be patient.

The first influence (**No. 2**) on this, Queen of Disks, shows the need to simply rest and be with what is happening. If she can combine this with the feeling of rightness indicated by No. 2 (Gain) in the first set, there is not a problem.

The other influence (**No. 3**), Indolence, suggests a space of not doing or not giving energy to. This is commenting on the No. 3 in the first set, which is about letting go. From this we understand that even though she thinks she wants to, or has, let go of the old, she needs to see that it is not the time to be putting energy into doing something about this situation, even letting it go.

Underneath this (**No. 4**), The Hierophant tells her that the foundation she needs to come from is that there is something to learn and understand, rather than move ahead enthusiastically (No. 4 in the first set). If we wanted to find out a bit more about what she needs to understand, we could pick another card and get Happiness (9C), which tells us that she needs to understand that she is coming from a place of hoping or expecting something from her brother. This could simply be that she is expecting to be able to complete the old situation or it could be that she has other expectations of him.

The final card, **No. 5**, Princess of Swords, shows that what she needs to move towards here is a process of clearing away, in this case the old hopes and expectations of trying to complete, rather than believing her version of the reality (the Devil in the first set).

To sum up her advice, she needs to understand that she is coming from a place of expecting something to complete or change with her brother and that actually there is nothing she can do about this situation right now. She is advised to be patient and open, while clearing away her old ideas and hopes.

3.

5. The Fool

2. Change (2D)   1. The Hermit (IX)   3. Tower (XVI)

4. Defeat (5S)

Third set. What results from this recognition is that she is thrown back into herself (Hermit, **No. 1**). The influences on this are Change and The Tower, cards that indicate much movement in how she will experience the situation. **No. 2** influence transforms the original feeling of positivity (Gain in the first set) into Change, and when we want to find out more about this change we pick Strength (9W). This indicates it is a change towards greater independence within herself about the relationship. The Tower (**No. 3**) shows that some of her old personality patterns of wanting to do something, or get rid of something, have to be thrown out.

The foundation of this (**No. 4**) is Defeat. From the understanding that she is expecting something from her brother (No. 4, second set), she now gets to realise this will not happen. She needs to allow the defeat of her hopes. From this comes **No. 5**, The Fool, which means staying in the moment and allowing things to happen spontaneously.

From this we see that the best place she can be with this situation right now is looking inside herself to allow strong changes and clearing to take place by giving up on expecting that she can make anything happen or get anything from her brother. Then she can just be in the moment with whatever may naturally and spontaneously occur between them.

Fourth set. Finally, we look at where Janet's brother is with her, because obviously this will help her to understand the situation. The **first card** here is Interference, showing that the brother is in a state of confusion about his relationship with her. He really doesn't know where he is or what is going on with it. The **influences** on this are both positive – The Star and the Lovers – showing that even though his mind is confused about what is happening, he trusts the situation as it is (the Star) and feels love for her (the Lovers).

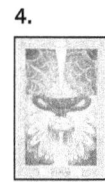

5. Ace of Cups

2. The Star (XVII)   1. Interference (8S)   3. The Lovers ((VI)

4. Peace (2S)

The foundation of this (**No. 4**) is Peace. The fact that he doesn't know what's going on is not a problem for him; he is at peace with his not knowing. The final card (**No. 5**) is Ace of Cups, showing that he is basically doing his own thing in a heartful way, following what he feels and needs for himself. We could presume that this indicates someone who is not into great analyses or working things out. He doesn't know what's going on inside of himself or with her in this relationship but his love is still there, (No. 3) and he trusts that what needs to happen will happen (No. 2). Meantime he is taking care of himself and getting on with his life (No. 5). (Note that the cards in the fourth set do not correspond to the other three sets because they are referring to a different person.)

To Summarise

In other words, the brother is fine with what's happening and doesn't need to work things out with her. It is up to Janet to work with this situation in herself and then wait to see what happens spontaneously with him from this deeper clarity.

CHAPTER FOUR – THE CHAKRA LAYOUT

This reading is designed for those who have some understanding of how the energy centres, or chakras, function in the body. It is particularly helpful for those who experience themselves more on an energetic level than a psychological one. By using the cards to map out what is happening in each of the seven centres, you can gain deep insight into the nature of the energetic process you are currently undergoing, as well as an understanding of how the individual energy centres are functioning.

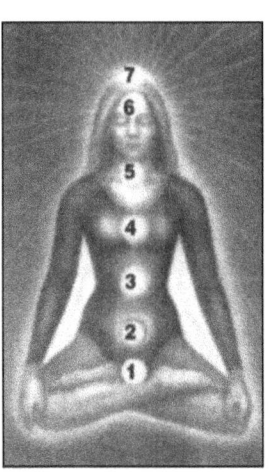

The Function of the Seven Chakras

1. The first chakra, sometimes called the root chakra, is situated at the base of the spine. It is our connection with the earth and the material world and is concerned with our survival programming: how we keep ourselves safe and protected in the world.

2. The second chakra, or hara, is situated about two inches below the navel. This is the centre of emotions and sexuality.

3. The third chakra, or solar plexus, is situated above the navel and just below the ribs. This is the centre of power in the body and controls how self-assured we are in going for what we want in the world.

4. The fourth chakra, or heart centre, is situated in the middle of the chest and is the centre of love and trust.

5. The fifth chakra, or throat centre, is situated in the throat and is concerned with expression and creativity.

6. The sixth chakra, or third eye, is situated just between the two eyebrows and is the centre for intuition, higher seeing and looking into ourselves.

7. The seventh chakra, or crown centre, is situated at the very top of the head and connects the individual with higher consciousness and purpose in life.

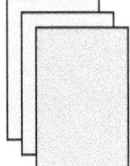

Picking the Cards

1. Spread the cards in front of you in the usual way. Bring your attention (and, if it feels good, the right hand) to the first centre in the body at the base of spine and pick the first card. If this card is not a major arcana card, continue picking one card at a time and placing them

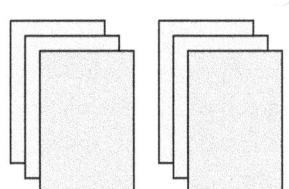

face up in a vertical line one under the other until you do pick a major arcana card. All the cards should be visible.

2. Now bring your attention (and, if it feels good, the right hand) to the second centre in the body, the hara, about two inches below the navel. Pick a card for this centre and continue picking and placing the cards one under another in a line until you pick a major arcana card. You should now have two lines of cards, one next to the other.

3. Now move your attention (and your right hand if this works for you) to the third centre, the solar plexus, above the navel and just below the rib cage. Pick the first card and continue picking and placing the cards in a vertical line until you pick a major arcana card.

4. Now pick the fourth line of cards for the fourth or heart chakra in the middle of the chest. Continue to place your right hand on the relevant chakra if this feels good for you. Again stop as soon as you get a major arcana card.

5. Again pick cards one at a time for the fifth centre in the throat, until you reach a major arcana card.

6. Now pick in the same way for the sixth centre, or third eye, just between the eyebrows.

7. Complete by picking for the seventh and uppermost centre at the very top of the head.

You now have seven lines of cards representing each of the chakras.

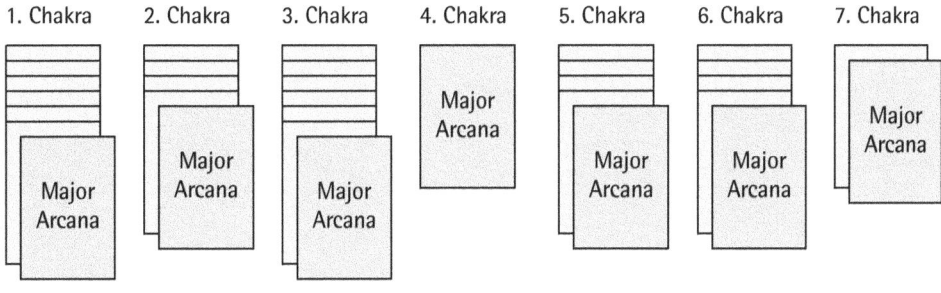

How to Read

The major arcana card at the bottom of the line represents the function of the chakra, its particular role in the whole of the being at this time. By looking at this card alone you can see what is happening in this energy centre.

The cards, if any, above the major arcana card show the process going on to reach or allow the pure functioning of this chakra. The more cards there are, the more complicated and involved the process you are going through in this area. If there are no cards above, in other words the first card you picked was the major arcana, then this centre is open and functioning with nothing in particular being worked out in this area. So at a glance you can see the centres where most of your processing is happening right now.

By looking more closely at the line of minor arcana cards, you can see the details of the process that is being worked out. To do this, start with the first card and let each one tell a story, step by step, of what is happening. It is like turning the pages in a book to reveal the next step. Even if you find reading the details difficult, it is relatively easy to get a feeling of what is going on, and very often it will correspond with sensations you have in your body.

It is not that the more cards you have, the more closed or blocked you are in that area; it is simply a matter of how much is processing there. In a time where nothing much is going on inside, you may have very few cards above the major arcana. In a time of great processing and change, there will be many.

Remember that the centres don't function separately from each other; they are interconnected and affect each other. By looking at where the long lines of cards are, you can easily see how these connections are working at that time. For instance, processing in the first and third chakras would indicate facing survival fears of owning your power and going for what you want, whereas activity in the second and fourth chakras could well indicate sexual relationship issues. Always keep in mind that you are looking at a mirror of the whole being, and from this reading you can get a sense of how the particular process you or the individual is going through psychologically is being reflected energetically in the body.

EXAMPLE OF THE CHAKRA READING

Yoko is a 50-year-old woman who feels that there is a positive inner change going on, but doesn't have any mental understanding of what it is. These are the cards she pulled.

The Reading

At a glance we can see that the main areas in which Yoko is processing are the Second and Fourth Chakras, the centre of emotion and the centre of love. From this we can deduct that she is working out limitations in the centres of intimate relating or connecting with others, even though there are none of relationship cards in the layout. This would lead us to presume that she is going through this process within herself rather than with anyone else.

The Cards

First Chakra
Victory, (6 W)
Knight of Swords
Tower

The **first chakra** function, The Tower, shows that there is a cleaning out of old restricting patterns around survival issues and the connection with the earth. It is probably this clearing that is releasing the energy that is being worked through in the second chakra. The details of this process are a feeling of positive resolution energetically (Victory) that has given clear focus (Knight of Swords) to allowing old patterns to fall away (Tower).

Second Chakra
Prince of Disks
Oppression, (10 W)
Virtue, (3 W)
Queen of Disks
Queen of Cups
Debauch, (7 C)
Pleasure, (6 C)
Failure, (7 D)
The Fool

The **second chakra** function, The Fool, indicates that the process going on in this centre is one of freeing up the emotional and sexual energy. The first card, Prince of Disks, shows that this is a relatively new process that has a clear goal. That goal is to experience the energy that is being repressed (Oppression) in a real and authentic way (Virtue), or to experience the authenticity of this energy that has been repressed. Through this, Yoko will more be able to rest in her own being (Queen of Disks) and allow her vulnerability (Queen of Cups). This will give her space to go into her emotions (Debauch) with enjoyment (Pleasure). From this space she is able to face the fear (Failure) of being open and spontaneous with her sexual and emotional energy moment by moment (The Fool).

Third Chakra
Works, (3 D)
Ruin, (10 S)
Lust

The **third chakra** function, Lust, reflects a lot of vital positive energy in the power centre. The process is one of creatively working towards (Works) letting go (Ruin). In this case of control, because it is the power centre, to allow the full aliveness and passion of the power energy (Lust) to be available.

Fourth Chakra
Satiety, (10 C)
Truce, (4 S)
Indolence, (8 C)
Queen of Swords
Ace of Wands
Knight of Wands
Wealth, (10 D)
Cruelty, (9 S)
Luxury, (4 C)
Futility, (7 S)
Knight of Disks
Adjustment

The **fourth chakra** major arcana card, Adjustment, which means watching, is a very cool, distant kind of function for the heart. It would indicate that all the passion and spontaneity of the first three chakras hasn't yet reached this part of the being, which would explain why there are no relating cards in the reading. The first card, Satiety, indicates that there is a feeling of enoughness, or boredom, with what she is feeling. But all she can do is accept (Truce) that there is nothing she can do about it (Indolence). From this space there is open-minded objectivity (Queen of Swords) that releases a lot of pure energy (Ace of Wands), which can then be directed (Knight of Wands) towards letting the process unfold in its own way one step at a time (Wealth). This will bring up the space to doubt and question (Cruelty) the way she keeps her heart emotionally secure (Luxury) and recognise the pointlessness (Futility) of doing this. From that comes the recognition that she is confident and strong enough (Knight of Disks) to be a watcher of her own heart (Adjustment).

Fifth Chakra
Fortune

In the **fifth chakra** function there is no processing or problems. There is simply a natural, uncomplicated flow with what is happening around the creative and expressive energy. This part of the being is not obviously affected by the processing going on in the first four chakras.

Sixth Chakra
Princess of Wands
Interference, (8 S)
Hierophant

The **sixth chakra** function is the Hierophant, showing that her intuition and higher seeing is involved in the process of experiential understanding. The first card, the Princess of Wands, shows that she is allowing and flowing with the not knowing and confusion (Interference) that is leading her towards this experiential learning (Hierophant). This would indicate that her mind is in the process of trying to understand what is happening in her hara and heart.

Seventh Chakra
Defeat, (5 S)
The Hanged Man

Yoko's highest purpose, shown in the **seventh chakra**, is to experience the uncomfortable changes (Hanged Man) going on in her life right now. Preceding that, Defeat indicates that this transformation through suffering comes from having to give up or admit defeat. This is the recognition in the highest part of her consciousness that there is nothing she can do, which is obviously connected with the letting go of control in the power centre.

Summary

There is a clearing out of old restrictive survival patterns that is enabling Yoko to start facing her fear of being more authentic and free in her emotional and sexual energy. This involves a letting go of control from the power centre that enables her to become aware of a complicated depth of old security patterns around the heart. The understanding of this process lies only through the experiencing and the giving up of trying to change or do anything about it.

PART FOUR

THE MEANINGS OF THE CARDS

The cards in the tarot are divided into two parts: the major arcana and the minor arcana. The major arcana, sometimes called Trumps, are the 22 stages or growth processes in the spiritual journey of man. The minor arcana are the different states of being human. This part of the pack is divided into four suits: Wands, Swords, Cups and Discs. Each of these suits represents a different element or aspect of the human makeup. Each suit has four court cards – the knight, queen, prince and princess – which represent different ways of relating to, or using, that aspect of the human makeup.

How this Reference Section Works

Each card will be presented in different sections. First is the 'Essence' of the card – the purity of its meaning. This is generally all you have to learn or remember. If you can absorb a 'feeling' of this essence in your being, you will have all the information you need to read the cards from an intuitive space.

The 'Descriptive Meaning' section goes into more depth about each card. It describes, in some detail, the state, or human condition, that the card represents to give a deeper understanding and clarity of the essence.

The 'Symbols' section gives some of the symbols used in each card and the astrological sign that represents it when one is given. There are over 1,200 symbols in the 78 cards, so it is not possible or necessary to go into all of them. Instead, we will look at the few major ones that are helpful for understanding the meaning of the card. Even these are presented only as background information that may be valuable and interesting. It is not necessary to learn all these to be able to read tarot. Refer to this section when you are first becoming familiar with a card, and when you are meditating on it later, but don't think you have to memorise the information. The same applies to the astrological symbols. They are only helpful for those already familiar with astrology. If you are not, don't bother with them.

In the minor arcana there are fewer symbols, so the 'Descriptive Meaning' and 'Symbols' sections are combined.

The last section, entitled 'Variations in the Current Life Reading', gives possible interpretations of the card in each of the thirteen positions in this layout. Apart from acting as a support that makes it possible for even a beginner to give accurate readings with this layout, it is an invaluable way of showing how the essence can expand into different shades and nuance of meaning as the card appears in different places or contexts.

CHAPTER ONE – MAJOR ARCANA

The major arcana cards represent the main life lessons or learning experiences that make up the spiritual path of man. These twenty-two principles are universal issues or processes that are experienced by every human being in different situations or times during their lives. In the purity of the tarot tradition, these cards portray the stages of man's spiritual journey. In daily readings they represent the encounter with one of these lessons. Because these cards stand for whole issues or processes they can be experienced in either a positive or negative way, depending on where we are with this issue.

The Spiritual Journey

Viewed in a very condensed way, we could see the spiritual journey represented by the major arcana in the following way.

In the beginning is the innocence of The Fool, the pre-ego space of the young child. Then comes The Magus, when we decide we want to do or say something about what is happening to us, and the ego, or sense of self, is born.

From here we move to The Priestess to find our intuitive knowing, our own inner voice, before we can move to the deeper caring and compassion of The Empress. Once we have learnt compassion for others and ourselves we are capable of taking responsibility on a higher plane for what is happening (The Emperor) both inside and out. Through this responsibility we are able to gain experiential understanding (The Hierophant) through the process of living. Now we are ready to explore the realm of love and partnership (The Lovers), through which we will have to learn the dynamics of how to use our power to get what we want, from others or in general (The Chariot). Once we know we are capable of this, we can move to a place of watching that comes from beyond the mind (Adjustment), and start to move our energy inside ourselves where we can explore our own inner beings (The Hermit). From this inner perspective, we no longer need to control what is happening and can allow life to flow in its own way (Fortune), and so rediscover the uncontrolled purity of our life force (Lust). This freed energy breaks through old conditioning patterns (The Hanged Man) and enables us to let go of whatever is dead or finished in life (Death). After this major let go we need time to integrate the subtle changes (Art) before we can really experience the reality and limitations of life and ourselves simply as it is (The Devil). This deeper perception and acceptance of what actually is allows outmoded concepts and security patterns to fall away (The Tower), and we are left with only our trust in ourselves and in existence (The Star). With this trust we are able to move into deeper layers of the unconscious and into the unknown (The Moon) to find the inner unity or source of the being (The Sun). From this feeling of unity we are reborn in the world with a much wider and more cosmic outlook on life (Aeon) and are ready to merge back into the whole (The Universe). Now, egoless and enlightened, we are again one with the spontaneity of life (The Fool).

0. THE FOOL

Issue: Freedom

Essence: Freedom, spontaneity, being in the moment, taking space, having the courage to take a risk, scattered.

Descriptive Meaning

This card is the beginning and end of the spiritual journey of the major arcana. At the beginning it is the energy of one who hasn't yet started the journey, one who is innocent or egoless like the child. His awareness is so in the moment that his energy may be scattered in too many directions, incapable of getting anything together or liable to do something stupid without thinking. He is the child, the simpleton, the fool. At this level he represents the negative abuse of freedom. At the end of the journey there is again this innocence and spontaneity, but now it comes from the space of being in tune with the whole and living beyond the control of the personality or ego. Here The Fool represents the ability and courage to respond energetically to the moment without the fear that comes from concerns for the future. It also represents the issue of taking the necessary space to feel free and spontaneous.

Symbols

The Fool represents an ancient tradition of wisdom through innocence or the chaos beyond reason. He has appeared in many different cultures in different ways, hence the complex wealth of symbols in this card. In medieval European courts he was the Fool or Jester who delivered his insights in a light-hearted way by playing at being the fool. Here he is presented as a slightly mad-looking version of Dionysus, the green god of Spring. His feet don't touch the ground but, rather, he hangs in space, open to move with each changing moment. His horns and the grapes are symbols of Bacchus, the God of Enjoyment and Ecstasy in Life. The Oriental symbol of fear, the tiger, is seen biting Dionysus's leg but, because he ignores it, it has no power over him. The crocodile is a symbol for both creativity and destruction – the beginning and the end. It also represents the reptilian or instinctual brain from which the lower level of this space functions. The umbilical cord that surrounds him and connects with his physical heart represents the innocence and freshness of the moment that comes from connecting with the wholeness of the universe through the heart. It winds around him in four spirals, each of them representing a different dimension of his connection with the whole, and each with its own symbols – too numerous to detail here.

Variations in the Current Life Reading

When this card appears in:

No. 1 – General Outlook: You view your life from the perspective of being free to move in any direction, or being open to whatever happens in the moment. You could also be feeling a bit scattered or without direction.

No. 2 – Communication: You are spontaneous in your way or relating to others and could be allowing your thoughts to be expressed as they come up – uncensored spontaneous talking.

No. 3 – Work: You could be feeling free of work responsibilities, or maybe just being in the moment with your work, waiting to see what happens without any fixed direction or goal. Or is it that you have this energy going in too many directions at once?

No. 4 – Inner Self: Your inner being is spacious, free, unrestricted and in the moment. It's also possible that there is the feeling of being without direction.

No. 5 – Sex Energy: This energy is very free, not bonded in relationship but available and alive to respond to whatever happens, or maybe whoever comes along.

No. 6 – Body: Your physical energy is alive and open to respond to whatever happens in the moment. If you are not centred, this could also indicate an uncomfortable feeling of being scattered and moving in too many directions at once.

No. 7 – Primary Relationship: Energetically you are not in a specific relationship, even if your mind thinks you are. You are free and available to make instant connections and respond to the moment without being restricted by relationship patterns.

No. 8 – New Perspective: How about just being in the moment right now and letting things happen spontaneously rather than trying to work it out.

No. 9 – Mind: You are thinking about freedom and space and probably wanting to have it. Or it could be that you don't want to make up your mind and are just waiting to see what happens by itself.

No. 10 – Peak Experience: The best thing you can do in the current situation is to be in the moment and let things unfold spontaneously. This might need a little courage to let yourself stay open and innocent to what's happening without planning.

No. 11 – Spiritual Message: Existence is encouraging you to take more freedom and space, to have the courage to live with the openness and innocence that allows things to happen moment to moment. It probably involves shaking off some of those polite personality habits that control the spontaneity of your energy.

No. 12 – Meditation: Being forced to live your life in an unplanned and spontaneous day-by-day way is the main area of growth in your life right now. You may find it scary, but it can also be great fun. Lots of spontaneous, unstructured dancing could be a wonderful help for you right now.

No. 13 – Overview: There is a general flavour of space or spontaneity in your life. In other words, you probably don't know where you are going but are living your life day by day. You may have the feeling that anything could happen, anytime.

1. THE MAGUS I

Issue: Doing

Essence: Doing or communicating, activity with intention, using available elements to make something happen.

Descriptive Meaning

Magus is another word for magician, which is the name of this card in most other tarot packs. He is the first male or yang principle in the major arcana, and so the first step out from the innocence and lack of direction represented in The Fool. When newly born, the child is simply a channel for the energy of existence, but at a certain stage in his development he naturally wants to 'do' things from his own volition. The Magus represents the ego or the individual will that wants to say or do something about a situation, or shape it in his own way. He is literally the juggler who takes and juggles all the elements or possibilities available to direct them towards what he wants to happen. Communicating or doing something with intention is the first step necessary for something to be created. The card represents any kind of directed doing or communicating. In a negative sense it can represent the habitual need to do or make happen instead of allowing things to be or to flow in their own way.

Symbols

ASTROLOGICAL SYMBOL: MERCURY

The Magus is represented by Mercury, the winged god of the Greeks. He wears a self-satisfied smile as he gracefully juggles the basic available elements and the different tools needed for doing or communicating. He stands poised delicately on a surfboard-shaped stand to illustrate the fine balancing required to make something happen effectively. His gaze is directed to the ibis's head which, because of the bird's ability to stand for long periods on one leg, is used both as a symbol for concentration and to represent Thoth, the Egyptian God of Wisdom. Above his head is the uraeus symbol, the Egyptian winged sun disk, with its protective snakes forming the caduceus or healing wand. Other symbols include the four basic elements of fire, earth, water and air along with the winged egg to show that what is born (egg) from the doing or communicating needs to be something on a higher (wings) level. The golden monkey represents both Thoth, the Egyptian God of Wisdom and Hanuman, his Indian counterpart. Here he is insisting on the importance of acting or speaking wisely as well as the necessity of flexibility, which is the quality of the monkey. The card is mainly deep blue, the colour of the throat chakra. Mercury himself is golden, the colour of the solar plexus or power chakra.

Variations in the Current Life Reading

When this card appears in:

No. 1 – General Outlook: There is an attitude of needing to do or communicate that means you are probably keeping yourself busy and may have difficulty just being still and quiet.

No. 2 – Communication: You are active and outgoing in your communicating, and probably direct and straight with what you want to say. Maybe you often have some purpose or goal in mind, something you are trying to make happen when you relate.

No. 3 – Work: You are putting an active and probably determined energy into your work, using whatever elements are available to achieve what you want.

No. 4 – Inner Self: You relate to yourself in terms of what you can do or achieve. Probably the focus of your energy is active and outgoing rather than looking in or being with yourself.

No. 5 – Sexual Energy: Whether in the sex act or in more general man/woman relationship energy, this is a yang force that is concerned with trying to do or make something happen.

No. 6 – Body: You are very active in your body. It could be because you are focused on doing something particular or it could be the energetic feeling of being driven to move.

No. 7 – Primary Relationship: You have an active, outgoing energy with your partner (or those closest to you) and maybe lots to say. It could be that you have some agenda about how the relationship should be, or are trying to make one happen. Or it could be that you have difficulty relaxing and being yourself in intimate connections.

No. 8 – New Perspective: Why not do or say something about the situation? It's no good expecting things to change without you making the move.

No. 9 – The Mind: You are thinking you need to do or communicate something.

No. 10 – Peak Experience: The best thing you can do in the current situation is actively say or do something about it. It's no good sitting there waiting; the movement needs to come from you.

No. 11 – Spiritual Message: Existence is encouraging you to be more active or yang in your energy. This may be by initiating and doing more, or by communicating more clearly and directly. In other words, get up and get busy.

No. 12 – Meditation: Your current meditation is to be aware of how you put your energy out – how you do things. It could be that you've been a bit lazy or that there are difficulties with communication that you need to work on right now. Either way, get moving.

No. 13 – Overview: The main issue in your life right now is around outgoing activity – what you are doing. Probably you are busy trying to make something happen or get somewhere in particular.

2. THE PRIESTESS II

Issue: Sensitivity

Essence: Intuition, subtle energy, refined yin energy or power, psychic or telepathic power. Spaced out, over-sensitive.

Descriptive Meaning

Being in contact with the intuition is a refined development of the subtle yin energy in the being. It is basically a receptivity or sensitivity to what is outside or beyond; the ability to pick up information in a way that is not of the mind or the senses, and ground it in this reality. It is like having an antennae to tune into subtle energies or thought forms that are always present but not accessible through the lower dimensions of the being. While there is dependence, this receptivity goes to others and we are not able to use yin energy on this level. In this way The Priestess is virgin or non-sexual yin energy. When we are in touch with our intuitive nature, there is an inner self-sufficiency and containment. We no longer need so much from outside of ourselves or are not so dependent on others; rather, we are able to draw on our own resources and trust our own inner guide. The Priestess represents the intuition or the ability to pick up on and work with the sensitive subtle energies around the body. It can also be telepathic, psychic or healing ability. In a negative sense it can represent being over-sensitive or the quality of being 'up in the air' or spaced out using this sensitivity or subtle energy to avoid being present in the body or feeling emotionally.

Symbols

ASTROLOGICAL SYMBOL: THE MOON

The Priestess is represented by Isis, the Egyptian Goddess of Intuition, and her Greek equivalent Artemis. The upper half of her figure is made up of soft curving lines that swirl upwards like an antenna to pick up from the beyond. The lower half of her body is solid and rock-like, covered by dynamic straight lines that move downward to ground her, and what she picks up from above, in the reality of the earthly plane. Across her knees lies the magical bow of Artemis who was also the huntress. The symbol can be seen as receptivity supported by grounding, softness and fineness supported by strength, and yin energy supported by yang, all of which are necessary for this highest and most subtle form of receiving. In the foreground of the card are symbols of what comes from this space – the seed pods show the beginning of forms and the flowers and fruits show the natural fulfilment. The crystals show the clarity of perception that happens with the use of this energy and the camel represents the resourcefulness and self-containment to travel long barren stretches, without nourishment or input from the outside.

Variations in the Current Life Reading

When this card appears in:

No. 1 – General Outlook: You are operating from a subtle, intuitive place, 'feeling' your way through life rather than trying to impose what you think on what is happening. It could also be that you are feeling a little over-sensitive or spaced out.

No. 2 – Communication: You are coming from an intuitive inner knowing in your relating to others. Maybe you are picking up on things that are left unspoken.

No. 3 – Work: You are intuiting your direction in this area of your life or maybe using this refined energy in whatever you are doing.

No. 4 – Inner Self: You are in a soft, delicate space with yourself, trusting your own inner voice and tuning into your subtle energies. You are probably self-contained and self-sufficient.

No. 5 – Sexual Energy: Probably you are not sexual right now. If you are, the energy will be refined, subtle and cool rather than hot and passionate. You are self-contained sexually, not in need, although you could be playing with a partner on a tantric level.

No. 6 – Body: Your energy is very subtle and delicate so you need to respect this and be gentle with yourself. It could be that your body is a bit over-sensitive or ungrounded and you pick up a lot from the outside.

No. 7 – Primary Relationship: It could be that you are feeling self-contained and not in need of a relationship but, if you are in one, your energy will be connected and tuned in to your partner in a very fine, sensitive way. Either way you trust what you know.

No. 8 – New Perspective: You could, right now, just trust your intuition and go where that leads.

No. 9 – Mind: Maybe you are thinking about intuitive or psychic powers, but it is more likely that you believe what you think your intuition is telling you.

No. 10 – Peak Experience: The best thing you can do in the current situation is trust your own intuitive knowing. You do know, otherwise this card would not appear here.

No. 11 – Spiritual Message: Existence is encouraging you to move deeper into this subtle, sensitive side of your yin nature to discover and trust your own inner voice. Intuition isn't reasonable, so it may take a leap in faith to put aside your rational mind and start listening to that part of your being that makes no logical sense. Using tarot is a good way to practice this, or an intuition or Reiki group may be helpful.

No. 12 – Meditation: Your growth right now lies in moving with or working with your intuitive or subtle energies. More and more, open into this sensitivity and trust what you pick up, even though it might sometimes feel risky or silly to do so.

No. 13 – Overview: Your intuition is giving you strong messages right now about the direction in which your life is moving. It seems you are listening to it, even if you are not sure what the consequences will be.

3. THE EMPRESS III

Issue: Compassion

Essence: Compassion, giving space to, mothering, empathy, sympathy, caring.

Descriptive Meaning

The Empress depicts the mature female archetype – fulfilled yin energy, the mother, the essence of pure caring. In its highest form, mother-love is the ultimate in nurturing, wise, unconditional loving. It is a compassionate energy that allows and gives space to what is being experienced. In day to day reality it is often not that. Mothering can suffocate with its need to give and control; it can be a concern with the other to avoid the self. In this way it can be the cover for an inability to receive or be vulnerable, a way of maintaining security in a relationship. This card can represent any of the different layers of 'mothering' in either man or woman. But in its highest and desirable form it is compassion: cool, empathetic, accepting, allowing, giving space to and therefore nourishing simply what is. It can be compassion for ourselves or for others, but we need to remember that we can't really have compassion for others unless we first have it for ourselves. Without this it is sympathy or pity, which has a slightly condescending sense to it. Self-compassion is basically the quality of allowing our own humanness in all its different colours and flavours.

Symbols

ASTROLOGICAL SYMBOL: VENUS

The Empress can be seen as the Greek Earth Mother, Demeter, or as Venus, the Goddess of Love and Beauty. She sits in a traditional passive position, her right hand holding a blue lotus, the flower of female power or wisdom, over her heart to show that she can share love wisely. Her left hand rests open, showing she is able to receive and does not protect her own heart. In this way she is balanced in her ability to give and to receive, and in her ability to take care of others and of herself. The birds represent different aspects of her female energy – the sparrow for sensuality, the dove for the peaceful way she faces life, and the pelican and babies for the ability to mother and nourish. The double white eagle emblem on the shield symbolises internal and external transformation. The fleur-de-lis at the bottom of this and the Emperor cards is both the western symbol for royalty and the eastern 'three-pronged flame' representing the union of body, mind and spirit. The background of the card is filled with a cool translucent light opening into the beyond, which illustrates the nature of compassion.

Variations in the Current Life Reading

When this card appears in:

No. 1 – General Outlook: There is an attitude of caring or being concerned with others that affects the way you look at your life.

No. 2 – Communication: You are sympathetic and empathetic in your way or relating and are able to give comfort and nourishment to others. Maybe check if it is at the cost of taking care of yourself.

No. 3 – Work: Your doing energy is involved with the concern or caring for others.

No. 4 – Inner Self: You are very accepting and compassionate with your own being right now, giving yourself space to be where you are.

No. 5 – Sexual Energy: This energy is more concerned with caring for the other than going for passionate connections. You are more the mother than the lover.

No. 6 – The Body: Your energy is very empathetic and nourishing. If this caring is going to others you may feel yourself energetically picking up a lot of what is happening around you. If you are directing it inwards, you are taking good care of yourself.

No. 7 – Primary Relationship: You have a lot of empathy and sympathy for whoever you are intimate with and are nourishing and caring to them. Check that you are not hiding behind a mother role to avoid your own vulnerability.

No. 8 – New Perspective: Why not just allow, accept, and give space to what you or the other is going through?

No. 9 – Mind: You are thinking about the need to be compassionate or caring, or it could be that you are thinking of your mother or your role as mother.

No. 10 – Peak Experience: The best thing you can do right now is be compassionate and caring, possibly with others but more likely with yourself. Try giving yourself a lot of space to be and feel where you actually are.

No. 11 – Spiritual Message: Existence is encouraging you to look and move into the female caring side of your nature. You need to explore the quality of compassion. It could include others, but first you need to learn how to take care of yourself and not give yourself a hard time.

No. 12 – Meditation: Your growth at this time lies in allowing, with caring and without judgement, whatever is happening in you or with another who is requiring this from you. Compassion is basically giving space to what is.

No. 13 – Overview: The main issue you are dealing with at this time is your compassionate caring nature. Maybe circumstances make this necessary, but possibly you are starting to become aware of how you can be too much concerned with others at the expense of yourself.

4. THE EMPEROR IV

Issue: Responsibility

Essence: Responsibility, authority, fatherhood.

Descriptive Meaning

Just as The Empress symbolises the role of mother, The Emperor, her mate, symbolises the role of father. He is mature yang energy, the one who makes decisions and who takes responsibility. The key word in this card is responsibility. When responsibility is identified as an external thing – being responsible for something or for doing the right thing – it becomes a restricting, controlled or controlling, burdening force. True responsibility is for the self and for the truth of our own beings; from this self-responsibility, true authority arises. It is not irresponsibility. It means that in any situation we take total responsibility for our own decision and its consequences. This invalidates the whole concept of blaming, feeling guilty, expecting or being caught in the expectations of society or of others. From this understanding we come from a place where everything we do is clean without expectations of others. We become our own person and that is the real quality of true authority. In general readings, this card can represent all aspects of the issue of responsibility.

Symbols

ASTROLOGICAL SYMBOL: ARIES

The Emperor is represented by a strong, powerful man holding a globe of the world topped with a Maltese cross, the same symbol of imperial dignity that is on the crown of The Empress. His legs are crossed in the traditional right-angle posture of law and order, which also forms the figure four, the number of this card. Beside him and on top of his sceptre are the heads of rams to represent his connection with the animal or physical world, and also the astrological sign Aries – the leader and individualist. The lamb resting at his feet with the white flag of surrender shows that his strength comes not from control or domination, but rather from peaceful submission to the higher cosmic laws of existence. On another level, the sheep is a domesticated version of the courageous wild ram and indicates the tame stupidity of those who always listen to the externally imposed responsibilities of society. The red colours of the card show the emperor's connection with the physical world as well as the fire of Aries. The symbols of the fleur-de-lis and the double eagles on the shield are repeated symbols from the card of The Empress. The Emperor and The Empress are a couple, looking towards each other and representing the polar opposites of mature male and female qualities.

Variations in the Current Life Reading

When this card appears in:

No. 1 – General Outlook: You see your life through the filter of responsibility. Probably you are feeling burdened by it.

No. 2 – Communication: You are coming from a serious and authoritarian space in your communications right now. Check if the authority is your own or what you assume by being a responsible person.

No. 3 – Work: Energetically you are in a strong place of authority and/or responsibility and can be counted on to do what is needed. Check if you are also listening to your own needs or just burdening yourself through your assumed sense of duty.

No. 4 – Inner Self: Your sense of yourself is tied up with a sense of responsibility: is it for yourself or for something outside of you? If it's for the outside, you have probably lost contact with your real feelings and desires or aren't paying them much attention.

No. 5 – Sexual Energy: Your energy with the opposite sex is dominated by a sense of burden or responsibility. Is it a habit to take responsibility for your mate?

No. 6 – Body: It could be that your sense of being burdened by external responsibilities is affecting your physical energy, or it could be that you are taking responsibility for doing something with your body at this time.

No. 7 – Primary Relationship: You are coming from a place of authority with the significant other(s) in your life and therefore feeling responsible. You are taking a kind of father role. This could be stopping you from feeling your own needs and vulnerability.

No. 8 – New Perspective: Have you considered that you could take responsibility for the situation you're in?

No. 9 – Mind: You are thinking about authority and responsibility – maybe wanting it, maybe wanting to get rid of it. Or it could be that you are concerned with your father or your role as father.

No. 10 – Peak Experience: The best thing you can do right now is take responsibility for the situation yourself rather than expect someone or something else to do it.

No. 11 – Spiritual Message: Existence is encouraging you to examine the nature of responsibility. Start by seeing that you are responsible for every aspect of your life right now and, if you don't like some things, look at what it means to take responsibility for making changes. The reality is that all you get out of blaming or expecting from others is resentment.

No. 12 – Meditation: Are you feeling burdened by outside responsibilities, or maybe being irresponsible? Real responsibility is something quite different. Life is creating many situations for you to look at this right now.

No. 13 – Overview: The main issue you are dealing with is responsibility. You are probably getting a lot of opportunities to become more aware of this aspect of yourself and to watch how the learning of true responsibility is unfolding in your life.

5. THE HIEROPHANT V

Issue: Understanding

Essence: Understanding, wisdom, experiential learning, knowledge.

Descriptive Meaning

True understanding is a transforming process that requires the uniting of the different parts of the being. When it just comes from the mind it is knowledge, not understanding, and this information will not have any real effect on our lives. The only way to acquire understanding and consequent wisdom is to live life experientially – having the courage to be present, to feel, to experience whatever happens, and then bring the intelligence of the mind into this experience to learn from it. Most of us either get lost in our own mental explanations of what we think is going on and try to fit what's happening into that, or drown in our emotions and forget the intelligence. Real understanding or wisdom comes when the head and the heart are united in an experience. It is the alchemy of feeling with reason. In its purity, this card represents the need to ground spiritual learning into what is real or actual in day-to-day life. In daily readings it symbolises learning or understanding in all its dimensions. Sometimes it will symbolise merely mental knowledge or trying to find answers just with the mind.

Symbols

ASTROLOGICAL SYMBOL: TAURUS

The Hierophant is symbolised as a religious figure seated on a throne made from a bull (representing Taurus) and two elephants that are the Hindu symbols for the same physical, practical energy as the bull. The figure can be seen as Osiris, the Egyptian God of Wisdom, and below him is his wife, Isis, the Goddess of Intuition. In the centre of Osiris' heart is their mythical child Horus, the God of Perception and Vision. These are the three ingredients of true learning and wisdom: understanding, intuition and feeling, and child-like innocence and curiosity. In the corners of the card are four cherubim representing the different elements or ways of being needed for true understanding to occur. The bull (Taurus) represents the earth, the practical, physical aspects of being; the Eagle represents Scorpio, water, the realm of emotions; the human face represents Aquarius, air, the mental plane; and the lion is Leo, fire, the energy of willpower and vitality. Here they appear as hollow masks to show the emptiness of theoretical knowledge. The three-ringed staff brings together the past, present and future in true understanding, and The Hierophant's left hand forms the devil's horns to show the dangers of empty knowledge. Above The Hierophant's head is the white light of expanded awareness in the form of flower petals, and above it the serpent of transformation.

Variations in the Current Life Reading

When this card appears in:

No. 1 – General Outlook: You are trying to filter your life through your mind to understand what's going on. You could be cutting yourself off from the experience of life in the meantime.

No. 2 – Communication: You are relating mainly from your intelligence, what you know. Is it your own knowing or borrowed? Or maybe you are in the process of understanding certain patterns around the way you relate with others.

No. 3 – Work: There is a process of learning or understanding in this area of your life. Maybe you are doing some kind of training.

No. 4 – Inner Self: You are genuinely trying to learn or understand something about yourself, but check that you are not lost solely in the ideas of your mind.

No. 5 – Sex Energy: You could be trying to intellectualise an energy that is basically instinctual and nothing to do with the mind. Or it could be that you are trying to understand some old pattern of relating with the opposite sex.

No. 6 – Body: You are trying to understand something that is going on in your body or physical energy and that could be hindering the process that wants to happen.

No. 7 – **Primary Relationship:** Whatever is going on here is a learning process for you, but whenever this card appears in an energy position you need to check that you are not lost in your head. Relationship is not an intellectual process.

No. 8 – **New Perspective:** Have you thought that maybe there is something to learn from your current situation?

No. 9 – **Mind:** You are thinking about wanting to learn or understand something right now.

No. 10 – **Peak Experience:** The best thing you can do at this time is simply be open to understanding. The current situation is a learning opportunity for you; stay grounded in the experience and use your intelligence.

No. 11 – **Spiritual Message:** It is time to open yourself in humility to the art of learning from your life. You can't do that while you think you already know, so put your ideas aside and bring your intelligence into what you are actually feeling or experiencing. This is your chance to get wise.

No. 12 – **Meditation:** It's probably difficult for you to understand what's happening in your life but you do need to; that's why this is your meditation right now. Start by letting things be as they are rather than trying to fit them into your concepts and belief systems.

No. 13 – **Overview:** The issue of learning or understanding is shaping the direction of your life right now. Be aware of the nature of real understanding and see if you are grounding your learning in the reality of what you are feeling and experiencing rather than just trying to work it out with your mind.

6. THE LOVERS VI

Issue: Love

Essence: Loving in all its dimensions and forms, loving relating.

Descriptive Meaning

The Lovers symbolises the learning through human relating that we experience in our search for love. It involves the principle of duality or opposites that is apparent in every aspect of existence, but which we experience most obviously in our search for wholeness by being with another. What is this energy that pulls us to the other, be it a sexual lover, a friend, a family member, a child? Why are we attracted to some people and not to others; why, in many cases, does the area of human relating make us either ecstatic or thoroughly miserable? Why does it 'get' to us so much? These are some of the mysteries of what we call love. Every relationship we have mirrors certain aspects of ourselves, often the parts that are underdeveloped or not recognised in our own beings. So it is through the joys and pains, the delights and the difficulties, the appreciation and conflicts of being with others that we learn about these disowned parts of ourselves. In intimacy we open and expose a deeper layer of our hearts than is possible in other areas of our lives. Unavoidably in this process we connect with our vulnerability and the basic childhood wounds that we otherwise unconsciously protect. It is through exposing these hidden parts of ourselves to the healing light of love that we become more unified and whole. Through this learning we move towards the source of love in ourselves from where we realise it was never the other we were looking for or needing, but rather the quality of being at one with ourselves and, through that, at one with existence. From this place we are no longer in need and our relationships can be truly based on love. In general readings, The Lovers can symbolise all dimensions and forms of our loving relationships with each other.

Symbols

ASTROLOGICAL SYMBOL: GEMINI

This card depicts the union of male and female – the yin and the yang, the dark and the light – wedded under the blessings of the faceless Creator. This cloaked individual can be seen as The Hermit, the symbol of inner wholeness and wisdom. The figure of cupid in the place of the Hermit's head illustrates the apparent randomness and lack of rationale on which love relationships are based. Everything in this card is in pairs. The royal couple, a black man and white woman, typify the attraction of opposites facing each other in the search for unity. The children represent the innocence and child-likeness that comes and is needed in intimate relationships. They hold in their hands the basic elements of relationships. The lion (Leo) represents male creative energy in nature, and the eagle represents Scorpio, the emotional depths of natural female energy, again two opposites unified through love. The winged Orphic egg surrounded by the snake represents both the transformation and the connection with the spiritual source of life that can happen in loving intimacy. The two statues are a Biblical representation of the light and dark sides of human nature. The bars in the background represent the danger of imprisonment and limitation that comes through attachment and possessiveness with love.

Variations in the Current Life Reading

When this card appears in:

No. 1 – General Outlook: You view your life through the filter of your loving relationships. Whether you're having a good day or not depends mainly on how you are getting on with those you love.

No. 2 – Communication: You relate with people in general in a loving way. You have the knack of communicating from your heart.

No. 3 – Work: If you are working, the focus of your energy is on your relationships to those you associate with in your job. If you're not working, probably your main concern is being with family or friends or working at your relationships with others.

No. 4 – Inner Self: There is a lot of inner concern with the love of another or others, and this could mean you are a little lost to yourself right now.

No. 5 – Sexual Energy: Sex and heart are meeting in a loving way. You are literally using your sex energy to make love whether you do it in a sexual way or not.

No. 6 – Body: It could be that you are in a loving space in your energy as a result of a close relationship with someone. Or more likely it is that your close relationships are effecting your energy. It is almost as though another or others are so close that they are *in* your energy system.

No. 7 – Primary Relationship: It is a time of loving with the other. Whatever is going on with your partner, positive or negative, it comes from the heart. Remember that love is not always 'nice'.

No. 8 – New Perspective: Maybe you could look at being more loving with others right now. Or is it that you have a heart connection with someone that you don't want to admit is there?

No. 9 – Mind: You are thinking about the beloved; it could be someone in particular or it could be that you desire to be in a loving relationship.

No. 10 – Peak Experience: There is love in your life right now; acknowledge it, go into it, and let yourself live whatever it brings up.

No. 11 – Spiritual Message: Existence is encouraging you to move on a path of loving and relating. Learn what it means to open your heart and let down your defences, even though it involves increased exposure and vulnerability. The path of the heart is very rich and never boring.

No. 12 – Meditation: Your loving relating might not be easy, but it's the major area of growth in your life. So stay present with what is happening, keep aware and you will learn much from it.

No. 13 – Overview: The major issue for you at this time is relating from the heart. It could be with one person or with many, but it is the main path you are moving along right now.

7. THE CHARIOT VII

Issue: Power

Essence: Power in all its dimensions; the ability to make things happen or achieve desires. Control.

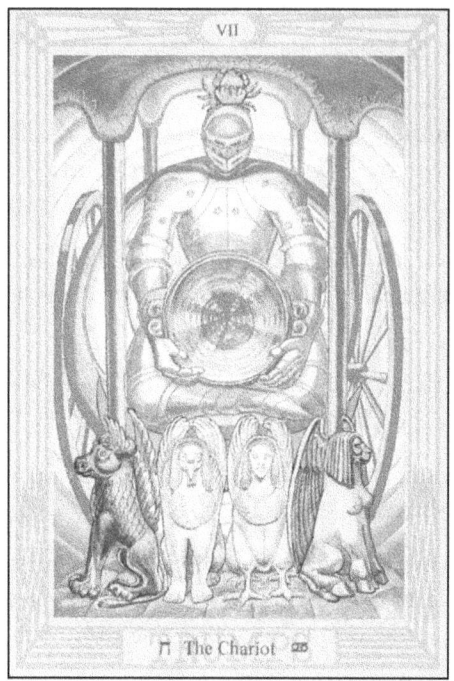

Descriptive Meaning

The dimension of power explains how we achieve our desires in the world; how we go about getting what we want. We tend to think of it as the ability to dominate a situation or a person, but this is not really power, it's control. True power is the balance between the male and female aspects of the being. The male or yang energy is the initiating, outgoing, driving and controlling force. It's useful for making things happen, but by itself it is a relatively crude level of energy and will burn out after some time. It is like breathing out all the time and never breathing in. Relating to others from this space is called, in therapeutic terminology, being the tyrant. When we relate to life from this space we are trying to control. Female or yin energy is the ability to be open, listen, allow and receive from others and from existence; to be available to and in tune with what is happening beyond the desires of the mind. On its negative side it can be lethargic, unable to move, giving power away to the other. This can be known as victim energy. Real empowerment happens when both the yin and the yang qualities are present and balanced. From this place we are strong enough to manifest or get what we want within the flow of existence rather than fighting against it to try and achieve private goals that are ultimately bound to fail. The Chariot represents all aspects of this power balance, but in a negative sense it often signifies control.

Symbols

ASTROLOGICAL SYMBOL: CANCER

The driver of the chariot is a powerful gold-armoured figure resting in a posture of meditation. He has no reins to control the four sphinxes that pull the chariot. Instead he holds the spinning Wheel of Fortune, the symbol for karma or the flow of existence, or what Crowley calls the Holy Grail, the symbol for the higher self. His power comes from his ability to tune into his higher being and flow with existence. The crab on his head represents Cancer, the astrological symbol for this card. The sphinxes are the same creatures as those pictured in The Hierophant and The Universe. They symbolise the four basic elements of existence, and show that all these ingredients (earth, water, air and fire) are necessary to have power or make something happen. They have exchanged bodies, representing the combination and unification of their energies that happens in empowerment. The great red wheels symbolise physical movement, the momentum needed to make something happen that can also be misunderstood as power.

Variations in the Current Life Reading

When this card appears in:

No. 1 – General Outlook: You are busy trying to control your life situation or to achieve your desires.

No. 2 – Communication: You are very strong and authoritative in your way of relating; check if you're being dominating or trying to control. Or do you work hard to control yourself?

No. 3 – Work: You probably have goals to achieve in this area; certainly you are going for it in some way. Be aware if you tend to push too much and burn yourself out, or lose contact with what's happening around and inside you.

No. 4 – Inner Self: You are dealing with inner issues of power and probably have yourself under control right now. Do you have any idea what would happen if you let go of that restraint?

No. 5 – Sexual Energy: You are empowered in your connections with the opposite sex, although probably there's not much room for receptivity or spontaneity. Check if you have a need to control this energy or to dominate the other.

No. 6 – Body: You have your body under control and may be feeling strong and powerful because of it. But you may also be tense and tight for the same reason.

No. 7 – Primary Relationship: You're coming from a power space here that could mean there's a power struggle going on between you and the other. Who is trying to control whom? Are you playing the victim or the tyrant? If you are not in an intimate relationship, be aware that while you are in this controlled space you may not be open to one.

No. 8 – New Perspective: Have you considered that you could get into your own power and go for what you want?

No. 9 – Mind: You are thinking about wanting to be in your power or to have the strength to make something happen.

No. 10 – Peak Experience: Claim your own power, stand up for yourself and go for what you want in this situation. It's not the time to sit on the wall or be a victim.

No. 11 – Spiritual Message: You are being encouraged by existence to explore what power means to you. Start becoming more aware of how you go about getting what you want in life. Do you tend to disown or ignore your desires and pretend you don't really care? Or do you push ahead and try to force life to give you what you want? It's probably one or the other and becoming more aware of it will start you moving towards the inner balance.

No. 12 – Meditation: You're having lessons around power right now and these are often not very comfortable. Generally we only learn how to use our power through power struggles with others, so be aware of where this is happening and learn from it.

No. 13 – Overview: Power is your issue right now. There could be concerns for achieving in the material world or conflicts with others. Wherever it is manifesting, be aware if you are trying to control yourself, or the direction of your life, and how that feels.

8. ADJUSTMENT VIII

Issue: Watching

Essence: Watching, witnessing, the state of meditative awareness; taking distance from.

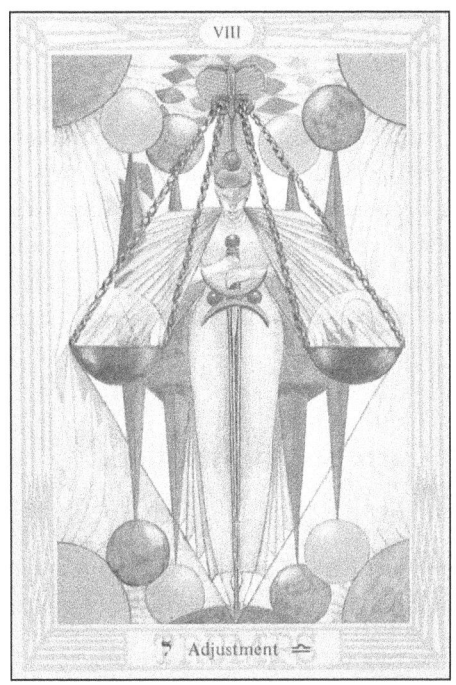

Descriptive Meaning

The practice of meditation is basically the knack of taking distance from the mind; of learning how to witness what is happening, both outside and inside ourselves, without being identified with it. From this higher awareness we are no longer caught into the dualistic mind that tries to work out the pros and cons, the rights and wrongs, of every situation. Rather, there is clarity of perception that leads to a natural balance and harmony. In some tarot packs this card is called Justice, as it carries the meaning of the higher justice or law that in reality everything exists in harmony or balance, even though this might not be apparent to the human mind. Generally, Adjustment depicts the practice of simply watching or taking distance from either what is happening or from the workings of the mind. In a negative sense it can represent avoiding involvement or feeling by standing back and watching.

Symbols

ASTROLOGICAL SYMBOL: LIBRA

The figure in this card is Maat, the Egyptian Goddess of Truth and Justice, who was responsible for judging the truth in the hearts of those who had just died. The whole card is an act of fine balancing. From above her head, and therefore beyond her mind, hang the cosmic scales containing the Alpha (the beginning) and Omega (the ending) that balance the truth of the universe. This also illustrates that real justice has nothing to do with the rights and wrongs of the dualistic mind; in fact, one opinion or thought and the whole balance will be lost. The Ace of Swords, upon which she delicately balances, represents the purity of mind. She is masked to show both her impersonal nature, and that her attention is turned inwards to maintain the stillness of mind and connection with higher self that is necessary for this incredibly fine balance above and beyond duality. The diamond shape in which she stands represents the awareness beyond the illusion of the mind. Outside this are circles representing formulated thoughts or bubbles of Maya, the Indian concept for the illusoriness of the world, perfectly balanced in dark and light.

Variations in the Current Life Reading

When this card appears in:

No. 1 – General Outlook: You tend to watch what's going on in and around you rather than participate in it. You could be feeling a little distant from everything.

No. 2 – Communication: Very cool, balanced, non-judgemental relating. You probably have objective awareness of all points of view, but are not very involved. Or you could be applying this awareness to your own relating patterns.

No. 3 – Work: You're coming from a balanced aware space with whatever you are doing, allowing and watching what's happening without getting too involved. This gives you a coolness and objectivity.

No. 4 – Inner Self: You have distance and are able to witness what is happening inside of yourself without being identified. It can be a very cool meditative space. Is it possible that the watching is avoiding feeling?

No. 5 – Sexual Energy: A very cool energy without passion. You are distancing yourself from your sexual energy or from the opposite sex, but not repressing. It could be that you are watching your connection with your sexual partner in a very objective way.

No. 6 – Body: Whatever is going on in your physical energy, you are not much involved in it. You allow the energy to move without identifying, which may make you feel a little distant from your body in some way.

No. 7 – Primary Relationship: You are just watching what's going on here. If there is an intimate someone in your life, you could be feeling a little distance from them. If not, there's no problem, but just be aware that you're not very open or available.

No. 8 – New Perspective: You could just take a step back and watch what's going on without being involved.

No. 9 – Mind: You either think you are just watching what's happening or that you need to take more distance.

No. 10 – Peak Experience: The best thing you can do in this situation is just watch; take a step back and allow what's happening without getting involved in it.

No. 11 – Spiritual Message: Existence is encouraging you to develop your ability to find the harmony in life that only comes from a higher awareness. Probably the best way to do this is through meditation, which is basically the art of taking distance from what you think and feel. If it's not part of your routine already, maybe it should be.

No. 12 – Meditation: There's probably a lot going on in your life that you need to take distance from and watch. If you don't know how to meditate, it could be time to find out.

No 13 – Overview: There is the feeling that you are standing up on a hill watching the direction of your life from an objective space. You could be feeling a little separate from what's happening.

9. THE HERMIT IX

Issue: Aloneness

Essence: Aloneness, introspection, going your own way, loneliness.

Descriptive Meaning

The Hermit depicts the quality of being with ourselves, of looking inside to find our own understanding and fulfilment. It is about withdrawing from superficial socialising, outward focusing and collective values to find our own depths and truth. When we know how to be with ourselves, the pain of loneliness turns into the joy of aloneness and the need to fit in, or to get things on the outside, becomes less. This space doesn't necessarily refer to being physically alone, although it can, but rather it is about staying in contact with our own inner being whether others are around or not. When awareness is directed inside rather than out, past experiences are completed with understanding and every situation becomes a medium for transformation and deepening wisdom. The Hermit is not only a light unto himself but also a light for others to follow. He can share his inner knowing; he is the wise man who can help others on their path. Usually when this card appears in a spread, we are being encouraged to take space for ourselves, or to find our own way or direction without outside influence; to trust our own truth without compromising to fit in with others. In a negative sense it can mean loneliness or isolating oneself from others.

Symbols

ASTROLOGICAL SYMBOL: VIRGO

The wise old man walks along carrying his own shining lantern to light his way. His concentration is on the Orphic egg in front of him, a symbol for the origin of all things or the mystery of creation, as well as the transformation and ability to give birth to new insights that comes from inner wisdom. The sperm cell also supports this image of connecting with the nature of creativity in its highest sense. His bent posture and white hair, along with the ripe sheaves of wheat around him, suggest that this is a space of fruition and maturity that has come as a result of growth. The three-headed dog at his feet is Cerberus, the guardian of the Greek Underworld, symbolising his ability to look into and learn from the depths of his own being. Apart from the bright light of his lantern, the colours of this painting are dull and uninteresting, showing that the outside world has no attraction.

Variations in the Current Life Reading

When this card appears in:

No. 1 – General Outlook: Your primary concern at this time is with yourself and what is happening inside of you. Or it could be that you're feeling either isolated or lonely.

No. 2 – Communication: You're not very sociable right now, either out of choice or necessity. If it's choice, you are enjoying being with yourself; if it's necessity, you could be feeling cut off and lonely.

No. 3 – Work: This could mean you are working by yourself, or doing your own project your own way. Or it could mean that your work right now is to do with looking inside yourself, of working on yourself.

No. 4 – Inner Self: You are very connected with your inner light and probably enjoying being with yourself. Maybe you are doing some soul searching about who you are or what your life is about.

No. 5 – Sexual Energy: This has little to do with the other so, if you are in a sexual relationship, you may be feeling a little separate and distant from the partner. This energy is moving internally and is not concerned with anyone else.

No. 6 – Body: Your energy is very inward turning and with yourself. It may be helpful to honour this and not try to push it outwards, even if you feel a little uncomfortable around others.

No. 7 – Primary Relationship: If you're in one, the other is either physically absent or you're feeling very separate from them. Whatever the external situation, you are actually on your own right now. This could be either that you are enjoying your aloneness or feeling lonely, depending or how connected you are with your inner being.

No. 8 – New Perspective: Have you considered just accepting that you're on your own right now, or that you need to look inside to find your own answers and understanding?

No. 9 – Mind: You're thinking about wanting to have more time or space for yourself, maybe wanting to go your own way.

No. 10 – Peak Experience: The best thing you can do right now is take some time for yourself; you need to look inside to discover your own answers. You're not going to find what you're looking for from someone else or anywhere outside of your own being.

No. 11 – Spiritual Message: Existence is telling you that it's time to go into your aloneness and find your own answers. Be prepared to face loneliness and keep moving inside yourself rather than avoiding that with outside distractions. If you can say 'yes' to what is there, you can enter deeply into your own being and become your own person.

No. 12 – Meditation: Whether you like it or not, and you probably don't, you're on your own. Don't try to avoid this reality but learn from it. Everything you're really looking for is inside yourself.

No. 13 – Overview: You may be living and working in the middle of the city and surrounded by close relationships, but still you connect principally with yourself and your inner world right now. You are looking in yourself to find your own way.

10. FORTUNE X

Issue: Flowing

Essence: Going with the flow, relaxing into life. Karma, fate or destiny.

Descriptive Meaning

From a dimension higher than what the mind can perceive, everything in life has its own time, its own meaning, its own reason. We often don't know what it is, but if we can just relax, allow things to be as they are, the current of life will take us wherever we are supposed to be. This can also be seen as the law of destiny or karma: the understanding that the future is simply a product of what has happened in the past and there is nothing to be done but accept and allow. This is not inactive resignation (although in its negative meaning it can be); rather, it represents a higher understanding that enables us to see the rightness of surrendering, or at least co-operating, with existence rather than trying to force life to fulfil our personal agendas. It is saying 'yes' to what is and making that work for us. The card indicates the rightness that comes from allowing life to unfold in its own way, from going with the flow without trying to impose our will or plan and control. In a negative sense it can be lack of direction, or avoidance of responsibility or action by taking the easy way out.

Symbols

ASTROLOGICAL SYMBOL: JUPITER

In the background of the card, lightning bolts strike and energy swirls like whirlwinds, but the ten-spoked Wheel of Fortune keeps on turning. This signifies that however dramatic or apparently difficult the events we are experiencing, it is all part of the natural flow of life. The three figures attached to the wheel are three Egyptian gods who represent the different aspects of the natural movement of life. These are commonly known as the three principals of Hindu mythology: Brahma the creator, Vishnu the preserver and Shiva the destroyer. They are also the three gunas or attributes – rajas (excitement, restlessness), sattva (calm, balanced) and tamas (inertia, darkness) – that describe the basic characteristics that make up cosmic substance. Each of these qualities is an essential part of the whole and life naturally revolves between them. To be able to flow with life we need to allow each to come and go in its own time.

Variations in the Current Life Reading

When this card appears in:

No. 1 – General Outlook: You have a relaxed, easy outlook on life right now. You're just flowing along with what's happening.

No. 2 – Communication: There are no problems – just an easy, allowing flow in your connections with people. There could also be a bit of an 'easy is right' philosophy in your way of relating.

No. 3 – Work: There is a positive ease happening in this area of your life. You are flowing along with whatever is happening without letting your private goals get in the way. Or maybe you don't have any and are just waiting to see what happens.

No. 4 – Inner Self: There is a feeling of relaxing into whatever is going on inside of yourself, of allowing the inner processes to evolve in their own way.

No. 5 – Sexual Energy: There is an easy connection with the opposite sex. You are allowing this energy to flow in its own way without making a problem out of it, whatever is happening or not happening.

No. 6 – Body: There is a positive synchronicity between mind and body. The physical energy flows easily and you are comfortable with your body.

No. 7 – Primary Relationship: There is an easy flow between you and the intimate other or others. You are probably allowing whatever comes up to be there and are flowing with it.

No. 8 – New Perspective: How about just relaxing into the flow of what's happening rather than trying to stop or control it?

No. 9 – Mind: You are thinking that you want to just allow things to take their own course. Whether you are actually doing that is another matter.

No. 10 – Peak Experience: The best thing you can do in the current situation is allow it to unfold in its own way. Don't get in the way; let destiny take its course.

No. 11 – Spiritual Message: You are being encouraged to drop control patterns and experience what it means to let go into the flow of life. Get out of your own way and let life happen through you.

No. 12 – Meditation: There are things going on that you can't do anything about and, whether you like it or not, events are moving in their own time in the only way they can. There is a lot for you to learn from simply allowing and flowing with what is.

No. 13 – Overview: There's the feeling that life is doing its own thing, in its own way and that nothing is required from you except allowing. Whatever needs to happen is happening on its own.

11. LUST XI

Issue: Energetic Aliveness

Essence: Life force, vitality, aliveness, total energy, passion for life, sex.

Descriptive Meaning

The meaning of this card is best understood when it's called 'Lust for Life'. It is not necessarily referring to the raw energy of sexual passion, although it can be, but rather to pure life force, the juice or vitality that makes everything in life a passionate affair. In traditional packs this card is called Strength as it refers to the strength that comes by surrendering to the life force or animal energy of aliveness that moves naturally through the body. When life energy, of which sex is the basic level, is controlled by moral or religious concepts, all the joyous passion goes out of life – the fire dies. This card symbolises the courage to put total energy into whatever is happening and live life to the fullest beyond these restrictive ideas. The animal part of the being is not tamed by control and repression but by acceptance and surrender, which allows this energy to move up into higher realms. The hero of *Zorba the Greek* is a great representative for the essence of this card. In a negative sense it can refer to a kind of 'sex, drugs and rock and roll' type energy that gets stuck in the over-indulgence of excitement or sensuality.

Symbols

ASTROLOGICAL SYMBOL: LEO

This card can be seen to represent the idea behind the myth of *Beauty and the Beast*, the parable of how raw bestial energy is made beautiful by innocent surrender to it. The beautiful naked woman lies back, apparently intoxicated or orgasmic, on the back of the multi-headed lion. She is totally relaxed into and surrendered to her animal energy. In one hand she holds an urn of fire, or the Holy Grail, from which stream the snakes of transformation that come through this surrender. It is this transformation that has her total attention. Her other hand holds a rein that connects to the lion's seven heads. These represent the different archetypes of personality that merge together into a single energy by this totality or passion. In other words, energy is one although its expression is various. The folded hands and shadowy faces in the background represent old religious and moral restrictions that are left behind with surrender to this vital energy.

Variations in the Current Life Reading

When this card appears in:

No. 1 – General Outlook: You have a juicy, vital outlook on life right now. You probably bounce out of bed with enthusiasm for the day.

No. 2 – Communication: There's lots of positive energy for relating right now so you're probably spending much time socialising or in passionate animated conversations with people. Just be aware that you could sometimes be a bit much.

No. 3 – Work: A positive area for you right now and probably your energy is going enthusiastically into whatever you're doing. Such totality is bound to bring good results.

No. 4 – Inner Self: You are feeling very vital and alive in yourself and it could be that you're capable of enjoying this energy on the inside rather than having to do something with it.

No. 5 – Sexual Energy: Basically you're hot! Whether you're making love or not, whether you're with a particular person or a number of people, you've got a lot of alive vital energy that's probably attracting and attracted to the opposite sex.

No. 6 – Body: Your physical energy is very free and alive right now. Used properly this vitality can make everything you do in every moment a delight. It can literally be a joy to be alive.

No. 7 – Primary Relationship: There's a lot of passionate energy for the other right now and it's anything but boring. It could be that much of this passion is happening in the bedroom; if not, you may well be wishing it was.

No. 8 – New Perspective: How about putting your total energy into whatever is going on, get some enthusiasm moving?

No. 9 – Mind: You are thinking about passion or vitality. It could be that you are enjoying it or it could be that you want it. If it is the latter, thinking about it isn't necessarily going to help.

No. 10 – Peak Experience: The best thing you can do at this time is put your energy fully into what is happening. It's not a time for control or understanding, just live it totally. Get into your energy.

No. 11 – Spiritual Message: Your spiritual path is about rediscovering your passion for life. What turns you on? What gets your energy moving? What gives you that buzz of excitement? You're not going to find it with your head, but by listening to your energy. If that means going places or doing things against your moral judgements, then maybe it's time you got rid of them.

No. 12 – Meditation: Totality is the meditative key for you right now. It doesn't matter what you do, as long as you do it with your total energy. The only thing you can do wrong is be partial or split.

No. 13 – Overview: It could be that you are passionately living whatever is going on. In this case, the experience of being fully alive is taking you wherever you need to go. Or it could be that it is the issue of having passion for life that is most occupying your attention.

12. THE HANGED MAN XII

Issue: Suffering

Essence: Transformation through difficulty or suffering, uncomfortable processing. Confronting outmoded conditioning patterns.

Descriptive Meaning

Change and spiritual growth is not always easy. This card reflects the energy of transformation, which is at best uncomfortable and at worst distinctly difficult. The process of becoming conscious involves having to bring light into the areas of darkness in the being that come from the old conditioning patterns of early childhood or previous lives. These patterns exist deep in the unconscious mind, so we are generally unaware of them even though they control how we act. At certain times we get the opportunity to confront them consciously, usually through being forced to experience how they manifest in limiting and destructive ways in our daily lives. The energy of The Hanged Man is the process of experiencing these negative blocks or 'hang-ups' with a surrendered awareness – which is the only way to change them. It's about having enough distance from the ego to see some of its games and let them go. It is being in the situation where the old no longer fits but we haven't yet found the new, so we feel we are hanging upside down in our world. It is the process of learning and growth through the difficulties in life. This processing can be physical, emotional or mental according to the situation and the individual. The negative side of this card is to suffer without learning or needless suffering.

Symbols

This card can be seen as the crucifixion of the ego, or particular ego trips. A naked man (the exposed ego) hangs nailed upside down, immobilised in his situation. His eyes, nose, ears and mouth are either absent or closed, depicting that his senses are all turned inwards to experience his inner process; he is forced to totally surrender to the situation. He hangs from an Egyptian ankh (the reversed cross), which is a symbol of the endless life force that is available for creativity or growth. The snakes that lie coiled beneath his head and around his foot represent the potential transformative energy (the snake's ability to shed its old skin to make way for the new) that is available through this process. The energy lines pouring from his head show that the transformation is going on largely in the mind. The body hangs in the shape of an equilateral triangle covering a cross – an ancient symbol for light descending into darkness to redeem it. The lattice of squares behind the figure represents the structure or 'squareness' of personal patterns and social conventions that no longer fit.

Variations in the Current Life Reading

When this card appears in:

No. 1 – General Outlook: You are not having a good time! Maybe everything seems wrong, regardless of what it is. Remember that this is just your attitude to life: check the other positions to see if your suffering has a basis in reality or is just how you view things.

No. 2 – Communication: You're having difficulties being with people. Expressing or making yourself understood is definitely an uncomfortable area for you. Maybe you can no longer play your old relating games and haven't yet found a new way to connect.

No. 3 – Work: Changes are going on in work that probably feel pretty bad. It could be that you no longer fit in the old situation or that something has changed in a practical sense that is difficult for you. Hopefully you are able to use the opportunity to learn.

No. 4 – Inner Self: You are confronting a lot of difficult stuff about yourself. Probably you are seeing old habits or conditioning patterns that simply don't work any more. Even though it feels bad, you could give yourself credit for having, on some level, chosen to see and deal with this.

No. 5 – Sexual Energy: You are going through some difficult process in your way of connecting with the opposite sex, or with your own basic life force. It could be with a sexual partner or with your own inner patterns.

No. 6 – Body: You're going through a major change right now that is manifesting mainly through your body. There may be some physical sickness, but either way you need to take special care of your health. It could be good to tune in more to your feelings and find a way to express them. Emotional energy that is repressed must be processed on a physical level and creates problems in the body.

No. 7 – Primary Relationship: This is a difficult time for you with the other. Know that probably the part of you that is suffering is connected with old conditioning patterns that you now have the opportunity to become aware of.

No. 8 – New Perspective: Have you considered that you could allow yourself to learn through the difficulties in this situation rather than repressing or resisting them?

No. 9 – Mind: You 'think' you're suffering but possibly it's all in your mind.

No. 10 – Peak Experience: The best thing you can do is allow yourself to experience and be with the suffering that is going on right now; much transformation can happen through this situation.

No. 11 – Spiritual Message: This is a time of great transformation in your life and it's probably not easy. Existence is encouraging you to be with and learn from what is happening without trying to make things okay or cover wounds with sticky plasters. Essential change is nearly always difficult in some way, but it is from this that we grow.

No. 12 – Meditation: Whatever the problem in your life right now – physical, emotional or mental – know that it is a great learning experience and make it your meditation. The biggest mistake you can make is to suffer without self-awareness so that you miss learning from it.

No. 13 – Overview: You are not having an easy time right now. That's just how it is. There is uncomfortable change happening as the old way no longer works or fits. It may be helpful to remember that if you use the difficulties in a constructive way they can transform the whole direction of your life.

13. DEATH XIII

Issue: Death

Essence: The end of something, death, the gap or void, let go.

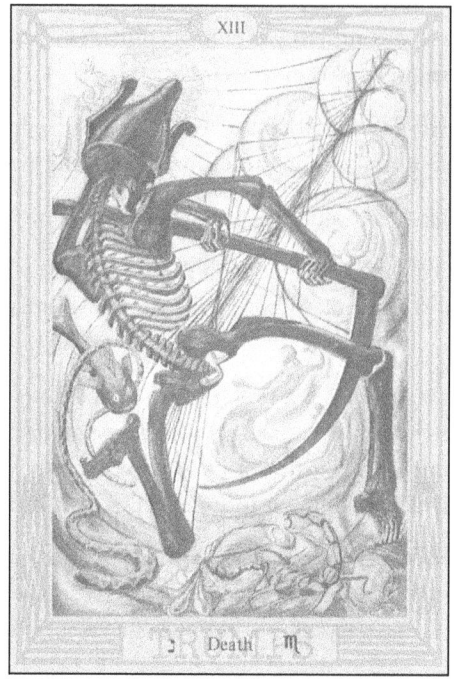

Descriptive Meaning

Life is a process of change, a movement from one event to another, from one relationship to another, from one stage to another and, ultimately, from one body to another. These changes cannot happen without becoming free of the old so that the new can be born. This card represents the act or stage of finishing one thing so that something fresh can come. Just as we tend to fear physical death, we tend to fear letting go of what is familiar or known because we have no concept of what will follow. But without allowing ourselves to move through these deaths, and to be in the gap that often follows them, life would become stagnant and stuck. To be relatively comfortable with this reality we need to see its inevitability. That means to trust that things leaving our lives are going because, in the greater scheme of things, they are no longer valid, even if we would not choose that to be so. This card can also refer to a process of grieving.

Symbols

ASTROLOGICAL SYMBOL: SCORPIO

The black skeleton poised with his sickle is the mythical figure of death harvesting his crop. At the same time the souls or spirits of the dead are moving upwards ready for birth in another form. The card represents the principle of purification: that the rotting of the dead provides the fertiliser for what is to grow. Death is represented astrologically by Scorpio, and the scorpion, which was reputed by early naturalists to commit suicide when in difficulty, is pictured at the bottom of the card, holding his tail ready to kill with its sting. The snake, which sheds its old skin, represents the letting go of what is dead, and the phoenix or eagle that emerges from Death's crown represents the transformation of the death process as well as rebirth into a higher form. Death's crown is an Egyptian funeral headdress that represents the expansion or consciousness that happens through letting go of the old concepts and ideas of the mind. The dying lily illustrates the transient nature of anything that lives, and the fish, a symbol for Christianity, represents resurrection as well as the passing of emotions.

Variations in the Current Life Reading

When this card appears in:

No. 1 – General Outlook: Maybe there has been a major loss or change in your life that is influencing your whole outlook. Or it could be that you're feeling very much 'in the gap' for other reasons.

No. 2 – Communication: There's some kind of cut off here. Maybe some old way of relating is no longer happening; you have let go of old patterns of behaving with people and are in the gap with how to connect. Or you could be feeling isolated and cut off from people as a result of actual changes in your social circle.

No. 3 – Work: Something has finished in your work or what you've been doing, whether you like it or not. It could be that you've lost your job or some part of it, but whatever it is it means major change.

No. 4 – Inner Self: Some deep inner 'let go' is affecting you strongly. You are looking within yourself at some kind of death.

No. 5 – Sexual Energy: There is a cutting off in this area of your life. Maybe a sexual partnership has finished, or you are feeling the absence of someone you have been bonded to.

No. 6 – Body: Either something dramatic has happened in your body or the letting go of something in your life is affecting your physical energy strongly. Take care.

No. 7 – Primary Relationship: Someone who has been close to you is no longer there. There is probably a sense of trauma at this loss.

No. 8 – New Perspective: Have you considered that whatever it is you're dealing with right now is actually dead, already finished?

No. 9 – Mind: You are thinking about the loss or ending of something or someone. Maybe it has happened or maybe you want it to happen.

No. 10 – Peak Experience: The best thing you can do is experience that something in your current situation is finished – it's over, it's dead. Let it go and then you will create space for the new. Don't let your fear make you avoid this powerful reality.

No. 11 – Spiritual Message: Existence is encouraging you to move into the gap. The past is no longer valid and the future has not yet come. It may feel a little bleak but it can lead to a powerful time of regeneration and spiritual growth.

No. 12 – Meditation: Something or some relationship is dead and there is much growth for you in going through the process of letting go and possibly grieving. Do it with awareness and make it a meditation.

No. 13 – Overview: There is a feeling of loss or the finishing of something in your life that is affecting every aspect of your being. Your future direction will unfold out of this death but right now you are probably in the gap.

14. ART XIV

Issue: Integration

Essence: Integration, synthesis, alchemical change, bringing things together. Refining, cooking, digesting.

Descriptive Meaning

This card depicts the process of integrating or synthesising disparate or different ingredients. It can be the joining of different sides of our nature or a situation into an integrated whole in a process of change so subtle that it can be termed alchemical. This can come as a result of major change (Death) when things in our inner or outer lives are so different that it takes time for us to digest or bring together the ingredients of the new situation into a solid state. This integrating process creates changes in the being that are so subtle or inner that we can't grasp what's going on, but out of them we experience major shifts in ourselves or our lives. Or sometimes it can be the feeling that 'something' is happening but the situation is still 'cooking', so we don't quite know what it is yet. It can be a process of refining the grosser elements of the being or a situation into a more refined cohesive whole. The traditional name for this card in other packs is Temperance, which refers to the refining of something, for instance metal. In a negative sense it can indicate a diluting or weakening, maybe through too much modifying.

Symbols

ASTROLOGICAL SYMBOL: SAGITTARIUS

The figure is an alchemist whose art was to synthesise opposites to create something higher and more pure. He is the final unity of the two beings who were married in The Lovers card. They have become a single androgynous figure, one side with a black face and white arm and the other the opposite, illustrating the synthesis not only of male and female, but of the different parts of the psyche. The dress is green, the colour of nature and creativity, and it is covered with the honeybees (one of natures great alchemists) and the snakes that were found on the gowns of the wedding couple. The supreme goal of the alchemist was to change base metal into gold. Here he is changing fire and water into steam, which rises from the golden cauldron in the shape of an arrow and forms a cloak over his shoulders. The symbols in this card are all about the unification of opposites. The lion and eagle, the astrological symbols for fire and water, have swapped colours in the alchemy so that the fiery Leo is the colour of water and the Scorpio eagle, a water sign, is the colour of fire. On the cauldron a bird, the symbol of life spirit, sits on the head of a skull, the symbol of death. The skull in also a reminder of the alchemical process of purification that follows death. The Latin sentence transcribed on the golden sun reads: 'Examine the inner realms of the Earth; by cleansing you will find the inner stone.'

Variations in the Current Life Reading

When this card appears in:

No. 1 – General Outlook: You probably feel as if some process is going on or some subtle changes are happening in your life, but you're not quite sure what it's all about.

No. 2 – Communication: There is some kind of subtle change going on in the way you relate. Maybe you are integrating ways of being with people that are still new for you.

No. 3 – Work: It's a time of integration either with what you do or how you do it. It may feel like trying to bring the different aspects of what you can do into an integrated state. Or maybe you are digesting certain changes that have been happening in the work situation.

No. 4 – Inner Self: There's a subtle inner integration or cooking happening inside of you right now that is probably leading to a refinement of your being.

No. 5 – Sexual Energy: There is an alchemical change happening in your sexual energy. It could be within your own life force and your programming, or it could be in your sexual connection with your partner. Whichever it is, it will lead to a more fine way of using this energy.

No. 6 – Body: Some subtle change is happening physically. The energy is refining as a process of digesting or synthesising happens through the body. If this is taking some physical manifestation, take care but don't worry.

No. 7 – Primary Relationship: Your way of relating with the primary other in your life or in intimacy in general is going through a refining process. Maybe a substantial change happened that you are still integrating, or maybe it is a natural adjustment in your energy and personality that comes from being with another.

No. 8 – New Perspective: How about giving yourself some time to just integrate what is happening?

No. 9 – Mind: You're thinking about how to bring the apparent paradoxes in yourself, or your life, together. Or maybe you believe that this is happening.

No. 10 – Peak Experience: The best thing you can do in the current situation is give yourself the time to digest and integrate whatever has been going on rather than trying to push ahead or make changes.

No. 11 – Spiritual Message: Existence is encouraging you to use this time in your life for inner alchemy. It may feel like nothing much is happening but, if you give plenty of space for this subtle synthesis to happen, you will find that certain gross aspects of your personality, or the extremes in your lifestyle, simply melt away and you emerge feeling more whole and integrated in yourself.

No. 12 – Meditation: You are probably faced with external situations that you need time to digest and integrate. Or it could be that there is the opportunity to balance certain extremes of your personality or your life. Whichever it is, make it a meditation not to get caught into the swings of what you think and what you feel.

No. 13 – Overview: The process of integrating and synthesising that you are currently going through is the doorway to your future.

15. THE DEVIL XV

Issue: Accepting Reality

Essence: The basic reality, suchness, accepting what is, dealing with limitation.

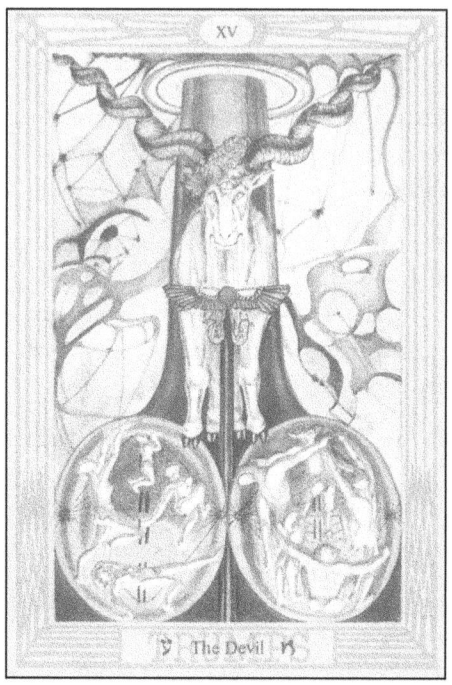

Descriptive Meaning

It is significant to note that this symbol is well along the spiritual journey of the major arcana. So much has happened in the previous fourteen cards and now we have arrived at simply what is. We might think reality is obvious, but in fact it takes a lot of clarity and awareness to see things as they actually are. When this acceptance is real and deep it is accompanied by humour, because how could things be other than what they actually are. Isn't it obvious! Intellectual man tries so hard to philosophise, understand, judge and consequently change life that he often loses contact with the simple reality. One of the most basic realities is the fact and limit of the physical body that keeps us in contact here and now with the earth, with what is actual. It makes us aware of the reality of birth and death, the suchness and pure physicality of life. This card symbolises the ability to accept and experience the actuality of what is and the clarity and insight that comes from that. It is pure experiencing without the interference of the mind and emotions. In a negative sense it can represent being stuck or limited to the physical.

Symbols

ASTROLOGICAL SYMBOL: CAPRICORN

The figure in this card is Pan, the Greek god of sensuality and humour. In the middle ages, when the Christian church, with its moralist judgements, started to dominate the western world, the qualities of physical enjoyment and other earthly pleasures were condemned. Because of this, Pan, the symbol for such pleasures, became associated with the devil, the dark force in opposition to the good of god. His wide-open third eye represents the ability to see with inner clarity that comes when we accept the reality that being in the body teaches us. The grin around his mouth shows the humour that comes from this acceptance. The column at the centre of the card is a phallic symbol that reaches from deep down in the brown earth and up through the female opening to the heavens, connecting this earthly reality to the spirit. The globes at the bottom are the testicles in which the sperm of four men and women are imprisoned in the body but ready to be born in the heavens. This represents the connection between the lower levels of reality and the higher, and the exalted state that is possible in the acceptance of this. The staff in front of Pan is the Caduceus wand found in many of the cards.

Variations in the Current Life Reading

When this card appears in:

No. 1 – General Outlook: You are seeing and dealing with things as they are.

No. 2 – Communication: You accept your way of relating as it is. Probably you are practical, down to earth and realistic with others even if you may sometimes feel limited. You say things like they are.

No. 3 – Work: Maybe you're feeling a little limited in what you're doing, but you are experiencing and accepting the reality of the situation as it actually is.

No. 4 – Inner Self: There is a level of self-acceptance in how you see yourself. You are experiencing your own inner reality and limitations – hopefully with humour.

No. 5 – Sexual Energy: It could be that you are facing a certain reality in your sexual partnership, or in your own patterns around sexuality.

No. 6 – Body: You are very physical and present in your body right now, even though that could involve the acceptance of certain physical limitations.

No. 7 – Primary Relationship: You are aware of the reality in your intimate relating, including the acceptance of certain limitations. In other words, you're not lost into any romantic dreams.

No. 8 – New Perspective: Have you thought about taking a reality check? Maybe things are not as you think they are.

No. 9 – Mind: You think you see things realistically.

No. 10 – Peak Experience: There is nothing to do in this situation but see and accept the actual reality of it. This is simply how it is and nothing can change until you experience this suchness.

No. 11 – Spiritual Message: Existence is encouraging you to take a major reality check at this time – not to try to do or change anything, but to look at all the different aspects of yourself and your life and experience what's actually happening. You may be amazed at finding certain very obvious things that you couldn't see before.

No. 12 – Meditation: You probably don't like what's going on right now or are feeling limited by it, so you're busy trying to pretend it's different or are doing something to change it. The fact is that nothing can change until you accept and experience the reality without your judgements and then much growth can happen for you from this situation.

No. 13 – Overview: You are experiencing certain realities about yourself or your life right now that are the keys to your future direction.

16. THE TOWER XVI

Issue: Disintegration

Essence: Major transformation, disintegration of the old, things falling apart, chaos, the destroying of old ego patterns to make way for deeper truth.

Descriptive Meaning

This is the major card of dramatic change and intensive transformation. It represents the time when old situations, old ways of being or old mind patterns no longer fit and are being destroyed to make room for the new to come in. It can be experienced as a time when external or internal securities are taken away, when previous ways of seeing the world are no longer appropriate, or when things are simply falling apart. It is a time when old habits or patterns in the mind are being ripped aside so that a clearer perception of the reality can happen. The mind tends to judge that something bad is happening at such times. This card is a reminder to allow the chaos and to trust that what are being taken away are internal or external forms that are outmoded and no longer needed. Sometimes it can be helpful to remember that this process comes as a result of awareness in the deepest part of our being; it wouldn't be happening if we were not ready for it on some level. In a negative sense The Tower can refer to blind or pointless destruction.

Symbols

ASTROLOGICAL SYMBOL: MARS

The collapsing tower building represents the form of the old that is being destroyed. This could be personality structures or old conditioning patterns, or some practical situation in life. In the lower corner, the mouth of a dragon roars powerful flames that will burn away this old, outmoded structure. The whole card is alive with the red colour of the burning. The four sketched geometric figures falling from the tower represent the superficial mental, emotional, physical and spiritual aspects of the being or situation that are no longer needed. In other words, the destruction is not of the real or essential. The wide-open eye at the top of the card can be seen either as the power of Shiva, the Hindu destroyer, or as the Eye of Horus, the Egyptian God of Perception, whose inner clarity is allowing this restructuring to take place. The lion–serpent with the halo is the deity Abraxas, who represents the expanded consciousness (the halo) of uniting form and spirit, life and death. The dove with the olive branch is a reminder that even in this chaos we can be at peace and be gentle with ourselves if we surrender with awareness to what's happening.

Variations in the Current Life Reading

When this card appears in:

No. 1 – General Outlook: Life appears to be chaotic right now. Probably nothing seems to be the way you think it should be and you're feeling quite disturbed, almost as though your whole life is falling apart.

No. 2 – Communication: There is a major disturbance in this area of your life and you certainly aren't getting on very well with others right now. Probably your usual relating patterns are simply not working any more and you're in the uncomfortable process of having to let them fall apart before you can find a more authentic way of connecting.

No. 3 – Work: Either the work you are doing, or your concepts about what or how you do it, are undergoing a major change. Probably you're not sure what's happening yet except that a lot of your old security is being taken away and everything is falling apart.

No. 4 – Inner Self: There's a major restructuring going on in your inner being. Old personality patterns are being stripped away to make room for a deeper connection with what is real and authentic in you. Right now it probably feels like chaos, and it may help to remember that it wouldn't be happening if you weren't ready for it.

No. 5 – Sexual Energy: Your old sexual conditioning patterns or performance games are undergoing major alteration. If you are with a partner it could be that the whole foundation of the relationship is falling apart. However this is manifesting, know that your connections with the opposite sex are transforming on a very basic level.

No. 6 – Body: There is a major restructuring going on in your physical energy. This may be causing disturbance or illness in the body. Whether you are aware of this or not, pay special attention to your body and do whatever is needed to take care of yourself.

No. 7 – Primary Relationship: There are great changes going on in your relationship or ways of relating intimately. The old habits of being with the other are no longer valid, so the security of the old games is falling away and hopefully you can trust that whatever happens out of this situation will be based on a deeper truth.

No. 8 – New Perspective: You would do well to just let things fall apart right now rather than try to keep them together.

No. 9 – Mind: You are having a hard time in your mind right now. Probably it seems like nothing fits anymore and you don't know what's going on. It could be that you think things around you are falling apart, or it could be an inner state.

No. 10 – Peak Experience: The best thing you can do in this situation is let all your ideas of how it should be fall away, and wait to see what remains. It is a time of intensive clean-out for you, and the more concepts and securities, or maybe attachments and possessions, you can let go of, the closer you are going to come to what is real and authentic in the situation.

No. 11 – Spiritual Message: This is a time of great change and healing for you. Move into it totally and allow yourself or certain aspects of your life to fall apart, if that's what wants to happen. Keep your focus on your fundamental commitment to grow, and trust that whatever is falling away from you right now is the non-essential.

No. 12 – Meditation: Don't succumb to the tendency to try and keep things together. Your meditation right now is to keep dropping your control and allow certain aspects of your life to be in chaos, as difficult as that may be for you.

No. 13 – Overview: It's a time of turbulence as a lot of old 'stuff' is falling away from you right now and your future direction is probably in chaos. Hopefully you can see that this comes from a place of higher awareness and letting it happen opens the doors to deeper truth in your life.

17. THE STAR XVII

Issue: Trust

Essence: Trust, self-trust, trusting existence.

Descriptive Meaning

This card symbolises the inner beauty and confidence that comes when true trust is experienced. This is not the trust of hoping that what we want will occur, but rather the higher trust that whatever happens must be right, simply because it is what's happening. This is the trust that takes us beyond personal opinions and mental judgements of good and bad. It is a state that transpires with the experiential understanding that our lives are not separate from what is greater or beyond. This can come from the trust in god or some higher power, or simply the awareness that, when we are in contact with our essential nature, we are in tune and at one with existence. From here we know that everything that occurs in the journey of life is being manifested from a place greater than the ego or personality. We don't have to do it alone. This gives a sense of great inner trust and relaxation in life as well as a clear perception of the reality of things. At this level The Star represents the state of pure trust, which happens when we are able put aside our personal desires and fears and let existence be manifested through us in the events of our lives. In general readings the card can represent trust in all its different dimensions, including the negative aspects of misplaced trust – destructive hope, naivity or the trust that is really avoiding taking responsibility. It can also mean dealing with issues of mistrust.

Symbols

ASTROLOGICAL SYMBOL: AQUARIUS

The figure here is Nut, the Goddess of the Sky, and also the astrological sign Aquarius, the water bearer. She is acting as a channel through which divine energy can be manifested on earth. In each hand she holds a cup from which spiralling vortices of energy pour down from the heavens on to the earth. Her focus is upward on the divine inspiration represented by the star reflected in the cup and, in total trust, without even looking, she allows the energy to fall to the earth in its own manifestation. As the energy or water reaches the ground it takes the form of crystals, representing the clarity that happens out of this trust. The flowers and butterflies at the side of the card symbolise the flowering and transmutation (butterflies) that come out of this process. It is interesting to note that every form of energy in this card is spiral, the shape that Einstein calculated as the basic movement of the universe. The colours are those usually used to indicate the higher chakras in the Hindu energy system.

Variations in the Current Life Reading

When this card appears in:

No. 1 – General Outlook: You have a very trusting outlook on life, allowing things to be the way they are. This can be beautiful, but check whether this trust is real or an avoidance of looking at and taking responsibility for things you don't want to deal with.

No. 2 – Communication: There is the feeling of harmony with those around you that probably comes from trusting yourself as well as other people. It is up to you to see if that trust is sometimes misplaced.

No. 3 – Work: You have a lot of trust and confidence in whatever you are doing or the work direction you're moving in. You could be feeling quite inspired, or are simply trusting whatever process you are in with this. Check the advice cards to make sure that this trust isn't a destructive hope.

No. 4 – Inner Self: There is a beautiful quality of self-trust and confidence in you right now. This is not the confidence that comes from the ego, but rather from getting out of the ego and allowing existence to be manifested through you.

No. 5 – Sexual Energy: It could be that you really trust in your own basic life force and, because of this, your sexual energy can move into love of its own accord. Then there is no need of the sex act or the other to move it, although you may well be enjoying both. If you are in a sexual relationship there is a deep trust of your partner on an energetic level. Or it could be that you are dealing with issues of trust around your own sexuality or with your partner.

No. 6 – Body: You are saying 'yes' to your physical energy; there is no controlling with the ideas of the mind. Literally, you trust your body and this probably gives you a confidence in yourself and grace of movement.

No. 7 – Primary Relationship: You have trust in your relationship with the most important person in your life. This quality will enable you to deal with whatever may come up between you. If you are not in an intimate relationship, you trust that is right, and probably that trust goes to those closest to you.

No. 8 – New Perspective: Have you thought of simply trusting what's happening instead of trying to work it out or to change it?

No. 9 – Mind: You have decided to trust what is happening, or at least are wanting to. Check with the card in New Perspective to see if this is a valid option for you right now. Sometimes trusting can be avoidance of responsibility or action.

No. 10 – Peak Experience: The best thing you can do in this situation is trust. Trying to understand or change what is going on isn't going to work. There is nothing wrong with what's happening even though your mind might want to tell you otherwise.

No. 11 – Spiritual Message: Existence is encouraging you to move deeper into trust, in yourself and the direction your life is moving. Maybe things are happening that make no sense to you, or maybe you don't know what's happening. There is no need to know; you can trust that you are in connection with something higher than your personal desires and fears, and that everything is happening as it must.

No. 12 – Meditation: There are probably things going on that you don't like or understand, or people around who you distrust. But your meditation right now is the act of conscious trusting. Keep bringing your awareness back to that feeling and move aside the doubts.

No. 13 – Overview: Hopefully you simply trust the direction your life is moving. Certainly, trust or lack of it, in yourself or what is happening in your life, is the main issue you are dealing with right now.

18. THE MOON XVIII

Issue: The Unknown

Essence: The unconscious mind, the unknown or unknowable, the mysterious or hidden.

Descriptive Meaning

The Moon is the symbol of the unconscious, the part of the mind that is literally not available to our conscious awareness. In reality, although we seldom recognise it, this – by far the largest part of our minds – rules us most of the time. It's just that we think we know what's going on, or why we are doing something, when in fact most of our moves, our motivations and our emotional responses come from the programmes and information stored in the unconscious. This vast reservoir of information contains everything we have ever learnt and every situation we have ever experienced, in this life and probably in others. The process of becoming conscious is the almost endless process of bringing the light of awareness into this basement of the being. The Moon also refers to the place when it is impossible to understand or to know what is happening, when we are forced to accept this not knowing and live in the sometimes vague and unclear space of the mysterious. For instance, before we can move into a new phase of our lives or our understanding, we have to move away from old familiar territory and into unknown terrain where we have never been before. This card symbolises the process where we are unable to understand what's happening or where we are going and are forced to live in the unknown. From this space we are more able to allow the unconscious mind to reveal itself and thereby become aware of hidden programmes or motivations that have been ruling us. In general readings it can refer to any aspect of the unknown.

Symbols

ASTROLOGICAL SYMBOL: PISCES

On either side of the painting, two guards stand in sentry boxes protecting the narrow path that leads towards the waning moon – the symbol of the unknown or unconscious mind. These guards, with their jackal heads, are the symbols of the Egyptian God of Death, Anubis, the mythical guardian who protects the path to the underworld. The wild dogs at their feet are poised ready to jump on anyone who tries to pass through the gates before they are ready. To move into the dimensions of the unconscious or unknown at the wrong time, for instance through the wrong use of powerful drugs, can be dangerous; it can literally lead to madness. The scarab beetle in the murky waters at the bottom of the card is the symbol for Khepri, the Egyptian God of Transformation and Renewal of Life. In life the beetle pushes a ball of dung in front of him: here he pushes the Sun, a symbol for the light that he is about to move into the darkness of the underworld so that the hidden can be revealed, the unconscious made conscious. The undulating shapes in this portion of the card are reminiscent of brainwaves on an EEG in the dreaming phase of sleep.

Variations in the Current Life Reading

When this card appears in:

No. 1 – General Outlook: Your life seems to be a bit of a mystery to you; you don't know what's going on or why. Maybe you're feeling vague or confused. This could be a fact, or it could be a habit of not wanting to look or see clearly.

No. 2 – Communication: There is something unfamiliar or unknown in your way of relating. Maybe you feel you just don't know how to connect with others or what is going on here. Or it could be that you are picking up unconsciously on things happening in the minds of others that they are not expressing, so you feel like you're getting a double message.

No. 3 – Work: This area of your life is unclear for you at the moment. Probably you're in a place where you're not sure what's happening or what direction to move in.

No. 4 – Inner Self: You are moving into deeper dimensions of yourself than you have been before. The door to your unconscious is relatively open to you right now and there is a readiness to explore the hidden depths of the mind. This can be fascinating so long as you move with awareness and don't try to find explanations or understand.

No. 5 – Sexual Energy: This is a receptive and mysterious energy to have in this area. You are in the depths of your yin energy and may be capable of moving into new and possibly 'strange' sexual dimensions. Or it could be that you're dealing with unconscious patterns around sex and simply don't know what's happening with this energy or with your way of relating to the opposite sex.

No. 6 – Body: There is something going on in your physical energy that you can't understand. Possibly it is something from your unconscious mind that is having to express itself physically because you don't want to see it or feel it.

No. 7 – Primary Relationship: Whether you are with someone in particular or not, there is a feeling of not knowing what's happening in relationship. The whole area of connecting intimately could feel like a mystery to you at this time. Maybe you have to let it be that way.

No. 8 – New Perspective: Have you considered that you could just relax into the mystery of allowing not knowing and stop trying to work things out?

No. 9 – Mind: Your mind knows it doesn't know, that it is in an area beyond its conscious comprehension. If you can allow this, maybe the unconscious mind can reveal itself.

No. 10 – Peak Experience: The best thing you can do in this particular situation is know that you don't know what's happening, and wait to see what unfolds. Whatever is directing your life right now is not in the control of the conscious mind. If you can relax with this, you may be ready to experience a deeper dimension of the mysteries of your own mind or move into unknown directions in your outer life.

No. 11 – Spiritual Message: You are at a point in your spiritual development where your conscious mind can no longer comprehend what is happening. The mind only knows what it has experienced in the past and you are moving into a space where the mind has not been. It may feel a little strange, but it's only a problem when you try to know what is simply not knowable right now. Much can be revealed to you, but only from a space of not knowing.

No. 12 – Meditation: As uncomfortable as it may be for you, your major growth right now lies in allowing your life to be a mystery to be lived rather than a problem to be solved.

No. 13 – Overview: Life is a bit of a mystery right now. Things may, or may not, be going on as normal, but underneath it all you are aware that you don't know what's happening or where you are heading.

19. THE SUN XIX

Issue: Wholeness in Relating

Essence: Learning to be whole in relationship, relating programmes; the patterns and limitation of contractual relationships.

Descriptive Meaning

The Sun deals with our ways of relating to each other. In its purity it represents the ability to include and illuminate all the different aspects of who we are in our expression in the world. It is the shining forth of our energy in a creative way with others. Our relationships are our main way of learning how to acknowledge and embrace the disowned or hidden parts of ourselves by looking into and learning through the mirror of our connections with others. When we unite with another in a true way there is an expansion in consciousness and creativity. However, in most of our relationships we are caught in certain contracts and agreements about how to behave, because this keeps us secure. In childhood we inevitably learn the right way to act with people, to fit in and get what we want from them. So, with the mother we learn to behave in a certain way, with the father a different way, with the teachers another way. Later, this same conditioning is carried into the right way to act in our adult relationships. While we are caught in these patterns we are stuck in stereotyped roles – the roles of mother, father, daughter, husband, student, teacher, boss – whatever it may be. This conditioned relating leaves us little room to be who and where we really are and, therefore, little room to connect with our authentic wholeness as it is mirrored by the other. This card symbolises the process of illuminating and expressing the different parts of our own beings through our relationships. In general readings, The Sun will often appear in the negative to represent our contractual relationships or relating patterns that limit true connecting. It is a reminder that bonded relationships limit our wholeness, inner unity and expansiveness.

Symbols

ASTROLOGICAL SYMBOL: THE SUN

The sun shines out from the centre of the card, illuminating all the twelve astrological symbols that represent the different parts that make up the whole. The uniting in freedom with another is symbolised by the two children dancing ecstatically together. Their butterfly wings represent the freedom that is possible and needed in relationship to avoid bonding; the green mountain on which they dance is the natural creative energy that comes from such a partnership. Even though this dance with another is such a joy, the wall at the top of the mountain, blocking the way to the sun, warns of the dangers and limits of contractual relationship. It illustrates that when we restrict our expression and expansiveness in relationships out of security concerns we are blocking our own path to unity and wholeness.

Variations in the Current Life Reading

When this card appears in:

No. 1 – General Outlook: You view your life through the mirror of your relationships with others. This could mean you find yourself playing a lot of roles.

No. 2 – Communication: You have strongly defined ways of relating with others. Check to see if this way of relating is stuck in old ideas of how you should communicate that are limiting your freedom to connect with spontaneity and truth.

No. 3 – Work: Your work energy is mainly involved in your partnerships with others. If these connections are authentic they could be producing a lot of creative energy to pour into the current project. But if you are relating out of security roles you are probably limiting your working potential and yourself.

No. 4 – Inner Self: Either you relate to yourself mainly through the mirror of your relationships with others, or you are taking a good look within yourself at the relationship roles you play.

No. 5 – Sexual Energy: You are probably in a committed sexual relationship where you play a certain role to keep the partnership secure. If you're not in a relationship, you are looking within yourself at your sexual roles.

No. 6 – Body: This could be a state of energetic inner wholeness, but it's more likely that your physical energy is reflecting the restrictions of your relationship patterning and roles.

No. 7 – Primary Relationship: You are in a solid, committed relationship energetically, which means that most of what you do will be affected by the other. If you are enjoying, good, but if not, check to see if the role you are playing to keep the relationship secure is limiting your personal freedom.

No. 8 – New Perspective: How about taking a good look at your relationships with others to see how much of your behaviour comes from playing out roles or ideas of how you should behave.

No. 9 – Mind: Your ways of relating are occupying most of your thoughts right now.

No. 10 – Peak Experience: The best thing you can do in the current situation is allow yourself to look totally into the mirror offered by your relationships with others and see what you can do about yourself and your patterns of relating. Don't hold back out of false independence.

No. 11 – Spiritual Message: Existence is encouraging you to bring your awareness into your ways of relating with others. There are things about yourself you can only explore through your relationships with others, so you need to be aware of any tendency to avoid connecting or showing what is real just because it feels more safe and comfortable.

No. 12 – Meditation: Relationships are your meditation right now. This probably means you are hitting conditioning patterns in yourself that are not pleasant to see, but accept that staying present and experiencing whatever comes up in this area is your major learning.

No. 13 – Overview: The main issue you are dealing with is your way of relating to others and you could be finding this doesn't leave much room for yourself. Examining what is true for you in this area opens the door to your future direction.

20. THE AEON XX

Issue: Higher Perspective

Essence: New perspectives that come from higher understanding, new beginnings or ways that come from that. Seeing the bigger picture, broader outlook, rebirth.

Descriptive Meaning

At certain times, often after intense inner or outer changes have happened, we are in a space where we can look at our lives from a higher or deeper perspective. It is as though our narrow, limited, personal judgements of things have been removed to allow a more timeless or far-reaching perception that goes beyond the smallness of the ego. We can see things from a broader, more universal, or higher viewpoint. It is the perspective we sometimes experience when we stare up into the starry sky at night and feel the vastness of the universe and the smallness and insignificance of our individual selves. From this awareness we have different priorities; we perceive things in a new way that gives a greater clarity and sometimes the feeling of being reborn with fresh vision and understanding. This card represents the ability to see things from a new higher perspective and move into new directions or find new ways of dealing with things as a result of this vision. It can also be simply seeing the bigger picture in a situation. In a negative sense it could imply getting so lost in the broader outlook that we lose touch with the details.

Symbols

The dark blue shape encircling the card is the stylised figure of the Egyptian sky goddess, Nut, who leans over the earth so that her body supports and provides a background for the stars. The large transparent figure can be seen as Osiris, the Egyptian God of Wisdom, who is depicted here in a childlike form to represent the innocence needed for wisdom and fresh perspectives. Behind this figure and inside the womb-like shape is a falcon-headed older form of the same god, showing the ancient wisdom that we can give birth to when we put aside personal opinions and beliefs. The three embryo figures at the bottom of the picture represent the new forms and perceptions that can be born out of this fresh understanding.

Variations in the Current Life Reading

When this card appears in:

No. 1 – General Outlook: Something has changed in the way you're viewing your world. You might not even know quite what it is; just the feeling of standing back and taking a broader perspective on what is happening.

No. 2 – Communication: There is something new happening in your way of relating with people. You have taken a step back from your old habits or subjective opinions and this has given you a wider viewpoint from which to see and connect with others.

No. 3 – Work: There is something new opening out for you here. It could be that your work or how you are looking at it is moving into wider or more far-reaching areas. Or it could be that you are simply looking at what you are doing from a different viewpoint. Either way it will probably bring about positive changes.

No. 4 – Inner Self: You are looking into yourself in a new way. Some old ideas of who you are or how you should be have been dropped so that you can see within yourself with fresh clarity. An inner door has opened.

No. 5 – Sexual Energy: Either there is someone new in your sex life, or you are starting to view or relate to your partner, or the opposite sex in general, in a different and more mature way. Be aware that your energy could be very fertile right now.

No. 6 – Body: There is a fresh, new way of experiencing your energy that could connect with a change in physical routine. Or it could be a shifting and opening in the patterns of the mind that is affecting the physical energy. Remember that body and mind are not separate, so what happens in one affects the other.

No. 7 – Primary Relationship: Maybe there's been a clearing of old judgements with your loved one, or maybe something has changed within you. Either way you have a new perspective around intimate relationship right now that is based on a higher, less personal viewpoint.

No. 8 – New Perspective: Have you considered that you could view your situation in a new way that takes into account viewpoints other than your own?

No. 9 – Mind: You are thinking about trying to find a better way to look at or deal with things. This probably comes from the recognition that something in the old needs to change.

No. 10 – Peak Experience: The best thing you can do in the current situation is find a whole new way of dealing with or looking at it. You need to get out of your tunnel vision so that you can view what's happening from a broader and probably less subjective perspective.

No. 11 – Spiritual Message: Existence is encouraging you to change your way of looking at your life to allow something new to happen. It is not enough to function through the smallness of your personal ego and its old opinions and beliefs. Life is a lot bigger than what you think it is and, if you need to remind yourself of this, spend a couple of hours staring up at the vastness of the starry sky. Some kind of workshop or adventure could be a good impetus to change your perspective.

No. 12 – Meditation: You need to keep remembering to look at whatever is happening from a less personalised space. Something new is starting to happen, but it takes awareness not to fall back into the subjective judgements and viewpoints that keep you stuck in the old.

No. 13 – Overview: You are moving in a new direction in your life, probably as the result of a fresh vision of what it's all about. You may feel that your priorities have changed and this is giving you a broader perspective. It could seem as though you've stepped back from your life and are therefore seeing it, or some part of it, in a different context.

21. THE UNIVERSE XXI

Issue: Completion

Essence: The organic completion or natural flowering of a situation. Unavoidable consequences. Dissolving into the whole.

Descriptive Meaning

This card completes the journey that began with The Fool. With his spontaneous stepping into the unknown a seed was planted that was picked up by The Magus and now comes to fruition in The Universe. This completion is as natural and organic as the growth of a seed that finally comes to flower. From the moment of its conception in seed form, the flower can only become what it now is. For example, a marigold seed can only produce a marigold flower; it is inevitable. So it is with the situation that this card represents. It has an inexorable inevitability and rightness – whatever it is. Things have come to a head; what was, is coming to completion, and it is unavoidable. It doesn't necessarily represent the end of something – there could well be another phase or stage – but the way things have been up till now will change as unavoidably as the petals of the flower must fall and the ripe fruit must drop. On the ultimate level in the spiritual journey this is the point where the drop falls into the ocean, the part merges with the whole, the individual becomes one with existence. This is the inevitable conclusion of the spiritual journey of all beings. From this place of completion, we are again The Fool: free and spontaneous, in the moment, at one with existence and ready to respond to whatever it may send. In general readings, The Universe is the organic completion or fruition of something.

Symbols

ASTROLOGICAL SYMBOL: SATURN

A woman dances naked in a womb-like space bordered only by a fine net that represents the insubstantial nature of what separates the individual from the whole. She holds a sickle to show her ability to cut through this flimsy mesh. The head of the sickle comes from the Eye of Horus, the symbol for the Egyptian God of Perception, indicating that it is only perception and awareness that is needed to cut through this web of separation. The woman stands on the head of a large snake, representing that the transformation (snake) is now tamed and complete. The pantheon sketched at the bottom of the card is the Greek symbol for the home of the gods. It depicts that at this stage of our development we are basically the same as the gods. The four cherubim in the corners of the picture represent the basic aspects of human nature that are united in this space: energy – Leo, the lion; body – Taurus, the bull; emotions – Scorpio, the eagle; and mind – Aquarius, the face. In The Hierophant these cherubim were the hollow masks of empty knowledge; here they are channels for existence.

Variations in the Current Life Reading

When this card appears in:

No. 1 – General Outlook: You are feeling that a phase of your life, or something in it, is naturally completing and that there is nothing you can do but allow this to happen.

No. 2 – Communication: You have reached a place where you are seeing that something in your way of connecting with people is naturally coming to an end.

No. 3 – Work: Something around your work situation or what you have been doing with your energy has reached a place of fruition. Whether or not you like this outcome or result, you are seeing the natural fulfilment of what has gone before and can recognise that it is the only way things could have worked out.

No. 4 – Inner Self: There is some flowering happening within your inner being. You recognise that there is nothing to be done but allow and see what develops. Trying to make something happen would be like pulling the petals off a half open flower to see what it would have bloomed into.

No. 5 – Sexual Energy: Your basic energy connection with your partner or with the opposite sex is reaching the natural flowering of a certain phase. You know that everything is perfect the way it is, and changes are happening of their own accord.

No. 6 – Body: Some natural energy cycle is completing. This could be something physical you have been doing or some way you have been relating to your body. Or it could be a natural time of change that has something to do with aging or some other organic happening.

No. 7 – Primary Relationship: You are reaching a natural change point in intimate relating. There is nothing wrong; it's inevitable that certain phases in any connection complete so that the relationship can grow and develop. You can trust the inevitability of change and let it happen.

No. 8 – New Perspective: Has it occurred to you that what's happening now couldn't be any different: it's just a natural development of what's gone before?

No. 9 – Mind: You are thinking about the fulfilment of something. Maybe you want this to happen, maybe not, but the mind is preoccupied by what it sees as this inevitability.

No. 10 – Peak Experience: The best thing you can do in this situation is allow things to take their own course and develop in their own way. There is a natural fulfilment or conclusion that needs to be reached and you are not at it yet. When this has happened you will know.

No. 11 – Spiritual Message: Existence is encouraging you to recognise that a certain phase of your life is reaching an organic completion. There is no point in trying to judge whether this is good or bad. Instead, you are asked to see the inevitability of what is happening, to be patient and allow this flowering to have its own timing.

No. 12 – Meditation: You need to give time to allow whatever is happening in your life to ripen, to reach its natural fruition. If you try to hurry up the process or cut it off, you will miss the growth that is still needed in this situation.

No. 13 – Overview: There is a feeling of something coming to a natural conclusion in your life right now. Probably you are accepting the inevitability of letting things take their own form and waiting to see what direction develops from this.

CHAPTER TWO – THE MINOR ARCANA

The minor arcana is divided into four suits: Wands, Swords, Cups and Discs. Each of these represents one of the basic elements in nature, which in turn represents one of the aspects of human nature. Wands are the symbol for fire that represents pure energy and the way of using it that incorporates will. Swords symbolise the air element and represent the mind and how it works. Cups are the symbols of water and represent the emotional, feeling states and their expression. Discs symbolise the earth element and represent the physical, practical, material side of life. The cards ace (one) through to ten are representations of states or experiences that happen in each of these different areas of the being. The court cards represent a certain way of using or relating to those states rather than the state itself; in other words, how you relate to your energy, your mind, your emotions and your body.

Before studying the minor arcana in detail, it is suggested that you lay out the cards in their suits and look at them all together. As you look at the court cards you will see very clearly how the colours and symbols in the pictures represent the different elements. Wands people are red and surrounded by fire, swords are grey and white and live in the air. The cups people are bluish and related to water, while the disks are full of the rich natural greens and browns of the earth.

As you look at the rest of the suit you will start to get a feeling of how the meaning of each is represented by the shapes and colours of the symbol involved and the way they are positioned on the card.

The Court Cards

The court cards represent a particular way of using or mastering the particular element.

The Knight, which is used in this pack instead of the King used in most tarot packs, represents the mature or established yang, or male quality or use of that element. Yang energy is outgoing, active or expanding. He could also be seen as the fire aspect of that particular element.

The Queen represents the mature and established yin, or female quality or use of that element. Yin energy is inward moving, receptive, still, or deepening. She could be seen as the watery aspect of that particular element.

The Prince, which is used in this pack instead of the Page used in many tarot packs, represents the younger, less mature or solid quality of the element that is outgoing, active or moving. He has a teenage quality and could be seen as the air aspect of that particular element.

The Princess, which is not used in most tarot packs, represents the younger, less mature or solid yin or female quality of the element that is ingoing, still, centred or receptive. She could be seen as the earth aspect of that particular element.

If you decide to use the cards in this way, the court cards can also represent particular people who currently mirror that element in your life. The Knights and Queens will tend to be around your age or older, and the Princes and Princesses will represent either children or people you feel to be considerably younger than yourself. This manual doesn't use the cards in this way.

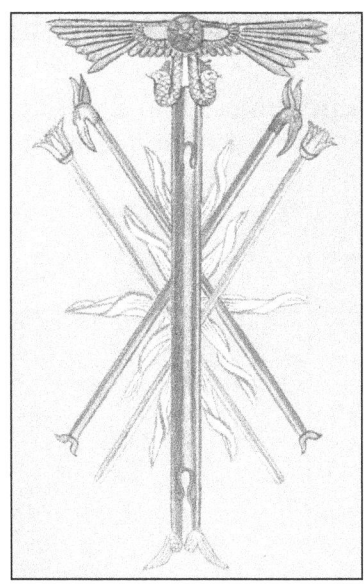

WANDS SYMBOLISE FIRE AND REPRESENT THE USE OF ENERGY, LIFE FORCE OR WILL

KNIGHT OF WANDS

Essence: Moving in a specific outward direction; focused or dynamic movement.

Descriptive Meaning and Symbols

The Knight of Wands represents the mature yang use of energy or will. He is charging ahead on horseback, a solid cloak of flames pouring outward from his shoulders and the burning torch of the Ace of Wands in his hand. He is using the pure energy of fire to burn away all obstacles that might limit his movement or his direction. He has the vision to know where he is going and won't let anything get in his way. He is established and mature in the use of his energy and in his ability to get where he wants to go. His reptilian armour symbolises his ability to leave behind all that is old or outgrown, like a snake sheds its skin, so that he can keep moving and growing. He represents the use of energy or will that is focused, strong and outgoing – the quality of moving in a particular direction. In a negative sense this can indicate compulsive movement or action, or the inability to be still.

Variations in the Current Life Reading

When this card appears in:

No. 1 – General Outlook: You have a determined outlook on your life that keeps you moving. Possibly you have some specific direction in mind and are energetically heading in that way.

No. 2 – Communication: You relate in an outgoing and probably forceful way. You know what you want to say or how you want things to be and are energetically strong and determined in your delivery.

No. 3 – Work: There is a mature, purposeful energy going into whatever you are doing right now. Things are moving. Or maybe it is you who are moving from one workplace to another.

No. 4 – Inner Self: You are in tune with your yang energy and use it to move actively in a positive growthful way. Probably your focus is more out than in and you relate to yourself in terms of what you do.

No. 5 – Sexual Energy: Whether you have a sexual partner or not, you have active confident yang energy with the opposite sex.

No. 6 – Body: Your physical energy is strong, active and outgoing right now; you're probably moving your body a lot in a purposeful way.

No. 7 – Primary Relationship: Whether you are with someone in particular or not, your relating energy is outgoing and determined. You know where you want to go or how you want things to be with the other.

No. 8 – New Perspective: Have you considered that you need to focus your energy and get yourself moving?

No. 9 – Mind: You are thinking about the need for movement or growth in a specific direction.

No. 10 – Peak Experience: The best thing you can do in this situation is to keep moving your energy out in a clear determined direction even if you're not quite sure why or where you are moving. Or it could be that you need to make a particular move.

No. 11 – Spiritual Message: Existence is encouraging you to get your energy moving in a focused way. This means finding the positive yang side of your nature and being prepared to leave behind old concepts and opinions that might be limiting your progress. Find that inner strength and maturity inside that enables you to go for what you want.

No. 12 – Meditation: You need to focus your energy in a positive direction, or literally get yourself moving. This must be difficult for you right now or you wouldn't have picked it as your meditation.

No. 13 – Overview: There is a flavour of determined positive movement that suggests you know where you want to head in your life.

QUEEN OF WANDS

Essence: Receiving or inward directed energy;
inner awareness of energy; using available energy for self-awareness.

Queen of Wands

Descriptive Meaning and Symbols

The Queen of Wands represents the mature yin way of relating to energy. She sits quietly on her throne of flames, her eyes closed to show that her focus is inwards. The flames around her move upwards into her being. She is taking in and experiencing the energy around her. The hand resting softly on the leopard shows her connection to her own natural energy and the loving inclusion of her instincts and passion. The rays that form a crown around her head indicate the inner understanding of the energy she experiences. This card symbolises the quality of relating to energy in a receptive or inner way. It is the yin or female way of using energy – taking in or being still with what is happening – which creates the space for inner awareness. The response of the Queen of Wands to a situation would be to take it in and experience it, while the Knight of Wands would be busy rushing off to do something about it. In a negative sense she could indicate passivity, a lack of movement or will.

Variations in the Current Life Reading

When this card appears in:

No. 1 – General Outlook: Your attitude to life is one of receiving and experiencing whatever is happening and being open to learn about yourself through it.

No. 2 – Communications: You are open, receptive and mature in your way of relating. Maybe you are a little passive and tend to listen more than you express.

No. 3 – Work: You have a receptive energy in work that allows you to be aware of what is going on inside of you and to learn from what you are doing.

No. 4 – Inner Self: You have a strong connection with your yin energy, and this allows you to be comfortable with your inner being and to stay in connection with your own instincts.

No. 5 – Sexual Energy: This is a receptive space that is open but not needy of the opposite sex when and if they are present. Check whether there is a tendency for passivity.

No. 6 – Body: You have a soft but powerful physical energy that enables you to stay connected with your inner self as you move with what's happening.

No. 7 – Primary Relationship: There is a receptive availability to the significant other or others in your life that comes from feeling comfortable with your own female energy. Check whether sometimes you hold back on your own desires.

No. 8 – New Perspective: Have you considered that you could say 'yes' to what's happening and use it for self-discovery?

No. 9 – Mind: You think you are receiving and using whatever is happening in your life for your own growth.

No. 10 – Peak Experience: The best thing you can do in this situation is find the place of maturity inside where you can allow yourself to take in what is happening and learn from it.

No. 11 – Spiritual Message: Existence is telling you it's time to look inside and experience your own natural yin energy; it's time to appreciate and live the maturity you have achieved by saying 'yes' to yourself. It's time to give space to the woman in you.

No. 12 – Meditation: Your main learning right now is to take in whatever is happening and use it as an opportunity for looking at yourself. This must be difficult for you or you wouldn't have picked it as a meditation.

No. 13 – Overview: You are allowing life to take you where you need to go. You are open to receive and respond to whatever comes your way and use it for self-awareness.

PRINCE OF WANDS

Essence: Enthusiastic or keen; intensity or urgency; fresh approach.

Descriptive Meaning and Symbols

The Prince is symbolised by a powerful young man who rides naked and unprotected. His arms are spread wide, exposing the open heart that is depicted by the open lotus on his chest. His chariot is pulled by a very determined-looking lion who symbolises the powerful animal energy that is free to move the innocent heart. The flames of his cloak are outward moving but much shorter and less dense than on that of the knight. He represents energy that moves outwards with intensity and enthusiasm, but not with as much substance and maturity as the knight. His phoenix wand shows that his is a state of fresh new energy coming out of the old. Because he doesn't have a set or rigid approach he is able to be creative about whatever is happening. He is the not fully developed yang use of energy; rather the enthusiastic teenager who hasn't yet learnt the caution that sometimes comes with experience and can't always be counted on to follow through or finish what he has started. In a negative sense he can be too impetuous or too intense.

Variations in the Current Life Reading

When this card appears in:

No. 1 – General Outlook: You look at your life in an enthusiastic and positive way. Check whether you are sometimes a bit impetuous.

No. 2 – Communication: You are outgoing and enthusiastic in your way of relating. Be aware if you sometimes get too carried away by your own intensity.

No. 3 – Work: There's an enthusiastic, creative energy going into whatever you're doing.

No. 4 – Inner Self: There is a freshness and innocence in your awareness of yourself and your approach to life.

No. 5 – Sexual Energy: You have an enthusiastic but innocent energy for the opposite sex, kind of like a teenager. Or maybe that enthusiasm is going into examining your sexual patterns.

No. 6 – Body: Your physical energy moves outwards in an intense but positive way.

No. 7 – Primary Relationship: Whether this is with someone in particular or not, there is an enthusiastic energy for intimacy. Maybe there is someone you would like to connect with; just be aware of your impetuousness.

No. 8 – New Perspective: How about putting a little more intensity or enthusiasm into whatever you're involved in.

No. 9 – Mind: You could be thinking in a fresh way or you could be considering the need for more enthusiasm for something in your life.

No. 10 – Peak Experience: The best thing you can do right now is simply put some more enthusiastic or intense energy into the situation.

No. 11 – Spiritual Message: Existence is suggesting that you give yourself a metaphorical kick up the pants to get yourself moving. Keep your energy level up, your heart open and move into life with innocent enthusiasm. If you don't know where or how to start, go and spend time with some kids, or do something a bit silly – Scottish country dancing for instance.

No. 12 – Meditation: Maybe you are feeling a bit lethargic, lazy, or jaded. Your main growth right now lies in putting more positive enthusiasm into whatever you are doing.

No. 13 – Overview: You have a fresh, open enthusiasm for your life right now that is taking you where you need to go.

PRINCESS OF WANDS

Essence: Flowing with the energy; saying yes to whatever is happening; drifting.

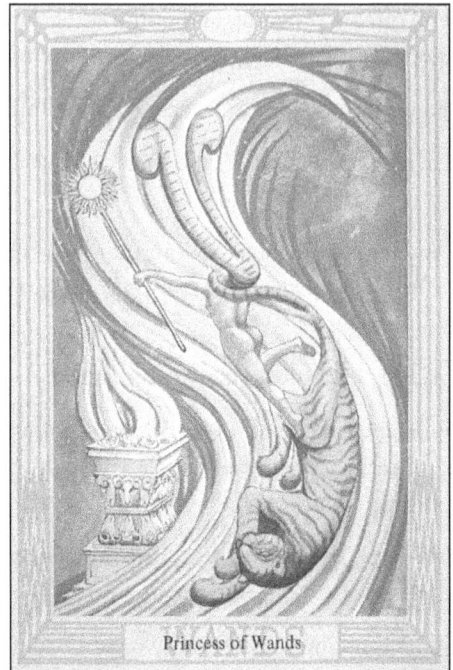

Princess of Wands

Descriptive Meaning and Symbols

The Princess of Wands represents the less established yin way of relating to energy. She is naked and unprotected in her fearlessness and relaxes effortlessly into the roaring flame that represents the energy surrounding her. She has released the energy blocks caused by fear; she literally has the tiger (the symbol for fear) by the tail and he follows powerlessly behind her. She has no need to defend or manipulate energetically but flows along with whatever comes. Her elongated antler-shaped headdress represents her heightened ability to tune into the energy around her in a practical grounded way. The sun on the top of her wand shows her connection with the source of energy. This card symbolises the ability to relax into the flow of whatever or whoever is around, to tune into and allow whatever happens without hesitation. It is the quality of saying 'yes' to, and going along with, the natural flow of energy rather than trying to control it. In a negative sense it can indicate being weak-willed or spineless, a tendency to drift with what is on the outside rather than standing in one's own energy.

Variations in the Current Life Reading

When this card appears in:

No. 1 – General Outlook: You are simply flowing along with whatever life presents. If you are feeling a little aimless, check if you need to listen more to your own energy rather than that outside of you.

No. 2 – Communications: You have an easy flowing way of relating to others without difficulty. Check if maybe you tend to agree or fit in too much or too easily.

No. 3 – Work: You're available to do whatever needs doing, saying 'yes' to whatever is happening.

No. 4 – Inner Self: You have a fresh, easy, flowing relationship with yourself. But just check whether you can be too easily swayed from the outside.

No. 5 – Sexual Energy: This energy is flowing, fresh and available to say 'yes' to whatever is happening.

No. 6 – Body: Your physical energy is free and flowing.

No. 7 – Primary Relationship: Whether there is somebody in particular or not, the energy of intimacy flows easily and without drama. Just be aware if you sometimes fit in a little too easily with the other rather than listening to yourself.

No. 8 – New Perspective: Have you ever thought of letting yourself relax a bit more, of just taking it easy and saying 'yes' to whatever is happening?

No. 9 – Mind: You are thinking that all you need to do is flow along with what's happening.

No. 10 – Peak Experience: There is little to do right now except say 'yes' to the situation and flow along with it.

No. 11 – Spiritual Message: Existence is suggesting you relax more into life and take it easy. Give yourself the opportunity to see what happens when you simply say 'yes' to what is happening rather than trying to make things happen. Maybe you could experiment with functioning from an 'Easy is right' attitude.

No. 12 – Meditation: Your growth right now lies in learning to say 'yes' and relaxing into the flow of life. It sounds simple, but it must be difficult for you otherwise you wouldn't have picked it as your meditation. If you find yourself getting uptight, try taking a deep breath and letting go of tensions and fears.

No. 13 – Overview: You are flowing into your future in a simple, uncomplicated way. If it's feeling good – great. If it's not, see if you need to find a sense of direction rather than drifting.

ACE OF WANDS

Essence: Pure, raw or strong energy; creative life force or will.

Descriptive Meaning and Symbols

This card represents the quality of pure energy before anything has been done with it or before it has taken form. It is the creative impulse or life force – the very quality that gives things life. The great torch, drawn in the shape of the Cabalistic Tree of Life, is like a burst of power that sends out flames in all directions. It is up to us how we use or transmute it, but this high energy is the raw ingredient needed to make things happen. It could be likened to the quality of raw electric power.

Variations in the Current Life Reading

When this card appears in:

No. 1 – General Outlook: You may not have a sense of direction but there's a strong energy and intensity in the way you approach your life.

No. 2 – Communication: You have a lot of raw energy going into your relating, which probably means you are coming on pretty strong. It could be that you are talking a lot and not saying much, but people are going to know you are there.

No. 3 – Work: You have a strong dynamic energy for your work or whatever you are doing. It could be that the impetus for some new direction hasn't yet taken form. With intelligence and awareness all this energy can be put to very creative use.

No. 4 – Inner Self: You are aflame within yourself. If you are allowing yourself to be still with this energy, rather than feeling restless and throwing it out, it will be a strong transformative force.

No. 5 – Sexual Energy: You have a lot of pure sex energy right now. In other words, you're hot! Remember it's just energy and, if you're not in a sexual relationship, allow it to be and it can transform into a creative or loving force as it moves up through your energy body.

No. 6 – Body: There is a large amount of energy in the body. Maybe you don't know what to do with it and it makes you uncomfortable, or maybe you are getting off on moving with it.

No. 7 – Primary Relationship: You have a lot of energy for intimate relating. Maybe you are focused on someone or wanting to find someone, but the relationship doesn't have a form yet. Just be careful not to come on too strong with all that raw energy.

No. 8 – New Perspective: How about giving yourself a good push to just get your energy moving?

No. 9 – Mind: Either you are restless and thinking about what to do with your energy or you want to have more energy.

No. 10 – Peak Experience: The best thing you can do in the current situation is keep your awareness with your energy and follow whatever it wants to do. In other words, don't listen to your mind or even your emotions. Tune into your basic life force and see where it takes you.

No. 11 – Spiritual Message: Energy is our basic life force and your message from existence right now is about tuning into and following it. Don't be concerned with understanding or feeling; just move your body. Dance, run, do active meditations, anything that will help you to reconnect with your pure energy.

No. 12 – Meditation: Experiencing the dimension of energy is your meditation. Maybe you have too much, maybe not enough, but keep your awareness on this way of experiencing your being and you will learn much. Make it a meditation to move your body in some unstructured way and with awareness.

No. 13 – Overview: There's a lot of energy moving around you and through you right now. You might not know what's going on or where you are going but you are in a hurry to get there.

TWO OF WANDS – DOMINION

Essence: New direction, dynamic new way.

Descriptive Meaning and Symbols

MARS IN ARIES

The word 'dominion' means to be in command of, in this case yourself or the situation. The two strongly-formed red wands are dorjes, the Tibetan symbol for a thunderbolt, which signifies divine power. Here they represent the personal power that comes from deep within the being in a very balanced, centred way. The demon masks with horses' heads at the top of the wands symbolise destructive energy, the eradication of the old. The snakes above the arrowheads at the other end show the regeneration and renewal that follows this destruction. The old must go for the new to come. The card symbolises the movement into a new direction or new way from a place of inner strength and centredness.

Variations in the Current Life Reading

When this card appears in:

No. 1 – General Outlook: You are viewing your life in a new way, or seeing it moving in a new direction.

No. 2 – Communication: You are relating with people in a new way. You may not even know what this is, but you are aware of something different happening in your connections.

No. 3 – Work: Something new is happening for you in your work. It could be that you are about to move into a whole new area, or it could be that you are doing the old in a new way.

No. 4 – Inner Self: You are relating to yourself in a new way or feeling your inner being moving in a new direction.

No. 5 – Sexual Energy: There's some change in your sexual energy. It could be that you are connecting with the opposite sex in general in a way that is new for you. Or it could signify a new partner or something different happening in your basic connection with your current partner.

No. 6 – Body: There's something different happening in your physical energy. It could be that you are starting to do something new in the way of diet or exercise, or that an energy change is coming from inside.

No. 7 – Primary Relationship: You are either moving into a new relationship or relating in some new way in your existing partnership. If you are not in one, you are looking at this area of your life in a new way.

No. 8 – New Perspective: How about moving in a new direction or finding a new way of being with what's going on?

No. 9 – Mind: You are thinking about taking new directions or making new moves in your life.

No. 10 – Peak Experience: The best thing you can do right now is find a whole new way of looking at or dealing with the particular situation you're in. The old way won't work any more.

No. 11 – Spiritual Message: Existence is telling you that you are ready and able to take a major new direction in your life. Recognise your inner readiness and know that there is nothing more to be gained from hanging on to the old, even though it may be familiar and comfortable.

No. 12 – Meditation: It could be that you're a bit resistant, but your growth right now definitely lies in going towards the new. Moving into unfamiliar territory may make you feel a bit shaky, but you must be ready for it or you wouldn't have picked this card.

No. 13 – Overview: There's a new direction, inner or outer, that is affecting the whole direction of your life.

THREE OF WANDS – VIRTUE

Essence: Integrity, authenticity, natural, ordinary, real.

Descriptive Meaning and Symbols

SUN IN ARIES

The three matching organic-looking wands in this card represent the body, mind and heart united in harmony and functioning together. From this inner unity a deep flowering starts to happen, which is represented by the flower-shaped flames that come from their point of connection and the budding lotus blossoms at the top of each wand. The state of being authentic or real means to function from a place in the being where thoughts, feelings and actions are all in alignment. From this space there can be no compromise with our own inner truth for any reason; we can only be what and who we are and allow whatever is natural to happen. This is essentially integrity or honesty. With this inner honesty comes an ordinariness and fresh vitality that is represented by the orange colour of the painting. Negatively it can imply a naivety.

Variations in the Current Life Reading

When this card appears in:

No. 1 – General Outlook: You approach life in a very natural, real way.

No. 2 – Communication: You are authentic and genuine in your way of relating with people. In other words, you are just being yourself, and you say things how they are without trying to hide or cover up.

No. 3 – Work: You maintain your integrity in your work situation and are not compromising your truth for any reason.

No. 4 – Inner Self: There is a scrupulous honesty and integrity in the way you look at yourself.

No. 5 – Sexual Energy: You are authentic and real in sexual matters. You will not compromise yourself to please the other or for any other purpose.

No. 6 – Body: You are in tune and natural with your physical energy and don't let your mind compromise the messages from your body.

No. 7 – Primary Relationship: There is a beautiful authenticity in your connection with the one (or ones) closest to you. You may not always be 'nice', but you are being real.

No. 8 – New Perspective: Have you thought of just being yourself, of just being honest?

No. 9 – Mind: You are thinking about integrity or authenticity; maybe you are wanting to be or maybe you think you already are.

No. 10 – Peak Experience: The best thing you can do in this situation is simply be real and natural with whatever is happening or whatever you are feeling. There is nothing to be gained by trying to do anything else.

No. 11 – Spiritual Message: Existence is encouraging you to drop your pretences and masks to move more and more into your authenticity. The message literally is: Get real! Integrity and natural ordinariness are what you are learning to live. This is not something you can develop but, rather, what is left when you get rid of all the games.

No. 12 – Meditation: It obviously isn't easy for you at this time, but you need to keep coming back to what is really happening inside of you and be it. Being what is simply real without trying to act different is your meditation.

No. 13 – Overview: You are facing your life in a real and authentic way and this is the doorway to your future.

FOUR OF WANDS – COMPLETION

Essence: Completing, resolution, finishing.

Descriptive Meaning and Symbols

VENUS IN ARIES
Here the wands are connected in a circle; there are no loose ends. Events are being brought to a completion. Aries, the male symbol of new beginnings represented by the ram's head on one end of the wands, comes together with Venus, the symbol for the female qualities of beauty and love, represented by the dove at the other end. Opposites are being resolved to enable a real completion of the old in a beautiful way from within the heart. This is necessary before the new can begin. This card represents the need to do whatever is necessary to complete something; it is the process of completing or resolving.

Variations in the Current Life Reading

When this card appears in:

No. 1 – General Outlook: You have a sense of completing certain things or a certain stage in your life.

No. 2 – Communication: Something in your old way of relating to people is finishing. You may find you are no longer able to act or speak as you used to.

No. 3 – Work: Something in your area of work, or what you are doing, is coming to the end. It could be the whole job or it could be just a certain phase or way of doing things that is completing itself.

No. 4 – Inner Self: You are in the process of resolving some inner situation and bringing it to completion.

No. 5 – Sexual Energy: Something in your old way of using your sexual energy or relating to the opposite sex is completing. Or maybe you are completing an old sexual bonding.

No. 6 – Body: There is a process in your body that is coming to the end. It could be some physical ailment that is curing, or it could be a more subtle process of the energy.

No. 7 – Primary Relationship: A certain phase in your relationship with the other is finishing. Probably there is another phase to come, but first it is necessary to complete this one with grace and understanding. If you are not in an intimate relationship right now, it is an old way of relating or an old relationship that is finishing to make room for the new.

No. 8 – New Perspective: Has it occurred to you that you need to complete something in this situation for yourself?

No. 9 – Mind: You are thinking about the resolution or completion of something.

No. 10 – Peak Experience: You need to do whatever is necessary to complete the current situation in a graceful way. Know that you haven't yet done this.

No. 11 – Spiritual Message: You are at a time of your life when things as they have been need to be completed. This may bring up uncertainty or insecurity, but know that you can't move into the next phase of your life until this one is resolved.

No. 12 – Meditation: There are certain things in your life that need resolving or completing right now, and this is your priority and major growth, even though you probably don't like it.

No. 13 – Overview: There is a sense of completion, maybe coming from inside or out, that is affecting the direction of your whole life.

FIVE OF WANDS – STRIFE

Essence: Problem, conflict, difficulty, blocked energy, being stuck.

Descriptive Meaning and Symbols

SATURN IN LEO

The three different wands used here appear in various configurations in the next three cards. The central wand, that Crowley calls the staff of the Chief Adept, is also used in the major arcana cards The Magus and The Devil. It carries the winged sun symbol used to signify kings in ancient Egypt and here portrays the strong energy that dominates and restricts the weaker dull-looking wands of energy behind it. On two of the smaller wands the phoenix heads, which symbolise purification and renewal, are facing away from each other. The lotus blossoms on the other two wands, that represent honesty of the heart (from Three of Wands), are also grey and dead looking. The vivid yellow background of the card shows that there is energy wanting to be expressed but that something is limiting or blocking it. The literal meaning of the card is blocked or stuck energy. It is usually experienced as a problem, conflict or difficulty, either inside yourself or in the outer world.

Variations in the Current Life Reading

When this card appears in:

No. 1 – General Outlook: You have a problem-orientated outlook on life. It could be that there are real problems you have to deal with, or it could mean that you view anything that happens as a difficulty.

No. 2 – Communication: There is conflict and frustration in your way of relating. You could be experiencing this as frequent disagreements or tension with people or simply as difficulty in expressing yourself.

No. 3 – Work: There are major difficulties in your work, or whatever it is you are doing. You probably feel restricted and frustrated.

No. 4 – Inner Self: There is a lot of inner conflict. Maybe you are fighting with certain aspects of yourself, or maybe you are dealing with some problem.

No. 5 – Sexual Energy: You are experiencing a block in your sexual energy. It could be that you feel it as a problem with your sexual partner or the opposite sex in general, but probably the roots of it lie in your own sexual conditioning.

No. 6 – Body: There is an obvious block in your physical energy right now. This needs experiencing and releasing or it could cause physical problems. If you are already experiencing a physical problem, know that it has something to do with blocked energy and either move your body or give yourself the space to express whatever emotions are coming up.

No. 7 – Primary Relationship: This is a difficult area for you right now. You are having problems with your partner or around allowing partnership, and it is hard to see what's happening as your clarity is clouded by the blocked energy.

No. 8 – New Perspective: How about simply accepting that you have a problem and dealing with it rather than trying to pretend it isn't there?

No. 9 – Mind: You are seeing something in your life as a problem and the mind is very concerned with it. This could be a reality or it could be an idea of the mind.

No. 10 – Peak Experience: There is a situation right now that you really need to deal with. Confront what is going on, face the restriction and problem directly. It isn't going to go away by itself.

No. 11 – Spiritual Message: Existence is encouraging you to deal with certain difficult situations in your life that you may have been avoiding for a while. You must be ready to do this or you wouldn't have pulled this card.

No. 12 – Meditation: Your meditation right now is to be present in the difficulties and problems that are happening. It's probably not fun, but it's definitely good for your growth.

No. 13 – Overview: There is some problem in your life that is colouring everything else that is going on. This is not an easy time, but you are probably dealing with stuff that needs to be seen to clear the way for your future direction.

SIX OF WANDS – VICTORY

Essence: Positive, fine, uncomplicated, no problems, okay.

Descriptive Meaning and Symbols

JUPITER IN LEO
The difficulties of the previous card have passed; the situation has been positively resolved. The wands are back in harmony and balance; they support one another, giving rise to the flames of energy where they cross. The same symbols appear on top of the wands as in Strife, but now the suns on the two central wands that represent conscious perception are no longer blocked, so clear vision is again possible. The phoenix heads, which symbolise renewal, are facing each other in harmony, and the lotus blossoms (open heart), like the wands, are golden and alive. The light violet colour of the background was used in ancient Egypt to represent victory. This card represents the energy of something that is happening in the right way or has been successfully resolved. Things are okay: the situation has worked out in a good way. It's not something momentous, just that there's no problem. Negatively it can imply a superficial state of avoiding dealing with deeper issues.

Variations in the Current Life Reading

When this card appears in:

No. 1 – General Outlook: You have a bright outlook on life. Whatever happens you are able to see it in a positive way.

No. 2 – Communication: There is a feeling of ease and wellbeing around your general way of relating with people. Maybe some difficulties have been positively resolved or maybe this is simply an area where you have no problems at this time.

No. 3 – Work: There is positive energy going into whatever you are doing. Maybe something has just been achieved or a problem settled, or it could be that you just feel fine about what's happening.

No. 4 – Inner Self: You are feeling okay about yourself. You are not dealing with any inner problems right now, even if they are there.

No. 5 – Sexual Energy: The sex energy is moving in an uncomplicated and unproblematic way.

No. 6 – Body: The body energy is moving in an easy, pleasant way.

No. 7 – Primary Relationship: Whether it's somebody in particular or a number of people, your intimate energy connections are even and without drama or difficulty.

No. 8 – New Perspective: Has it occurred to you that you could look at the bright side of what's happening, that maybe it doesn't have to be a problem?

No. 9 – Mind: Your mind is positive and easy with whatever is happening.

No. 10 – Peak Experience: The best thing you can do in the current situation is look at it in a positive way. You may think you have a problem when you don't.

No. 11 – Spiritual Message: 'Easy is right' could well be a motto for you from existence. You are being encouraged to see that there is no need to make problems or dramas; everything is okay the way it is. You might want to practice living the Australian philosophy: 'No problems mate!'

No. 12 – Meditation: Maybe you feel more familiar with problems and struggle, but right now your growth lies in finding a simple okayness with whatever is happening. Be aware of a possible tendency to make things difficult and see if you are ready to let it go.

No. 13 – Overview: There's a general sense that your life is working. Maybe you don't even know why or what, but simply that there are no problems facing you in the foreseeable future. Everything is fine.

SEVEN OF WANDS – VALOUR

Essence: Courage, being forceful, making an effort.

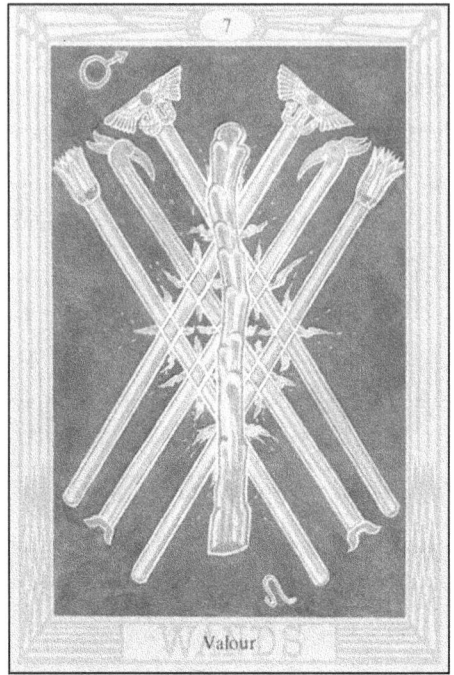

Descriptive Meaning and Symbols

MARS IN LEO

The same wands that have appeared in the Five and Six of Wands are seen here in their final development. From the blocked energy in Strife, and its positive resolution in Victory, there is now the necessary energy to move into areas that require more courage or effort. The new central wand shaped like a rough club has a powerful organic feel and is chipped with the experience of living. It shows the need to trust what we know even though the path is not easy; it takes effort and valour to move from the relative ease and comfort of Victory. The peaceful, pale violet background of the last card has darkened and intensified as the male, warrior energy of Mars comes into play. This card symbolises a strength and determination to move on, regardless of the difficulties; and this movement takes effort and/or courage. Negatively it can also mean forcing energy against its natural flow.

Variations in the Current Life Reading

When this card appears in:

No. 1 – General Outlook: You look at life as though everything is a bit of an effort; or maybe you feel that it takes courage for you to keep going.

No. 2 – Communication: Relating is a bit of an effort for you right now. Maybe you are trying very hard to express yourself, even though it is taking courage to do so.

No. 3 – Work: You are making a great deal of effort to do or achieve something in the area of your work. This may feel like a bit of a strain.

No. 4 – Inner Self: You're not in a relaxed state with yourself right now. There's a certain striving or pushing that probably doesn't feel comfortable. Maybe this is a positive facing of certain inner difficulties, or maybe it comes from not accepting yourself.

No. 5 – Sexual Energy: There is a pushing or effort in your sex energy that could come from trying to make something happen with someone. Or it could be that you are using courage and effort to cut through old sexual conditioning patterns.

No. 6 – Body: You are forcing your physical energy against its natural flow. Maybe this is necessary in your particular situation or maybe it isn't.

No. 7 – Primary Relationship: You are probably trying very hard to make something happen with the one you feel closest to right now. Or it could be that it is taking courage to stay with or share what is real for you in intimacy.

No. 8 – New Perspective: Have you considered that you could apply more effort or find a bit more courage to do something about what's happening?

No. 9 – Mind: You are thinking about making the effort to do something.

No. 10 – Peak Experience: The best thing you can do in the current situation is have the courage to make a necessary push or effort. It's no good waiting for things to happen by themselves.

No. 11 – Spiritual Message: Existence is encouraging you to develop the warrior side of your nature. Possibly you've let things slide for long enough. It's not the time to give way, even though there may be fear or difficulties. Effort and courage is needed.

No. 12 – Meditation: Finding the courage to do what is necessary is your major growth right now. Every time you start to give in, push yourself again.

No. 13 – Overview: There's a certain effort required to make your life the way it is right now. This may be necessary to take you where you need to go, or it could be keeping you away from flowing with what is.

EIGHT OF WANDS – SWIFTNESS

Essence: Change of gestalt, new perspective, finding the knack.

Descriptive Meaning and Symbols

MERCURY IN SAGITTARIUS

This card symbolises the solution to a difficulty, and the instantaneous release of blocked energy that happens when there is a new clarity or new perspective of a situation. This change of gestalt, or way of looking at what's happening, allows something to be done or said that enables the situation to move and the desired results to happen. The blocked energy is symbolised by the square shape which, when turned slightly, becomes a crystal diamond that releases red bolts of energy that can be seen as brainwaves. The rainbow above represents the fulfilment of dreams or desires that is possible when this switch happens. Sometimes in life we imagine we have an insurmountable difficulty with someone or something, but if we can find the knack of letting go of old concepts or ideas and looking with fresh clarity in the moment, we find a new perspective from which the difficulty simply disappears. This can be felt as an 'Ah ha!' experience, where everything suddenly falls into place; or something as simple as struggling to get a key into a lock and suddenly realising we are holding it upside down.

Variations in the Current Life Reading

When this card appears in:

No. 1 – General Outlook: You have a fresh new way of looking at your life.

No. 2 – Communication: Something has switched in your way of connecting with others; maybe you are seeing certain patterns in your way of relating in a new light.

No. 3 – Work: The switch may be internal or external but there's a new perspective of whatever you are doing in work. Suddenly your situation looks or feels quite different; maybe some difficulty is no longer there.

No. 4 – Inner Self: There has been some inner revelation in the way you see yourself. Maybe there was something about yourself that you saw as a problem, but when looked at from another perspective, it no longer was, so now you are ready to move on.

No. 5 – Sex Energy: There has been a switch, or an energetic change in your sex energy. This could be in your relationship with your sexual partner or it could be in your connection to the basic life force within yourself that will affect your way of relating to the opposite sex in general.

No. 6 – Body: Some block that has existed in your physical energy has been freed, probably giving you the feeling of release in the body. Or it could be that you have a new perspective about something that is happening physically.

No. 7 – Primary Relationship: There has been a switch or movement in your intimate relating that is allowing you to see something in a new way. This could be helping you to be more clear with what is happening or what you want.

No. 8 – New Perspective: Have you thought that maybe there is a different way to look at this situation that stops it from being a problem?

No. 9 – Mind: You are thinking you have found a new way of looking at what you are doing or how you are relating to some situation in your life.

No. 10 – Peak Experience: The best thing you can do in this situation is simply change the way you perceive what's happening. Then you will find things change of their own accord.

No. 11 – Spiritual Message: Existence is suggesting that you look at your life from a fresh perspective. A simple change in outlook could make previous problems seem at the worst like learning situations, at the best like blessings. In times like this it could be helpful to get some outside input, maybe from some kind of counsellor. Do you know anyone who can give you a good card reading?

No. 12 – Meditation: You are being confronted by an old habit pattern of seeing or dealing with something in a particular way. Keep reminding yourself that it's not really the problem you perceive it as, and that you actually know a better way of dealing with it that enables you to achieve what you want.

No. 13 – Overview: There has been a change in how you look at your life that is having a profound effect on your whole future direction.

NINE OF WANDS – STRENGTH

Essence: Independence, individuality, the strength that comes from standing in your own energy.

Descriptive Meaning and Symbols

SUN IN SAGITTARIUS

The strong central wand connects the moon, the symbol for the unconscious and inner parts of the being, with the sun, the symbol for the externalised and conscious parts. This represents a state of true unity when the inner and the outer, the conscious and the unconscious, are connected and functioning in accord. The eight background arrows are positioned in fours, harmoniously supporting the central wand. They are the four different parts of the being – mental, physical, emotional and spiritual – that when unified create the state of inner wholeness and strength. Each of these arrows is tipped by an upward-turning crescent moon, demonstrating that this strength is something that comes primarily from an inner space. The card symbolises the state of being unified within ourselves and therefore not in need from the outside. From this inner wholeness comes the ability to be oneself independent of anyone and anything else. When we are standing in our own energy in this self-sufficient way, we are strong enough to be the individuals that we are without trying to protect, control or defend. In a negative sense the card can also represent the state of independence that is a defence of vulnerability or anti-dependent space.

Variations in the Current Life Reading

When this card appears in:

No. 1 – General Outlook: You see yourself functioning in life as an individual, independent of the views and influences of those around you.

No. 2 – Communication: You stay rooted in your own energy when you relate with others. This probably means you maintain your own opinions and outlook and are not unduly influenced by others.

No. 3 – Work: Whatever you are doing around work, you are doing it by yourself or for yourself. Even if you are working for someone, you are an independent agent in this area of your life and probably not into being told what to do.

No. 4 – Inner Self: You feel very whole and at one within yourself. There is an acceptance of your own individuality.

No. 5 – Sexual Energy: Even if you are in a sexual relationship with someone, your sex energy is very much your own and not bonded or compromised by partnership.

No. 6 – Body: You are centred in your own physical energy and don't easily get lost into other people. This gives you a quality of inner strength and wholeness.

No. 7 – Primary Relationship: Your intimate energy is operating independently of anyone else. If you are in a relationship, check whether this comes from a genuine inner wholeness or if you are closing yourself off from the other, refusing to be open and vulnerable.

No. 8 – New Perspective: Have you considered that you could do what you want to, independent of anyone or anything else?

No. 9 – Mind: Your mind is occupied with thoughts of being more independent and centred in your own space and energy.

No. 10 – Peak Experience: The best thing you can do in this situation is come back to your own energy and experience yourself as a whole, independent person. Don't be influenced by others; decide what you want regardless of the opinions of anyone else.

No. 11 – Spiritual Message: Existence is encouraging you to find the space inside yourself where you are not influenced by and dependent on your relationships, or even your society; where you can start to experience yourself as an independent individual. It is time to go your own way.

No. 12 – Meditation: Claiming your independence and individuality is your meditation right now. Maybe you're feeling wobbly at having to stand on your own. Maybe you're coming out of a dependent relationship and have to keep remembering that it is time to bring your centre back to yourself.

No. 13 – Overview: You are on your own path right now, finding your own way independent of anyone else.

TEN OF WANDS – OPPRESSION

Essence: Oppressed or repressed energy; the state of feeling held back or constricted; restraint, depression.

Descriptive Meaning and Symbols

SATURN IN SAGITTARIUS

The two wands in the foreground are repeats of the Tibetan dorjes or sacred power objects from the Two of Wands. In Dominion they were working in harmony to promote the new; here they are hard and metallic and holding back the eight weak insubstantial wands behind them. Instead of allowing energy to move into new directions, they are restricting movement. The orange colour and the central burst of flames show the intensity of the energy that is being held back. When the ability to experience and express is blocked, energy that might have moved into emotional, physical, mental or spiritual dimensions, represented by the groups of four wands, is oppressed and we lose connection with ourselves. This restricted energy can turn sour inside us and either becomes self-destructive or makes us depressed. This card represents the state of feeling repressed, restricted or limited in any way, either from the inside or the out. It can also indicate the state of depression.

Variations in the Current Life Reading

When this card appears in:

No. 1 – General Outlook: You are feeling constricted or limited, or possibly even depressed with life in general. This may be caused by a practical external situation or it could just be a state of mind.

No. 2 – Communication: You are either repressing yourself or allowing others to restrict your expression. There is much that wants to be said or shown that you are holding back.

No. 3 – Work: You are feeling confined and restricted in your work situation. Probably you can't move ahead in the way you would like to.

No. 4 – Inner Self: You are feeling constricted or maybe depressed within yourself. Maybe you are repressing so much you can't feel yourself, let alone your own power to move.

No. 5 – Sexual Energy: Your sexual energy is being repressed, so you are withholding this connection from the opposite sex.

No. 6 – Body: Your physical energy is being held back or constricted, which probably feels very tight or heavy inside your body. This could be coming from a practical limitation, but if it comes from the inside, be aware that you can make yourself sick this way. You may need to make an effort to move your physical body and release whatever is being repressed. Dance, go for a run, do exercises, shake yourself – anything to get the energy moving and the emotions out.

No. 7 – Primary Relationship: You are withholding your energy from the one closest to you, or from the possibility of someone coming close to you. You may be interested to find out exactly what it is you are trying to hide.

No. 8 – New Perspective: Have you considered that you could restrain yourself a little; there is no need to keep racing ahead into whatever it is?

No. 9 – Mind: You are thinking about being constrained or restricted.

No. 10 – Peak Experience: The best thing you can do in the current situation is hold yourself back from moving in the direction you have been heading. A little restraint right now is just what you need.

No. 11 – Spiritual Message: Existence is holding a restraining hand over your life at this time. You may be longing to continue in your usual 'doing mode' but are being encouraged to break this pattern, to literally hold yourself back.

No. 12 – Meditation: You are in a restricted space right now and not liking it. But that's simply how it is: you are stuck, repressed, confined in some way. All you can do is keep experiencing that and make it a meditation. You may be grateful for this learning later.

No. 13 – Overview: There is a repressive energy limiting your direction that may or may not have specific causes or reasons. Whether the restriction comes from external situations or internal causes, it could well be feeling heavy and depressing.

SWORDS SYMBOLISE THE ELEMENT OF AIR AND REPRESENT THE DIFFERENT STATES AND WAYS OF USING THE MIND

KNIGHT OF SWORDS

Essence: Concentration, focused thinking, mental determination, single pointed.

Descriptive Meaning and Symbols

The Knight of Swords represents mature male or yang mind. He is charging through the air at full gallop with the intensity of one who knows where he is going and is motivated by a determined direction or goal. He represents the quality of mind that is focused, concentrated and very quick. To have such determination, there needs to be a certain passion behind the thinking that comes from the unification of body, mind and heart, represented here by the three swallows that fly in formation next to the knight. The propellers above his helmet that keep him in the air represent the loftiness of his thinking, which in a negative sense can sometimes mean he is not connected with reality. This card represents a use of the mind that is focused, concentrated and determined in its positive form, and aggressive or narrow minded in the negative.

Variations in the Current Life Reading

When this card appears in:

No. 1 – General Outlook: You think you know where you're going but your tendency to be focused on mental goals or directions in your life could mean that you're feeling a bit speedy or driven, possibly without even knowing why.

No. 2 – Communication: Your way of relating with others can be intense and passionate. Check if you may sometimes be a little aggressive or single pointed in your views as well.

No. 3 – Work: There is a lot of determined, focused mental energy going into your work. You probably have some ideas or goals and are passionate about achieving them.

No. 4 – Inner Self: You relate to yourself through the intensity of your mind right now, which could mean that you spend your alone time concentrating on what you are thinking.

No. 5 – Sexual Energy: It would be hard for you to follow your sex energy right now because your mind has such strong ideas about the direction this energy should be taking. Or it could be that you are taking a good focused look at some of your sexual patterns.

No. 6 – Body: Your physical energy is being affected by the focus of your mind. If you think you should be doing something, you'll probably do it, regardless of the messages from the body.

No. 7 – Primary Relationship: You are conducting your intimate relating through the focus of your mind, which probably means that there is a lot of mental exchange and maybe ideas of how things should be. Be aware that nothing other than mind is possible in this state.

No. 8 – New Perspective: Have you considered that you need to be clearer about your intentions or focus?

No. 9 – Mind: You are thinking about focusing or concentrating, probably on something in particular.

No. 10 – Peak Experience: The best thing you can do right now is use your mind for some determined, focused thinking about your current situation. You need to really look at what's going on and get rid of fuzzy thinking.

No. 11 – Spiritual Message: Existence is encouraging you to develop more mental focus or purpose. In other words, you need to find your strength of mind. Without this mental determination and concentration on the matters at hand you can't move along your spiritual journey.

No. 12 – Meditation: The art of keeping your mental focus is your meditation right now. Maybe you have to make a determined effort to stop your tendency to loose concentration or get spaced out.

No. 13 – Overview: You are very focused about the direction your life is moving in. Probably you have some purpose or goals that you are concentrating on. Just check if this single-pointed outlook sometimes cuts you off from seeing what is actually happening around you.

QUEEN OF SWORDS

Essence: Open minded, clarity, objective thinking, the mask cutter.

Descriptive Meaning and Symbols

The Queen of Swords represents mature female or yin mind. She sits in the air on a throne made of clouds with a sword in one hand and a mask in the other. She has taken off her own mask and so is able to use the sword to cut away the masks, the outer appearances or personality layers, of what she looks at to see the reality underneath. The large crystal crown on her head represents the clarity and insight of this state of mind. The child's head above shows her return to the freshness and innocence of the child mind. Just as children are often able to see more clearly than adults, so we need to cut through the clouds of our own ideas and belief systems to be able to see what is really there. This card represents the quality of mind that could be associated with the role of a counsellor. There is the innocence and openness to receive what is happening without defence, and the objectivity not to get emotionally involved. From this comes the clarity to cut through pretence, and the authenticity to see and to be with what is real. In a negative space this energy can be sharp or bitchy.

Variations in the Current Life Reading

When this card appears in:

No. 1 – General Outlook: You have an objective, clear outlook on your life right now. You are seeing what's happening without defence or pretence.

No. 2 – Communication: Your way of relating with others is honest, objective and very clear. You can be counted on to see and say what's actually going on authentically and openly. Be aware if you sometimes get too sharp or bitchy with it.

No. 3 – Work: Whatever work you are involved in, you have a clear, objective view of what's happening.

No. 4 – Inner Self: You are looking at yourself from an objective perspective right now, which enables you to get beneath the masks of your personality and see yourself as you are.

No. 5 – Sexual Energy: You are clear and rational in your perspective of whatever is happening in your sexual energy or in your sexual relationship, but in your mind rather than your energy.

No. 6 – Body: You have an objective clarity about your body or the processes going on in it right now. Maybe this keeps you at a certain distance from your body but you see the physical situation realistically.

No. 7 – Primary Relationship: You have an open and clear vision of what's happening in your intimate connections, but only with your mind. There is probably a lot of talking or thinking about intimacy going on.

No. 8 – New Perspective: Why not put aside your beliefs and take an open and objective look at what's really happening?

No. 9 – Mind: You think you are looking at life clearly and objectively.

No. 10 – Peak Experience: The best thing you can do in this situation is put aside your own ideas, defences and masks and be open to taking a rational objective look at what's going on.

No. 11 – Spiritual Message: Existence is encouraging you to take a fresh, clear look at your life. It's time to see what's really happening, or who you really are, without any pretence or hiding.

No. 12 – Meditation: You need to make a meditation of being open minded and objective and you won't be able to do this if you are hiding behind your own masks and the beliefs you use to keep yourself safe.

No. 13 – Overview: You are looking at your life and the direction you are moving with clarity and objectivity. It may feel a little dry but you are seeing what is.

PRINCE OF SWORDS

Essence: Cutting through limiting ideas or thought forms; critical, impatient.

Descriptive Meaning and Symbols

The Prince of Swords symbolises the less established yang way of relating to the mind. He is represented by a powerful young man swinging a sword with intensity and urgency. He is attacking the figures pulling the chariot that represent the thought forms and attitudes from the past that limit his freedom to think in a fresh creative way. He is a young energy that reflects impatience with any kind of confinement or restraint on his freedom of mind. The crystal on the front of his chariot symbolises his increasing clarity of perception as he clears away the old. His green colour symbolises the creative possibilities of this use of the mind. The card can represent the recognition and cutting through of old ideas or mental patterns that are limiting our lives. These patterns are usually old beliefs from childhood that we are still hanging onto and believing. In general it is a way of using the mind to clear away unwanted or restrictive thoughts. In its negative aspect it can symbolise a cutting or critical mind that is impatient and intolerant with other outlooks or ideas or with any feeling of limitation.

Variations in the Current Life Reading

When this card appears in:

No. 1 – General Outlook: You tend to be impatient with the attitudes of your own or others' minds that limit your freedom and space. You could have a generally critical outlook on life.

No. 2 – Communication: You are probably not very tolerant of other's views right now and could tend to be impatient or critical in your relating. Or it could be that this impatience is directed towards yourself and your own limitations around relating.

No. 3 – Work: The energy going into your work has a mental urgency as you try to clear away the restrictions of your own or others ideas.

No. 4 – Inner Self: There is probably a feeling of dissatisfaction in your inner being as you become aware of old belief systems that limit you from being or doing what you want.

No. 5 – Sexual Energy: Your sex energy is being filtered through the mind in a way that may be making you impatient or irritable with the opposite sex. Or it could be that you are trying to clear away old ideas that you feel are limiting you in this area.

No. 6 – Body: Your physical energy probably has an uncomfortable irritable feel. Maybe you are becoming aware of thought forms that are restricting the natural flow of your energy.

No. 7 – Primary Relationship: Your energy connection with the one or ones closest to you has an edge of impatience in it, and you could be a little critical or intolerant as you try to get out of old restricting patterns.

No. 8 – New Perspective: Have you considered that you could simply clear away old restricting ideas and patterns that are limiting you and get a fresh look at what is happening?

No. 9 – Mind: You are thinking about cutting through limitations or restrictions and may be feeling impatient.

No. 10 – Peak Experience: The best thing you can do in the current situation is make a determined effort to clear away old ways of looking at it so that you can find a fresh creative approach.

No. 11 – Spiritual Message: Existence is encouraging you to cut through old ideas about yourself and your life that are restricting your way of being in the world. You wouldn't have picked this card if you weren't ready to do this, so put some urgency into getting rid of all those old beliefs that were never really yours anyway.

No. 12 – Meditation: Your meditation right now is to keep cutting away old ideas and attitudes that stop you from moving ahead in a new creative way. Sometimes impatience is a good thing.

No. 13 – Overview: You are moving ahead in your life with a certain urgency or impatience as you try to cut through things or ideas that you feel are limiting your direction.

PRINCESS OF SWORDS

Essence: Clearing away the clouds covering practical or realistic thinking; the mood fighter; mental windscreen wiper. Cloudy or nervous mind.

Descriptive Meaning and Symbols

The Princess of Swords is the young yin or female way or relating to the mind. She leans on her solid pedestal or altar that is covered with coins or disks to represent that she is grounded in the earth or the practical. The air around her is tumultuous with mental disturbance. She is using her sword to clear away the rain and clouds that represent the moods or useless petty thoughts that cover her clarity. She symbolises the mental capacity to sweep aside the thoughts, emotions or moods that cloud the ability to see reality and think practically. She can function as a kind of windscreen wiper that clears the water and the mist from the window of the mind so that we can see where we're going. Instead of allowing moods to colour our clarity, the Princess sweeps them aside so that we can see what's really happening. In the negative she can represent a moody or restless, nervous mind.

Variations in the Current Life Reading

When this card appears in:

No. 1 – General Outlook: Your general outlook is a bit cloudy, but you are trying to clear away the mental haze so that you can see what's really going on in your life.

No. 2 – Communication: It could be that you are feeling a little nervous and restless around people. Or maybe you are trying to clear away superfluous thoughts and moods that cloud your ability to be clear in your relating.

No. 3 – Work: Possibly you are not quite sure what's going on with your work energy, but you are trying to wipe away a lot of superficial mental disturbances so that you can be more realistic and practical.

No. 4 – Inner Self: Your perception of yourself is a bit cloudy or unsettled, but you are trying to clear away moods or emotions that stop you from seeing more clearly where you are.

No. 5 – Sexual Energy: You are trying to clear away a certain moodiness covering your sexual energy so that you are able to see more realistically what's happening with you and the opposite sex.

No. 6 – Body: There is a layer of cloud or moodiness interfering with the clarity of your connection with your physical energy. You could be experiencing this as a feeling of fogginess or as petty physical irritations that you are trying to get rid of.

No. 7 – Primary Relationship: It's a little difficult to see what's really happening for you in intimacy right now because of the superficial moods and clouds that cover your perception. Probably you are trying to clear away these disturbances.

No. 8 – New Perspective: Have you considered that you could wipe aside your superficial thoughts and moods so that you can see the real?

No. 9 – Mind: You want to clear away moods or uneasiness that cloud the mind.

No. 10 – Peak Experience: The best thing you can do in the current situation is keep clearing away the mist of superficial moods and emotions so that you can deal practically and realistically with what's happening.

No. 11 – Spiritual Message: Existence is encouraging you to stop wasting your time with petty ideas and moods that cloud you from seeing what's going on in your life. It's time to make a concerted effort to clean up your perception so that you can see what's real.

No. 12 – Meditation: Your meditation is to keep wiping aside the mental clouds and moods that cover your ability to see realistically what's happening and what needs to be done. Don't indulgence in this kind of thinking. You do know when you are doing it or you wouldn't have picked this card.

No. 13 – Overview: There is a certain moodiness or lack of clarity hanging over you right now that you are trying to move aside so that you can see where you are going.

ACE OF SWORDS

Essence: Making a decision, pure clarity of mind, flash of insight.

Descriptive Meaning and Symbols

This card symbolises the sharpness or pure clarity of mind that happens when all doubts and confusion, represented by the clouds at the bottom of the painting, have been cleared away. The sun of consciousness rises above the sea of unconsciousness and burns away the uncertainties. The handle of the sword is made up of crescent moons, representing the unconscious mind, that are united by the suns, or conscious mind, to create a transformation of consciousness, represented by the coiled snake. The tip of the sword entering the crown (higher consciousness) symbolises that this transformation is of expanded or higher awareness. On the blade of the sword is engraved the Greek word for clarity or will. The Ace of Swords can be seen as an 'Ah ha' experience: a new insight, or awareness that has become clear in the mind. As this usually precedes a decision, this card will often represent the act of making or having made a decision. It is good to remember that sometimes we make decisions about things in our lives without even realising it, and these decisions have far-reaching effects on our reality.

Variations in the Current Life Reading

When this card appears in:

No. 1 – General Outlook: A decision you have just made, or need to make, is affecting your whole outlook on life.

No. 2 – Communication: Probably you have made a decision or had an insight about your way of relating with people. Check if this decision is getting in the way of your spontaneous expression.

No. 3 – Work: Either you have just made a decision or had an insight about your work. Or it could be that you are trying to make a decision.

No. 4 – Inner Self: You may have had an insight about your own inner nature, or it could be that you have made a decision that is, consciously or unconsciously, affecting how you relate to yourself.

No. 5 – Sexual Energy: You have made a decision with your mind that is affecting the reality of your sexual energy or way of relating to the opposite sex. You may or may not be conscious of this.

No. 6 – Body: You have made some decision about something concerning your body, or it could be that you have made a decision that is having a strong effect on your physical energy. This is neither good nor bad, but be aware that your will is ruling your energy.

No. 7 – Primary Relationship: It could be an insight or it could be a decision, but certainly you have reached some conclusion about your relationship with the primary other in your life, or your availability for having a relationship.

No. 8 – New Perspective: Have you considered that you need to make a clear decision about what is happening right now?

No. 9 – Mind: You want to make a decision or get clear about something in your life.

No. 10 – Peak Experience: The best thing you can do in the current situation is make a clear decision and stick to it. In other words, stop dithering around.

No. 11 – Spiritual Message: Existence is saying that you are capable of dropping the doubt and confusion that have been clouding your mind and need to make some conclusions or decisions that will have far-reaching effects on your life. Maybe it is that making decisions is generally difficult for you and the resulting procrastination is holding back your spiritual growth.

No. 12 – Meditation: There is a decision or maybe a number of them that you need to make. This is probably not easy for you, but be aware that having to make this commitment is your major growth situation and take it as a meditation.

No. 13 – Overview: You have had an insight or made a decision that is guiding the direction your life is moving in right now.

TWO OF SWORDS – PEACE

Essence: Peace of mind, allowing fate, keeping the peace.

Descriptive Meaning and Symbols

MOON IN LIBRA

The two swords meet together through a blue white rose of wisdom and love. The mind has come to rest in the heart. The praying angels that come from the handles of the swords indicate that decisions are out of the realms of the personal mind and in the hands of fate, or the gods. The yellow and green background colour of the card symbolises spiritual peace and the renewal or regeneration that comes from this. The four graceful shapes radiating from the centre of the card show the ease and harmony with which the body, mind, heart and spirit unite in this place. The card symbolises the belief that decisions have been or are being made, either by you or for you; there is no need for the mind to do anything but rest and relax. It is the place where human will hands over control to fate so that the mind is not needed and can be at peace. In its negative aspect it can also indicate the space where the mind ignores or avoids dealing with issues that need to be looked at.

Variations in the Current Life Reading

When this card appears in:

No. 1 – General Outlook: You are at peace with your world right now, at least on the surface. Check that you are not avoiding things by maintaining a superficial state of *laissez faire* or okayness.

No. 2 – Communication: You are very laid back and easy in your way of relating; you do not need to be heard or to prove. You may want to check if this comes from a need to keep the peace at the cost of your own truth.

No. 3 – Work: Whatever you are doing in the work area of your life, if anything, is not an important issue. You are probably easy going and happy with the way things are.

No. 4 – Inner Self: You are at peace with yourself right now. It could be a genuine inner serenity, maybe after a time of conflict or indecision. Or it could be that you're avoiding looking deeper into yourself.

No. 5 – Sexual Energy: There's not much happening in the area of your sexual energy. There is no conflict but no great passion either. Basically, whatever is happening, all is well.

No. 6 – Body: There is a certain sense of relaxation in your body – no conflict or problems. You are at peace with yourself on a physical level.

No. 7 – Primary Relationship: No great problems in the area of your primary relationship. You are at peace with your partner or with being without one. Or is it that you are invested with maintaining the peace with your partner.

No. 8 – New Perspective: Why not give yourself a break from worrying or trying to work things out? Maybe it's time to consider that things are not in your hands and leave it to fate.

No. 9 – Mind: It could be that you are thinking about wanting to find some peace of mind, or it could be that your mind is really at peace right now.

No. 10 – Peak Experience: The best thing you can do is stop worrying and let the mind be at rest with the situation the way it is.

No. 11 – Spiritual Message: Existence is encouraging you to stop trying to understand or make decisions in your life. Maybe you have a habit of worrying and judging that keeps you in a state of anxiety. It may help to give yourself permission to believe that life will continue just fine if you don't try to work out what's happening or where it's going.

No. 12 – Meditation: Your meditation is peace of mind, which presumably means that you are having difficulty finding that. Keep reminding yourself that there really is nothing that you can do with your mind right now, and hopefully that will help you relax.

No. 13 – Overview: You have a sense of peacefulness with the direction your life is taking; there's no conflict or problems as you look into your future.

THREE OF SWORDS – SORROW

Essence: Pain, frustration, anger, negativity.

Descriptive Meaning and Symbols

SATURN IN LIBRA

All three swords are piercing the very centre of the rose of the heart, injuring it and causing its petals to fall. This symbolises the negative energy of the mind that goes deeply into the feeling part of the being and causes sorrow. The swords are not balanced or in harmony: the two smaller ones are bent and insignificant, showing that the negative mind is discordant. The dark and gloomy colour of the card and the sharp or swirling irregular shapes in the background further indicate a state of emotional heaviness. This card represents the negative states of pain, anger and frustration. These emotions are all strongly related. Anger is active, outgoing pain – the state when we think we can do something about the situation. Pain or sorrow is negativity or anger that is powerless or helpless and turned inside. Behind every anger is pain. Frustration, resentment or irritation is a kind of half-formed anger that is not being fully owned. This card can represent any of these negative states.

Variations in the Current Life Reading

When this card appears in:

No. 1 – General Outlook: You look at your life through a filter of negativity. It could be that there is some real cause for this pain or anger, or it could be that you simply have an attitude problem. Either way it's not an easy space to be in.

No. 2 – Communication: Relating is very difficult for you right now. It could be that there is a general frustration around communicating, or it could be that you often find yourself angry or hurt by others.

No. 3 – Work: You are having a frustrating or otherwise difficult time with whatever you are doing with your energy. The problem could be with the job itself, or it could be from conflicts with people at your work. Whichever, it's not easy.

No. 4 – Inner Self: There is a lot of pain or anger in your inner being. No doubt you are not happy within yourself right now. Hopefully you are able to experience this without adding the extra burden of judging yourself for it.

No. 5 – Sexual Energy: There is anger or pain sitting in your sex centre at this time. Probably it is directly related to your relationship with a current or an ex partner. Or it could be old pain or frustration from early sexual conditioning that is starting to surface as a dislike for the opposite sex.

No. 6 – Body: There is pain in your physical energy. This could be literally physical pain in the body or it could be anger or emotional pain that has surfaced to the physical level because it hasn't been owned. Either way this is something that needs immediate attention, and either care or expression, otherwise it could become physical sickness.

No. 7 – Primary Relationship: You are either angry or in pain around your primary relationship. Check carefully in the advice areas of the reading to see what you can do about this without making the situation worse.

No. 8 – New Perspective: Has it occurred to you that it's okay to feel your pain or anger?

No. 9 – Mind: There are a lot of negative thoughts going on in the mind.

No. 10 – Peak Experience: The best thing you can do in this situation is get into the pain and/or anger that is there. It's not a time to try and make things better or make yourself feel good, but rather to let yourself experience the negative reality as it is.

No. 11 – Spiritual Message: Existence is encouraging you to feel the pain, anger and frustration that you may have been avoiding for years, if not life times. We tend to suppress these so-called negative emotions because we have been taught they are bad. But in fact, pain is often the doorway into the depths of the being, and anger the doorway to claiming our power.

No. 12 – Meditation: It's natural not to like it, but your major growth right now lies in allowing and owning the pain or anger that is going on in your being. Literally make it a meditation and you will learn much from it. You may find it helpful to consciously allow yourself time to cry, beat a pillow, gibber or do something active with the body that allows this energy to surface and be expressed.

No. 13 – Overview: Life is hard right now. There is a layer of negative energy that is affecting your whole life and there is no way around that. Let the experiencing of it be your teacher and know that it is taking you where you need to go.

FOUR OF SWORDS – TRUCE

Essence: Accepting what is, allowing the reality, isness.

Descriptive Meaning and Symbols

JUPITER IN LIBRA
Four swords of equal size and strength meet together in the rosette, the sign of official approval. The slanted Saint Andrew's cross behind the swords represents difficulty, but its green colour shows the creativity that has led to, and can come from, the acceptance of this situation. The blue colour of the background is a symbol of clarity, but the intricate webbing design on it shows that there are still conflicts or complications around. This is not a settlement or resolution, but a truce, a respite that comes from agreement. For agreement to happen one must be open and flexible like the Jupiter sign at the top of the card, and be ready to maintain a sense of balance without fixed position like Libra at the bottom. The four represents the unification of body, mind, heart and soul necessary for true acceptance. This card symbolises the state of allowing things to be the way they are. It indicates a place of acceptance in the mind that is not judging or trying to change but is simply able to acknowledge what is. It is the state of mental 'suchness'. In a negative sense this can contain an aspect of resignation, or it can be the acceptance that is an avoidance of doing something.

Variations in the Current Life Reading

When this card appears in:

No. 1 – General Outlook: You are simply accepting your life the way it is, whether you like it or not. It could be that this is a genuine acceptance, or it could be that it is easier to accept than do something about it.

No. 2 – Communication: Relating is not a very exciting area of your life right now. It's the kind of state that might have you saying, 'Is that so,' or 'How interesting!' a lot when communicating. You may feel a bit flat around people.

No. 3 – Work: There is a simple acceptance of your work situation; it is not very exciting but not a problem either. Is this really the reality or are you avoiding looking?

No. 4 – Inner Self: There is an acceptance of yourself as you are, which could, though not necessarily, mean a lack of willingness to look deeper or change.

No. 5 – Sexual Energy: If you do have a sex life right now, it's not a very thrilling one. It's more likely that you have resigned yourself to what is or isn't happening with the opposite sex and put it to one side.

No. 6 – Body: This card in the body energy could mean the acceptance of some physical state, or it could mean a resigned state of mind that is making the physical energy feel a little flat.

No. 7 – Primary Relationship: Whether there is or isn't an intimate relationship in your life, you have accepted the state of affairs as it is. This is not a problem, but it is not very joyous or juicy either.

No. 8 – New Perspective: Has it occurred to you that you could simply accept things the way they are?

No. 9 – Mind: You are thinking about accepting what is, which could mean part of you is fighting. Or it could be a resigned state of mind.

No. 10 – Peak Experience: The best thing you can do in the current situation is simply allow things to be the way they are. Nothing can be achieved by fighting the reality of what's going on. Facts are facts.

No. 11 – Spiritual Message: Existence is encouraging you to face the 'suchness' of your life right now. Accept the reality as it is without trying to fight or change. You can only start the journey by being where you are now.

No. 12 – Meditation: Simple acceptance of what's happening is your meditation, which probably means that is what is difficult for you right now.

No. 13 – Overview: You are accepting the course of your life as it is. There are no problems but not much enthusiasm either.

FIVE OF SWORDS – DEFEAT

Essence: Defeat, failure, without hope.

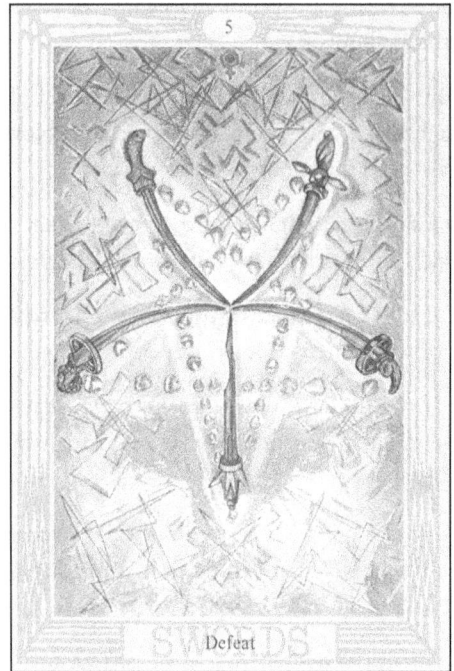

Descriptive Meaning and Symbols

VENUS IN AQUARIUS
The five swords are bent, chipped and out of balance, showing a lack of clarity and harmony in the mind. They have completely destroyed the pink rose at the centre, illustrating that this mental state destroys all the love in the heart. The petals are strewn around in the shape of an inverted pentagram, a symbol of unstable negative thinking that touches the deepest fears of loss, helplessness and abandonment. This card represents the point of recognising failure, of having to admit that you have lost, that what you wanted has not happened. There is no hope left; you admit defeat. At the same time there is light starting to shine through from the centre of the card and a tinge of creative green in the background, showing that when the mind gives up its old ideas, there is room for something new to happen.

Variations in the Current Life Reading

When this card appears in:

No. 1 – General Outlook: A sense of defeat is colouring the way you look at your life. There could be a specific reason for this or it could just be a defeatist attitude of mind, which may in fact cause everything to fail.

No. 2 – Communication: There is the attitude of defeat around your way of relating. Something of your old way of connecting is not working. Or it could be that you have given up trying to be heard or understood.

No. 3 – Work: The energy around your work is one of defeat or having lost. Whatever it is that you have been doing or wanting to do hasn't worked out, and this could be making you feel rather helpless.

No. 4 – Inner Self: There is a sense of failure or hopelessness in your inner being. You could be dealing with old abandonment issues or the feeling of not being good enough. You may find that until you deal with this inner state nothing on the outside can work.

No. 5 – Sexual Energy: There is a feeling of failure in your sexual energy, which means either that some sexual relationship hasn't worked out, or that you have a sense of defeat around your sexual identity.

No. 6 – Body: The sensation of failure in your body could be the reality of a physical disability that you can't do anything about. Or it could be an old sense of helplessness that is surfacing in the physical energy.

No. 7 – Primary Relationship: You are in a state of defeat around intimate relationship. Things have not worked out as you wished and you are forced to face failure. It could be a feeling of having lost, which may indicate that your attitude has been one of trying to win or to make something happen in a certain way.

No. 8 – New Perspective: Has it occurred to you that it's time to give up and admit defeat?

No. 9 – Mind: You are thinking about some situation where you feel defeated.

No. 10 – Peak Experience: The best thing you can do in the current situation is admit defeat. There simply isn't anywhere else to go or anything else to do about it. It's not working.

No. 11 – Spiritual Message: You are being encouraged to find the space in your mind where you stop fighting with life. Allow yourself to feel a deep inner sense of failure and know that however painful this may feel, what is being defeated is merely on the ego level of your being. Only by giving up on individual desires or goals can you tune in with the higher flow of existence.

No. 12 – Meditation: You are being forced to face a sense of defeat or failure that you are probably trying very hard to avoid. Let yourself really go into this and it could become a transformation.

No. 13 – Overview: A feeling of defeat or hopelessness is colouring your life right now. There is nothing to be done but be aware of it and see where it leads you. This could be the darkest hour before the dawn of something new in your life.

SIX OF SWORDS – SCIENCE

Essence: Objective clarity, analysis, scientific investigation, impersonal thinking.

Descriptive Meaning and Symbols

MERCURY IN AQUARIUS

The six swords in this painting are finely drawn, matching, balanced and in harmony. They meet in the middle of the rose of the heart at the centre of the cross, indicating authentic realisation. The cross, which is featured on the back of this tarot pack, is the symbol of the Rosicrucian's desire to bring the rational objective mind into the esoteric and mystic. The circle surrounding the cross symbolises the holistic mind or the ability to see things in a wide or universal way. The cool grey background of the card is covered with tiny well-formed shapes that illustrate the fine preciseness of this mental state. Science represents the mind that can be clear and rational in all dimensions. It is the ability to bring objective thinking into whatever is happening – the capacity to analyse in a detached, scientific way.

Variations in the Current Life Reading

When this card appears in:

No. 1 – General Outlook: You are looking at your life from a very cool, impersonal space.

No. 2 – Communications: You are rather cool and matter-of-fact in your relating. You could be quite analytical when you communicate, maybe probing and investigating to find the facts. Or it could be that you are looking at your relating patterns in this way.

No. 3 – Work: There is a rational and objective approach to your work. Maybe you are investigating something right now, or maybe you are simply seeing your situation in a very clear analytical way.

No. 4 – Inner Self: You are looking into your inner being with inquiry and objective clarity. This is quite an achievement but might feel a little dry and distant.

No. 5 – Sexual Energy: You are experiencing what is happening around your sexual energy from a clear mental perspective. It's great to be able to see what's going on rationally but is usually not very exciting.

No. 6 – Body: There is an objective awareness of what is happening in the physical energy, which may mean you feel a little distant or detached from your body.

No. 7 – Primary Relationship: You are fair-minded and rational in your intimate relating, which makes you very objective and clear to be with but not very exciting or warm. Or this could be the way you look at your own ability to be in an intimate relationship.

No. 8 – New Perspective: What would happen if you inquired into the situation from a rational, objective point of view?

No. 9 – Mind: You think you are being rational and analytical, or want to be.

No. 10 – Peak Experience: The best thing you can do in the current situation is take a step back from your subjective opinions and feelings and see what is happening from a cooler and more objective perspective.

No. 11 – Spiritual Message: Existence is encouraging you to take a good analytic look at your life from an objective perspective. This is a time when you need to see what is happening in a clear and impersonal way, which probably means putting aside a lot of your old opinions and judgements.

No. 12 – Meditation: Your meditation right now is to maintain objective clarity, which probably means you're having difficulty doing just that. See how identifying with what you feel or what you want can take away your clarity.

No. 13 – Overview: You have a cool rational perspective of what is happening and where you are going in your life. This could indicate a sense of objective inquiry into whatever is going on that will affect your future direction.

SEVEN OF SWORDS – FUTILITY

Essence: Futility, pointlessness, waste of time.

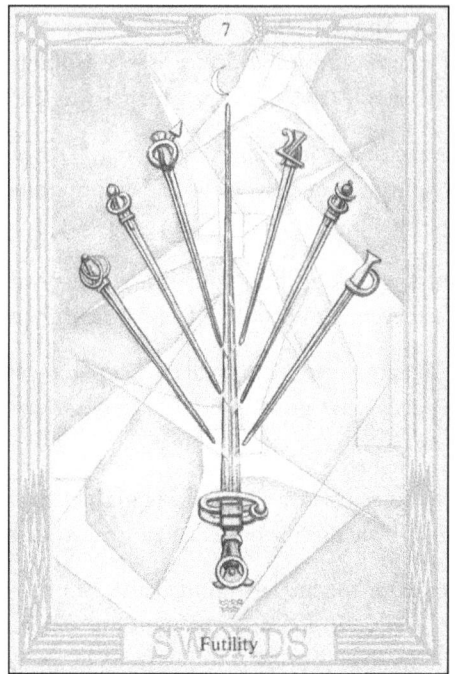

Descriptive Meaning and Symbols

MOON IN AQUARIUS

The central sword that represents clarity, or knowing what you want, is being attacked by six smaller swords which represent different negative ideas of mind that are sabotaging the clarity or sense of purpose. The six swords have different planetary symbols on their hilts, representing various unconscious tricks of the mind for why things won't work: 'I am not lucky enough', 'I am too tired', 'I can't be bothered', 'It's too difficult', 'I'm not sure'. The card symbolises the aspect of the mind that cuts motivation by telling you, 'It doesn't matter anyway – what's the point'. It creates a state of flatness in life where things can seem a waste of time or futile. This needn't necessarily be a negative space. There are times when doing something or going somewhere *is* a waste of time, or pointless, and experiencing this creates space to direct the energy into things that are more worthwhile.

Variations in the Current Life Reading

When this card appears in:

No. 1 – General Outlook: Your general outlook on life is gloomy and flat. It probably feels like there's no point in even getting out of bed in the morning. This could just be an attitude of mind, or it could be that you are genuinely recognising that a certain way of looking at life no longer has any point.

No. 2 – Communication: You can't be bothered to relate right now. Maybe you feel no one will understand or wants to know, so what's the point. Or maybe you can see a certain aspect of your way of relating that you don't want any more.

No. 3 – Work: Whatever you are doing in your work is feeling pointless and a waste of time. Or maybe you are not doing anything and it is feeling very flat. Certainly there's little motivation right now.

No. 4 – Inner Self: There is a sense of futility deep in your inner being that is probably making you feel dull and flat in yourself and could be causing you to question certain aspects of your life.

No. 5 – Sexual Energy: Something around your sexual energy is feeling futile. Maybe it's the particular relationship you're in, or maybe certain aspects of your own sexual programming. Or it could be the act of sex itself.

No. 6 – Body: There is lethargy in your physical energy that is probably making your body feel dead and lifeless. Maybe you feel there's no point in doing anything or even moving.

No. 7 – Primary Relationship: Whether it's with someone in particular or intimate relating in general, it all feels a bit futile right now. There's a feeling of, 'Why bother.' Or there may be the sense that there's no point in doing anything because it's not going to work anyway.

No. 8 – New Perspective: Has it occurred to you that something you're doing is completely without point, a waste of time?

No. 9 – Mind: You are thinking that something, or maybe life, is futile.

No. 10 – Peak Experience: The best thing you can do in the current situation is see its futility. You are wasting your time. Be with that awareness.

No. 11 – Spiritual Message: Existence is encouraging you to give space to the state of futility that is around you. Sometimes this sense of pointlessness is an existential reality, which is necessary to enable you to move beyond superficial desires that have previously seemed important to find a deeper motivation. Hang in there, even though it probably feels flat and pointless.

No. 12 – Meditation: This futility that you are experiencing is a great growth for you. Keep coming back to and embracing it rather than trying to avoid the feeling or find more desires to fill the gap.

No. 13 – Overview: There is a flat, pointless feeling around your life right now. Maybe you are looking ahead and seeing that to continue in the same way would be futile.

EIGHT OF SWORDS – INTERFERENCE

Essence: Confusion, not knowing, indecision, conflicting ideas.

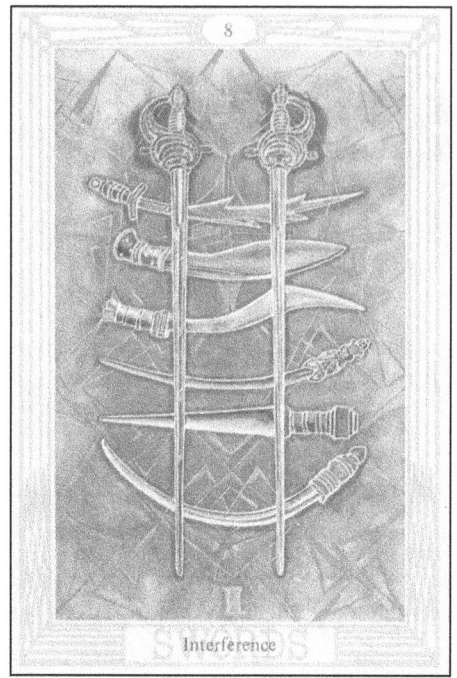

Descriptive Meaning and Symbols

JUPITER IN GEMINI
The mind, by its very nature, moves between opposites. It cannot exist without two extremes or limits to fluctuate between. Right/wrong, yes/no, up/down, in/out, black/white etcetera. This is how it functions. The two central swords can be seen either as these polarities of the dualistic mind or simply as two alternative ideas of apparently equal merit. The six swords of various sizes and shapes behind, represent the different thoughts that come up to substantiate first one alternative then the other. This is the mind in confusion or not knowing, often because there are two or more possibilities to choose from and so many disconnected ideas behind them that clarity is impossible. It is the state where the doubting mind gives reasons both in favour of a possibility and against it. The more we try to analyse the situation, the more confused we get. With deeper understanding we come to realise that this is simply the nature of the mind, and when we are caught in this space it is simply not possible to find an answer. It is allowing this space of not knowing and confusion to be there that creates room for clear insight or intuition to happen.

Variations in the Current Life Reading

When this card appears in:

No. 1 – General Outlook: You have a confused outlook on life right now, which probably means you don't know what's going on but are trying to.

No. 2 – Communication: You don't really know how to be with people right now, maybe because old ways of relating are no longer working. It could be that you get confused when you try to express yourself and everything comes out sounding wrong.

No. 3 – Work: There is a lot of confusion around your work or doing energy. Maybe you're trying to decide between two alternatives, or maybe you're just not knowing what to do. The more you try to figure it out, the more confused you are likely to get. The reality is: you don't know.

No. 4 – Inner Self: There is confusion deep in your being right now. You may be feeling you don't know who you are or you don't understand what is happening in your life.

No. 5 – Sexual Energy: Your connection with your sex energy or sexual partner is one of profound confusion. There are so many ideas in the mind that you can't begin to feel the truth of the energy.

No. 6 – Body: It could be that you are confused about something that is happening in your body. Or it could be that the confusion of the mind is stopping you from tuning into your physical energy. This could manifest as physical problems if you don't stop listening to your mind and just be with the reality of the physical energy.

No. 7 – Primary Relationship: You are in a state of perplexity with intimate relating. Whether it is with a current partner or with the issue of intimacy in general, your mind doesn't (and probably never will) have the answers for you. Maybe you need to come back to the reality of the energy and feelings to find out what's happening.

No. 8 – New Perspective: Have you considered that you could simply admit that you don't know and see what happens from there?

No. 9 – Mind: You are concerned with your confusion or state of not knowing.

No. 10 – Peak Experience: The best thing you can do in the current situation is admit that you don't know and allow the mind to be in confusion without trying to understand or find the solution.

No. 11 – Spiritual Message: Existence is encouraging you to relax into a state of not knowing. Sometimes it is necessary to give the mind permission to be in confusion so that you can find a place of knowing beyond the mind. Only when you know you don't know, is it possible to find this deeper place.

No. 12 – Meditation: Being in the state of confusion and not knowing is your meditation right now. Don't try to avoid it by attempting to work things out, no matter how tempting that may be. Just keep coming back to this reality and trying to rest with it.

No. 13 – Overview: You don't know where you are going or what's happening in your life right now. If you accept this, you can allow your life to be a mystery to be lived rather than a problem to be solved.

NINE OF SWORDS – CRUELTY

Essence: Self-doubt, self-judgement, guilt, mental insecurity, self-examination.

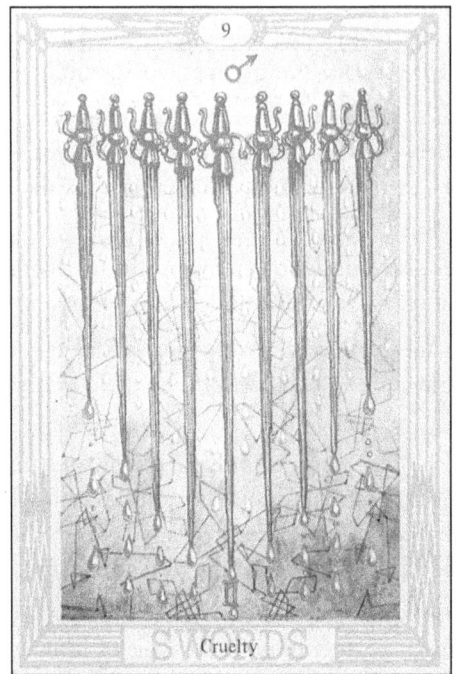

Descriptive Meaning and Symbols

MARS IN GEMINI

The nine chipped and rusty-looking swords hang downwards to different lengths. Blood drips from their ends and tears fall in the background. This signifies the wounds and pain that are caused when the mind is turned against the self in doubt and judgement. It is generally experienced as an attitude of self-criticalness that comes when we don't trust what we think or feel and so are constantly in a state of insecurity and uncertainty. It can also be experienced as guilt when we think there is something wrong with what naturally occurs in our being and believe we should be different. The roots of this state of mind usually come from internalising the criticism and judgements we received when we were young children. In a positive place this card can also symbolise the need for self-doubt – the need to question something about our beliefs or certainties.

Variations in the Current Life Reading

When this card appears in:

No. 1 – General Outlook: You are looking at the world through a veil of uncertainty and self-doubt, which probably makes it difficult for you to see reality at all.

No. 2 – Communication: You don't trust yourself or what you want to say when you are around others, so it is probably difficult for you to relate right now. You may experience this as a shyness or social insecurity.

No. 3 – Work: There is a lot of self-doubt and uncertainty with whatever you are doing. Maybe you feel that you have done something wrong or are just not good enough. Whatever it is, you are very much lacking in confidence.

No. 4 – Inner Self: You are hurting your being with your judgements and doubt about yourself. This probably makes you feel so insecure and uncertain that it is hard for you to be clear about who you really are. If this pattern is an old one, use this opportunity to see it for what it is and maybe try to understand where it comes from.

No. 5 – Sexual Energy: You are either insecure about your own sexual nature, or about your sexual connection with a particular person. Either way, this insecurity probably comes from ideas of the mind and is not the truth of your vital energy.

No. 6 – Body: The tendency of the mind to criticise and judge your own being or body is interfering with your physical energy and can cause real physical symptoms if it is not dealt with more consciously. Or it could be that you are feeling fragile and insecure because of something physical that is happening in the body.

No. 7 – Primary Relationship: There is so much negative energy turned against yourself at this time that it is almost impossible for anyone to get close to you in an intimate relationship. Be aware that this self-doubt is creating a wall between you and the one(s) closest.

No. 8 – New Perspective: Has it occurred to you that you may not be perfect or right all the time; that you could do with questioning yourself and your beliefs right now?

No. 9 – Mind: You are questioning or doubting your own thoughts. Or maybe it is that you are thinking about your lack of self-trust or guilt.

No. 10 – Peak Experience: The best thing you can do is question your concepts and beliefs about your current situation. It looks like you have been functioning under some misconceptions that you are now ready to see.

No. 11 – Spiritual Message: Existence is gently pushing you to question and doubt the very fabric of what you have considered your life. It is a time for serious self-examination and re-evaluation of who you are, what you are doing, or where you are going. You are learning how to do this without judging yourself for being or doing wrong.

No. 12 – Meditation: Your meditation at this time is to be with the feelings of self-doubt or guilt without trying to push them away. It probably feels awful, but just letting yourself be consciously aware of this part of your mental makeup, without trying to suppress it, is an important learning for you.

No. 13 – Overview: You are in a state of insecurity and uncertainty about your direction in life. That's how it is, so that's how it needs to be right now.

TEN OF SWORDS – RUIN

Essence: Let go, the point of giving up, cutting attachment.

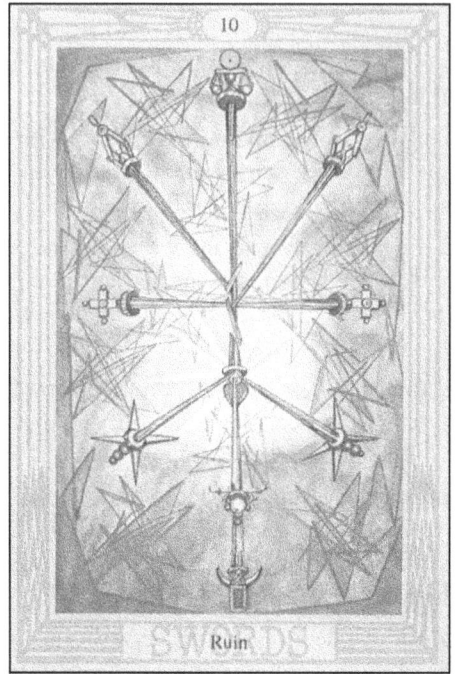

Descriptive Meaning and Symbols

SUN IN GEMINI
Nine of the swords have turned their points against the tenth sword in the middle and completely destroyed it. This is the mental state where there is nowhere else to go with the mind; there is nothing else to do but give up or let go. The mind has run out of possibilities or potential; it has tried everything and now it can only resign. This devastated sword bears the symbol of the heart; the giving up has pierced deep into the heart and the very sense of self. Like Death (XIII) in the major arcana, this card indicates the end of something. But Ruin is the letting go with the mind, the cutting of mental attachment rather than the actual event of something being finished that is indicated by Death. The letting go of the attachment of the mind doesn't necessarily mean the event has finished. We could, for instance, let go of our attachment to a relationship and still be in it for the rest of our lives – but in an unattached way.

Variations in the Current Life Reading

When this card appears in:

No. 1 – General Outlook: You are looking at your life from the point of having let go of something. You probably know what this is but, if it's not something obvious, look inside to see what attitude or hope you have let go of recently and realise it is colouring your whole attitude to life.

No. 2 – Communication: There is a sense of giving up around relating. Maybe there have been arguments or discussions in some direction, and you are at the place of letting go of trying to win or express. Or maybe whatever way you have tried to connect with people in general hasn't worked, so you are giving up trying.

No. 3 – Work: You are in a place with your work, or something that you have been doing, where your mind is ready to give up. Maybe you have tried to work out all the possibilities and now there is nowhere else to go with it but let go.

No. 4 – Inner Self: You are in a space within yourself of let go or giving up. This might be of something material, a specific mind trip that has been happening, or just a sense of giving up on trying to understand something about yourself with your head.

No. 5 – Sexual Energy: Probably you are letting go of a sexual connection or bonding with somebody. If not, you are letting go of some old ideas or trips around your connection with the opposite sex.

No. 6 – Body: This may indicate a letting go of some mental control over the body that you may be feeling as a physical release. Or it could be a deep let go on a mental or emotional level that is being reflected in the body.

No. 7 – Primary Relationship: You are probably in the process of dropping attachment to an intimate relationship, or some aspect of it. If not, there is a letting go of some hope or programme around intimate relating.

No. 8 – New Perspective: Has it occurred to you that it's time to just let go, give up?

No. 9 – Mind: You are thinking about letting go, which could mean you are still holding on.

No. 10 – Peak Experience: The best thing you can do in the current situation is just let go, give up. There is nothing else you can do with your mind, nowhere else to go. Literally take your hands off.

No. 11 – Spiritual Message: Existence is encouraging you to let go, to stop trying to control, understand or otherwise do something about your life. Maybe you have tended to hold on too tightly to what you know, and this is stopping the natural flow of your life. It is only by giving up with the mind that you can create the space for something new.

No. 12 – Meditation: Your meditation right now is the process of letting go, probably of something particular that you are attached to. Know that this is where your growth lies, and keep coming back to allowing this state again and again. Letting go is never easy and you are learning how to do it.

No. 13 – Overview: The letting go or giving up on something is affecting your whole life. It could be something on the outside of you or an inner process. Either way, it is having a profound affect on your direction.

CUPS ARE THE SYMBOLS OF WATER AND REPRESENT THE EMOTIONS OR FEELING STATES OF THE BEING

KNIGHT OF CUPS

Essence: Giving, expressing or sharing feelings; putting your heart into something.

Knight of Cups

Descriptive Meaning and Symbols

The Knight of Cups sits on a galloping white horse and has wings on his back to represent the active outward movement of his emotions. He holds the chalice or cup of his feelings stretched out in front of him for all to see. The Cancer crab in it symbolises both his security and enjoyment of sharing his heart. The faded peacock, the symbol of vanity, indicates that he takes pride in doing this, that he likes to be seen as a giving, sharing person. He is the only knight without a helmet, illustrating his willingness to expose who he is and what he is feeling. This card symbolises the quality of putting out, expressing or exposing emotions, or sharing from the heart – the mature yang aspects of emotion. In the negative this can include the quality of taking pride in being a giving, loving person, as well as the giving that happens out of the need for security or to be liked.

Variations in the Current Life Reading

When this card appears in:

No. 1 – General Outlook: You view your life through your role of being a giving, sharing person. This could come from a genuine, heartful space and wanting to share what you feel, or it could be the belief that you have to give to others to keep yourself safe and get what you want from them.

No. 2 – Communication: It could be that you are very giving and sharing in your way of relating with others, or else exposing a lot of what you feel. Either way, your energy is emotional and outgoing.

No. 3 – Work: You are pouring your heart energy into your work or whatever it is you are doing right now.

No. 4 – Inner Self: It could be that you are giving a lot to yourself right now, but more likely that you relate to yourself mainly through your ability to give to others. If the latter, you might want to look at why you feel the necessity to always give.

No. 5 – Sexual Energy: Your sexual energy is in a loving, giving space. Probably this is with someone in particular, but it could be a more general feeling of lovingness that you want to share with the opposite sex.

No. 6 – Body: Your physical energy is being shared in a giving, outgoing way. This can be beautiful, but check if the giving is always really the truth of your energy or something you think you have to do.

No. 7 – Primary Relationship: You are in a giving, sharing space in your intimate relationship. Maybe you are simply sharing the truth of what you feel, or maybe it is a habitual need to give in order to feel worthy of being loved.

No. 8 – New Perspective: Have you considered that maybe you could share more of what you're feeling?

No. 9 – Mind: You are thinking about exposing your feelings or sharing your love. Or it could be that you are considering what you want to put your heart into.

No. 10 – Peak Experience: The best thing you can do in the current situation is put out whatever it is you are feeling. There is nothing to be gained by trying to be reasonable or repressing what is going on.

No. 11 – Spiritual Message: Existence is encouraging you to learn what it means to share and expose what is going on with you emotionally. Maybe your upbringing taught you that it was unsafe or rude to express your feelings, but you are in a time in your spiritual development where you need to start taking that risk.

No. 12 – Meditation: Your meditation is to share whatever is going on with you. This probably means it's not easy for you, but often it is only through the process of expressing or exposing that we become clear about what is there.

No. 13 – Overview: The way in which you share yourself and express your heart in the world is the main issue for you right now. Maybe you are looking for something to put your heart into, or maybe it is your role as a giving person that is affecting your future direction.

QUEEN OF CUPS

Essence: Openness of heart, receptivity, vulnerability. Dependence, victim.

Descriptive Meaning and Symbols

The Queen of Cups represents the mature yin way of relating to emotions – principally the ability to receive and reflect. She is so much an open receptor that she appears only as a delicate, misty figure almost hidden behind a swirl of light beams. In this way she also illustrates the indistinct and mysterious nature of feelings that can take over the being. Her head is the most hidden, showing that the mind is unimportant in the area of emotion. Her reflection on the still water in front of her is almost perfect. This symbolises both the quality of owning feelings and allowing them to be reflected to the world outside, and the ability to put the self aside and allow who or what is outside to be reflected. The white lotus blossoms are a symbol of love; they grow out of the mud of the lake just as love grows out of the depths of the unconscious. The stork illustrates the connection with mother love and the willingness to open to the new. This card represents the female aspects of the emotions, which are principally openness, receptivity, sensitivity, vulnerability and softness. In the negative it can carry the destructive sides of the yin heart: getting drowned in emotions, passivity, dependency, giving away power and being a victim.

Variations in the Current Life Reading

When this card appears in:

No. 1 – General Outlook: You are looking at life from a very vulnerable and open place. It could be beautiful, but not always comfortable, to see yourself as so sensitive. Check to see whether you are feeling like a victim of life.

No. 2 – Communication: You are receptive and sensitive in your way of relating with others. You could be quite shy and find it hard to express yourself from this space, so you mainly listen and fit in with others.

No. 3 – Work: There is a sensitive openness around your work energy, which could be beautiful, or could mean you are giving your power away and being too passive.

No. 4 – Inner Self: You are feeling soft and sensitive in yourself. Maybe you can stay with this inner vulnerability without feeling the need to protect, or maybe you are feeling dependent or a victim of others as a result.

No. 5 – Sexual Energy: Whether you are male or female, you are open and available on an emotional level to the opposite sex or more likely to someone in particular. This is not hot passion but a sensitive, loving energy that could tend toward dependence on the other.

No. 6 – Body: Your physical energy is vulnerable and open right now. You probably need to take care of this delicate sensitivity.

No. 7 – Primary Relationship: You are open in your intimate relating. This can be beautiful, but don't forget that your surrender is to love and not to the other person or you will give away your power and become a dependent victim.

No. 8 – New Perspective: Has it occurred to you that you could simply be open and available and see what happens from that?

No. 9 – Mind: You are thinking about being vulnerable or dependent, or maybe about feeling like a victim.

No. 10 – Peak Experience: The best thing you can do in this situation is stay soft and receptive, and allow yourself to feel whatever comes up. Keeping the heart open is the only way to know what we feel, but often we try to find out with the mind.

No. 11 – Spiritual Message: Existence is working on your heart right now. You are being encouraged to drop your defences and be vulnerable, to be more concerned with taking in and feeling than with putting out. Receiving is a more subtle art than giving because it negates the ego.

No. 12 – Meditation: Your growth lies in staying open and vulnerable, which is probably something you would prefer to avoid. Literally make it a meditation not to close down and protect, even though that may feel threatening.

No. 13 – Overview: You are living your life from a very open, passive place right now, which could be making you feel a bit lost and helpless. Basically you are just allowing whatever is happening without trying to, or being able to, control.

PRINCE OF CUPS

Essence: Emotional desire, wishes, hopes, dreams, fantasy.

Descriptive Meaning and Symbols

The Prince of Cups represents the less developed yang way of relating to the feelings. The naked young man is being pulled along above the water in his shell-shaped chariot by a giant eagle. This illustrates that he doesn't actually go into his emotions (the water), but rather they are propelled upwards in the air or mind as wanting or desiring. He is not present to the reality of what he feels, but rather looking ahead at what he wants. The eagle can also be seen as the symbol of Scorpio, the astrological sign for passion and desire. The prince holds the lotus of love in his hand, but it is turned down in neglect. His attention is focused on the snake in his cup, in other words on the transformation he is hoping to get through what he desires. The snake can also be seen as the serpent that tempted Eve in the Bible. This card symbolises the energy of the heart that is projected outwards from the mind as desiring or wanting. Right desiring is like seeds being planted in existence; what we ask for is what we will move towards. Wrong desiring is dreaming or fantasising to escape from what is really happening.

Variations in the Current Life Reading

When this card appears in:

No. 1 – General Outlook: You are so full of your desires and hopes that you probably can't see what's happening. You are living in a bit of a dream.

No. 2 – Communication: You have hopes or ideas about how you would like to relate to people that may have some basis in fact or may be just hot air and fantasy.

No. 3 – Work: You have a desire about what you would like to do or achieve in your work area.

No. 4 – Inner Self: Your time with yourself is spent in fantasising about what you would like to happen or how you would like to be. In other words, you are day dreaming.

No. 5 – Sexual Energy: There is an emotional desire in your sex energy that might be for someone in particular or may simply be desire for romantic sex.

No. 6 – Body: There is a quality of dreaminess in your body that stops you from being present and probably makes you feel a little spaced out. Or maybe you desire to make changes to your body in some way.

No. 7 – Primary Relationship: There is desire around intimate relationship; it could be that you are wanting something from someone in particular or simply that you wish and hope for intimacy in your life. Be aware if this dreaming stops you from being present to whom or what is actually there.

No. 8 – New Perspective: Has it occurred to you that you need to check out what it is you actually want?

No. 9 – Mind: You are thinking about what it is you want, which probably means you don't know and are lost in dreams.

No. 10 – Peak Experience: The best thing you can do in the current situation is recognise your desires and feel where that takes you. What is it that you really want?

No. 11 – Spiritual Message: Existence is encouraging you to check out what your desires are in life, what direction you want to move in. It could be time for a priority check: what is the highest thing you could aspire to right now. Let it come from the depths of the heart; you are planting seeds for your future direction. What you ask for, you will get.

No. 12 – Meditation: Your meditation right now is to keep becoming aware of what it is you want.

No. 13 – Overview: You have ideas or dreams about where you want to go or what you want to happen in life that are occupying much of your attention. You may like to check whether those desires are based on reality or are an escape from reality.

PRINCESS OF CUPS

Essence: Emotional freedom, unattached to feelings, friendliness, love with freedom.

Princess of Cups

Descriptive Meaning and Symbols

The Princess of Cups is represented as a light, dancing woman dressed in a seashell gown with crystals along its hemline to show the clarity of her feelings. She holds the lotus, which represents her heart far out from her body. This shows that she has a distance from what she feels. In the other hand she holds a turtle in a seashell as a symbol of being at home and secure in her emotions. Because of this she has no need to control or possess in her relationships; she has moved beyond jealousy and manipulation. The open-winged swan above her head emphasises her ability to be free and independent in and of what she feels. The fish indicates the depth of her feelings and her ability to communicate them with clarity. This card symbolises the less established yin way of relating to emotions that is open and secure but not drowned in or attached to what is being felt. It is also the state of non-possessive love, or the capacity to feel the heart without trying to manipulate, hold on to or get caught in expectations. It is love that is based on freedom rather than bonding. This can be called friendliness – the capacity to be intimate with whoever or whatever, without judgement or expectation, which creates a lightness of the heart. In a negative sense the card can indicate the tendency to not take feelings seriously – to keep distance from them, or protect them.

Variations in the Current Life Reading

When this card appears in:

No. 1 – General Outlook: You have a friendly outlook on life that allows you to be in a light, heartful connection with what is happening around you without getting lost in old emotional patterns.

No. 2 – Communication: You relate in an open and friendly way with people – very heartful but light and easy to get on with. Maybe sometimes you could be a little frivolous.

No. 3 – Work: This is a positive, light-hearted energy to bring into your work. It could be indicating your feelings for what you are doing, or it could be showing that your open, friendly relationships with the people you work with are the most important thing there for you.

No. 4 – Inner Self: You are friendly with yourself, which means you are able to accept yourself lovingly, whatever is going on inside, without judgement.

No. 5 – Sexual Energy: Your relationship with your sexual partner or with the opposite sex in general is loving, open and non-possessive.

No. 6 – Body: You have a loving friendliness with your body, which enables you to say 'yes' to whatever energy is happening in it without judgement or holding.

No. 7 – Primary Relationship: This is a lovely card to have for intimate relationship. You are loving and open, but secure enough in yourself not to need contracts or control. Maybe there is a tendency to be too flippant sometimes.

No. 8 – New Perspective: Has it occurred to you that you could simply be friendly with whatever or whoever is foremost in your life right now?

No. 9 – Mind: You are thinking about wanting to be more friendly with something or someone.

No. 10 – Peak Experience: The best thing you can do in the current situation is simply be friendly to whatever is going on. Or, if it is a relationship situation, you need to start moving to a new and higher space with this person where you can love in an open, spacious way rather than with contracts and possessiveness.

No. 11 – Spiritual Message: Existence is encouraging you to find a space within yourself that is friendly with whatever is happening to you, both inside and out. Literally to befriend every emotional state or external happening without judgement of what it is. The key is to stay in the heart but not to be attached to what you feel, recognising that all emotional states will come and go.

No. 12 – Meditation: Your meditation is to move in the direction of bringing love and freedom together in your relating or with your emotions. This is never easy as it literally involves freeing up your own heart from the need for contractual security.

No. 13 – Overview: There is an overview of emotional freedom and friendly well-being in your life, which probably means you are having a pretty good time right now and have a positive, free outlook on your future.

ACE OF CUPS

Essence: Pure love energy, self-love, saying yes to yourself and what you feel. Trying to prove yourself.

Descriptive Meaning and Symbols

The wide-open cup sits on the base of a white lotus blossom, the symbol for pure love. The cup is filled by a light that comes from above, and continues out through the bottom; this is the energy of the divine that pours through the heart of man and onto the earth. The design in the upper and lower parts of the painting is the same: the realm of the spirit is reflected below in the emotional realm of water. This card symbolises the quality of pure love, the love that takes us beyond separation, which makes us one with each other, with the divine. This symbol could be based on the statement: 'God is love.' The chalice could be seen as the Holy Grail. It is through his connection with this pure energy of love that man connects with and becomes one with god. Our basic experience of this love is in loving and honouring ourselves, in realising that the love we feel, even for others, is our love. It has nothing to do with 'acting loving'; it is about being love. We cannot truly love another until we know the quality of love in ourselves by loving ourselves. So this card will usually represent the quality of self-love, of honouring our own beings and our own emotions, whatever they may be. In the negative it can be interpreted as trying to prove oneself.

Variations in the Current Life Reading

When this card appears in:

No. 1 – General Outlook: Your main concern in life is yourself right now. It could be that you are enjoying a space of genuine self-love and acceptance, or it could be that there's the need to try and prove yourself to others, which comes from non-acceptance of yourself.

No. 2 – Communication: It could be that you are giving yourself a lot of space to be who you are in your relations with others, or it could be that your behaviour is based on a need to prove yourself to them. Check to see which is relevant for you.

No. 3 – Work: You are probably doing what you want, your way, for yourself in this area of your life. But if you feel you are pushing yourself a bit, check if there is the idea of trying to prove something to someone.

No. 4 – Inner Self: You are enjoying the space of self-love and acceptance in your inner being right now. If you are feeling a bit selfish, remember that love for others will come naturally in its own time and way when you nurture this love within yourself.

No. 5 – Sexual Energy: Your sexual energy is strongly connected with your heart and, even though you may be sharing it with someone, your centre is in yourself and not with the other.

No. 6 – Body: You are in a space of loving your body and therefore centred energetically in your own heart.

No. 7 – Primary Relationship: You are in a heart space with the intimate other(s) in your life, but your concern is more with your feelings than those of the other. This can be beautiful too.

No. 8 – New Perspective: Has it occurred to you that you could start listening to your own heart, being with your own emotions, loving and saying 'yes' to yourself rather than to anyone else?

No. 9 – Mind: You are thinking about wanting to go for yourself.

No. 10 – Peak Experience: The best thing you can do in this situation is bring your focus back to yourself and what you want. Love yourself and honour what you are feeling, whatever it is.

No. 11 – Spiritual Message: Love of self is your path right now. It could be that you feel blocked with mental programmes that tell you there is something wrong with you and certainly something wrong with being selfish and thinking of yourself first. This is your time to learn to say 'yes' to yourself without being too concerned with the effect it has on others.

No. 12 – Meditation: Loving yourself and feeling your own love is your meditation. However difficult it may be, keep coming back to your own heart and feeling what you feel, or what you want, and saying 'yes' to it unconditionally. This is something that most of us have to learn.

No. 13 – Overview: You are going your own way right now and saying 'yes' to who you are and what you want. This is beautiful, but check that it is really what you want and not what you are trying to prove.

TWO OF CUPS – LOVE

Essence: Being or falling in love; romantic love.
The conditioning programmes around emotional need and love.

Descriptive Meaning and Symbols

VENUS IN CANCER
This card depicts the quality of the heart that is involved with the other. The self-containment of the Ace is now split so that there is the pull and need for the other half. The water of emotion flows from the one enormous lotus and fills the two cups to overflowing; one love fills two hearts, and to feel that love we need the other. The two fish wind around the lotus of love to illustrate the entwining and enmeshing quality of such love. This card can sometimes represent the quality of falling in love but, as most of us have experienced, this state tends to be a short-term illusion, a bubble that will burst in time when we inevitably move back up to the reason of our minds. Then we have to deal with the reality of the patterns and programmes that come up for us around the issue of love and this need for the other. These imprints are made in our beings by our parents, family and the environmental circumstances in the first seven years of life. The resulting mental programming affects not only the way we relate, but how we feel about ourselves for the rest of our lives. Very often this card will represent these early conditioning programmes that are based on the need for the other and can affect all aspects of how we function in life.

Variations in the Current Life Reading

When this card appears in:

No. 1 – General Outlook: You are looking at your life through the filter of an old conditioning programme, which means you are not seeing the reality as it is.

No. 2 – Communication: Your way of relating is affected by some old programme that is making you connect in a trippy way. You probably recognise the habit.

No. 3 – Work: Something around work has pushed a button that is bringing up dysfunctional emotional and mental programmes. Recognising that whatever you are going through here is your own movie rather than a reality will make you more objective.

No. 4 – Inner Self: You are very much in contact with, and could be lost in, some of your basic emotional patterns right now.

No. 5 – Sexual Energy: It could be that you have fallen in love (or lust), in which case you will be very aware of it. If not, you are confronting old conditioned behaviour patterns around the opposite sex.

No. 6 – Body: Early childhood experiences are literally patterned into the cells of the body. Right now your physical energy is being affected by that programming.

No. 7 – Primary Relationship: It could be that you have fallen madly and joyfully in love. You'll know if you have. If not, you are caught in your own conditioned programme around intimate love. You'll probably know that too, because it's a behaviour pattern you've experienced many times before.

No. 8 – New Perspective: Are you aware that whatever you are experiencing is coming from your own conditioning patterns rather than the reality?

No. 9 – Mind: You are thinking about, or are aware of, being caught up in old habit patterns.

No. 10 – Peak Experience: The best thing you can do in this situation is know that you are caught in your own patterns and go totally into whatever emotions are coming up. Don't be reasonable, but jump in and let yourself feel whatever is there – with awareness.

No. 11 – Spiritual Message: You are getting a strong message and opportunity to deal with some of the basic conditioning patterns that have been controlling your life. These patterns only change when we allow ourselves to feel and go through them with awareness. So don't judge or try to repress, but experience with consciousness.

No. 12 – Meditation: Bring your total awareness to seeing old emotional patterns that are running your life right now and let yourself fully experience them. Only full awareness of the programme allows freedom from it.

No. 13 – Overview: The direction of your life is largely influenced by habitual conditioning patterns right now. In other words you are in a rut. Being aware of this reality gives you the chance to see and change the patterns.

THREE OF CUPS – ABUNDANCE

Essence: Playfulness, non-seriousness, light hearted, overflowing abundance, celebration. Superficial, frivolous.

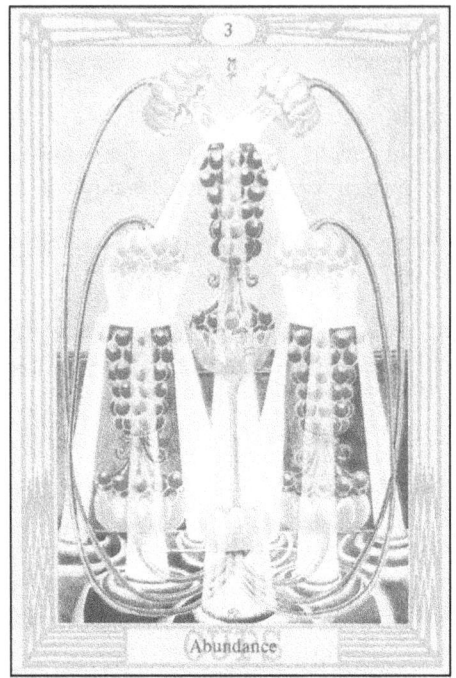

Descriptive Meaning and Symbols

MERCURY IN CANCER

The many yellow lotus flowers are pouring out streams of light golden, emotional energy into the overflowing red pomegranate cups. Pomegranates are rare fruits that were traditionally associated with riches and royalty in certain countries. The whole feeling is one of bountiful abundance. There is also a quality of lightness and playfulness in the red and yellow colours, which shows the fun and celebration that naturally results from abounding heart energy. The card represents the quality of emotional energy that is light and ebullient, so full and abundant that it can't help but share and communicate with others in a non-serious way. The young of any species are most often in this space. It's the feeling when we can't take anything seriously; everything feels like a play, a game or a celebration. In a negative sense it can represent the superficial frivolity or social behaviour that happens when the personality is used to hide the real.

Variations in the Current Life Reading

When this card appears in:

No. 1 – General Outlook: You have a light, playful outlook on life that probably means you can have fun with whatever is happening.

No. 2 – Communication: There is a light and bubbly sharing with others that probably means you're fun to be around but not very serious and possibly even a little superficial. Check to see if you have the habit of playing social games.

No. 3 – Work: There's a playful energy going into whatever you are doing. If you are not enjoying yourself, be aware that you are probably functioning from a superficial place in yourself rather than being real. In other words, you are playing some kind of a role or game.

No. 4 – Inner Self: There is a lightness in your inner being, which could mean you are enjoying your own being. It could also indicate that you are not into deep and meaningful self-examination.

No. 5 – Sexual Energy: Whether or not you have a sexual partner, you are capable of having fun with members of the opposite sex. But it could also be that you are into sexual roles or games.

No. 6 – Body: There is a bubbly abundance or energy in your body that probably makes you feel happy and playful.

No. 7 – Primary Relationship: There is much light, easy playfulness around your intimate relating, but you probably don't want to get into anything too serious. If you are in a relationship, check if you are hiding behind a superficial performance.

No. 8 – New Perspective: Have you thought that maybe you could be more playful, that you don't have to take things so seriously?

No. 9 – Mind: You are thinking about being playful and easy, certainly not wanting to be serious. Or maybe you are aware that you are playing a game in some area of your life.

No. 10 – Peak Experience: The best thing you can do in the current situation is not take it too seriously but keep things light and playful.

No. 11 – Spiritual Message: Existence is encouraging you to literally 'lighten up'. Maybe you have a tendency to take yourself and what's happening too seriously. Life doesn't have to be the serious, heavy thing that you might think it is. Start allowing yourself space to be a little more silly and less intense and meaningful.

No. 12 – Meditation: Your meditation at this time is to find a way to celebrate whatever is going on. See if you can have a good laugh about yourself or whatever is happening, and don't take things so seriously.

No. 13 – Overview: You are moving along in your life in a light, playful way, probably being social and having a good time. If this doesn't fit, check if you are so caught up in playing roles and games that you have lost touch with where you really are or what you really want.

FOUR OF CUPS – LUXURY

Essence: Emotional security issues, keeping things comfortable and safe.

Descriptive Meaning and Symbols

MOON IN CANCER

Here the four cups are made of metallic gold and are filled by a single pink lotus. There is a feeling of comfort, satisfaction and emotional security. But the cups are no longer overflowing because there is only one source of the emotional energy. The roots of the lotus flower are knotty and complicated, the sky above is starting to darken and the water below is a little rippled. This is the state where limits and compromises are imposed on the heart and feelings to ensure that things stay comfortable and secure, or when stability and safety are our main concerns. We are no longer available to take risks or be in the moment with what we feel because of the strong investment in keeping what we have, or ourselves, safe. The card can represent the state of being emotionally secure, but most usually represents the issues and compromises to truth that come up when security is our priority.

Variations in the Current Life Reading

When this card appears in:

No. 1 – General Outlook: Your general outlook on life is mainly concerned with the maintenance or acquiring of security. You don't like to take risks.

No. 2 – Communication: You play it safe in your relating with others. You aren't likely to say or do anything that might disturb the status quo, and you probably limit yourself to ways of behaving that you think are expected.

No. 3 – Work: There is a security concern around your work. This could be a result of instability in the job itself, or it could be an inner feeling of insecurity that makes you limit your behaviour through lack of self-confidence.

No. 4 – Inner Self: You are dealing with issues of security within yourself. It could be that you are concerned with maintaining security, but more likely that you are feeling insecure and wanting to get rid of it. Either way, you don't have much self-confidence right now.

No. 5 – Sexual Energy: The main concern around your sexual energy is emotional security. This could mean that you want to maintain a safe, secure situation with your sexual partner, or that you are keeping yourself secure by not exposing yourself or letting anyone close.

No. 6 – Body: There is an issue of security around your body. It could be that you are feeling insecure about your body, or that the need for emotional security is being experienced as protectiveness in the physical energy.

No. 7 – Primary Relationship: Your main issue in intimate relating is security, which probably means that you are compromising your truth to find or maintain emotional safety.

No. 8 – New Perspective: Has it occurred to you that you could feel secure and safe in this situation, or look at the reason why you are not?

No. 9 – Mind: You are thinking about security and keeping safe.

No. 10 – Peak Experience: The best thing you can do in the current situation is accept that you're dealing with your security issues and become aware of the price you pay for trying to keep things safe.

No. 11 – Spiritual Message: Existence is encouraging you to find the real inner security that comes from the trusting heart and has nothing to do with anyone or anything else. As long as your security is based on outside factors, there will always be a level of insecurity and compromise.

No. 12 – Meditation: You are probably being pushed into a situation that makes you feel insecure. Recognise that this is your major growth and experiment with feeling comfortable with your insecurity.

No. 13 – Overview: Your main issues right now are to do with security. It could be that you are feeling insecure about your future, or that you are aware of and wanting to change the compromises in your life that come from trying to maintain security.

FIVE OF CUPS – DISAPPOINTMENT

Essence: Disappointed expectations, dissatisfaction, unfulfilled. Yearning of the heart.

Descriptive Meaning and Symbols

MARS IN SCORPIO

The cups in this painting are made of fragile, breakable glass; the lotus flowers are withered and dying and nothing flows from them into the empty cups. The water below is green and murky with stagnation. This is the symbol of emotional disappointment. Something that was wanted and hoped for hasn't happened; some yearning has not been fulfilled. The heart is left feeling empty and fragile; the emotions are stagnant and murky like the water. The roots of the lotus are knotted into the shape of a butterfly to illustrate that transformation is possible from this state. In an advice place, the card can also indicate the yearning that such emptiness creates in the heart, which can sometimes act as a guiding force towards higher states of consciousness. The awareness of being unfulfilled or empty, feeling that there must be something more but not having a specific desire in the mind that we believe would make us content, can be the beginning of the spiritual search.

Variations in the Current Life Reading

When this card appears in:

No. 1 – General Outlook: You look at your life through a veil of disappointment and unfulfillment. Maybe there is a particular reason for this right now, or maybe it is a habitual attitude of dissatisfaction that colours everything in your life and makes it not work. Either way it's probably feeling pretty empty.

No. 2 – Communication: Relating is not easy for you right now. Maybe you are feeling so empty in yourself that you have nothing to give or say, or maybe certain hopes or expectations of others have not been met and you are disappointed.

No. 3 – Work: Your work, or lack of it, is unfulfilling for you at this time. Maybe something you were hoping for didn't work out or maybe there is just a feeling of lack of satisfaction.

No. 4 – Inner Self: You are feeling empty or unfulfilled in yourself. It may be the result of some particular disappointment or it may be an inner emptiness with no reason that you know of. With awareness it can turn into something else.

No. 5 – Sexual Energy: You are feeling unfulfilled or a sense of disappointment in your sexual energy. It could be that you are not getting what you want or expect from your sexual partner, or it could be the result of not having one.

No. 6 – Body: Your body needs something. On some level you are not properly nourishing yourself.

No. 7 – Primary Relationship: You are unfulfilled in the area of intimate relating. It could be that there is the lack of a mate, or else some hopes or expectations of your partner haven't been fulfilled. If it is the latter, you may need to remember that no one has any obligation to fulfil your expectations and look at what you need to do to fulfil yourself.

No. 8 – New Perspective: Has it occurred to you that allowing yourself to feel disappointed or unfulfilled is okay?

No. 9 – Mind: You are thinking about your emptiness or lack of fulfilment.

No. 10 – Peak Experience: The best thing you can do is recognise that you are disappointed or unfulfilled in this situation rather than trying to avoid the feeling or fill it with something else.

No. 11 – Spiritual Message: Existence is encouraging you to recognise the emptiness or yearning that you feel inside rather than trying to avoid or hide it with the superficialities of life. Don't be concerned with trying to find out what you are yearning for because your mind probably doesn't know; rather allow yourself to stay with the feeling and your heart will pull you where you need to go.

No. 12 – Meditation: Your meditation right now is to keep bringing your attention to and allowing the dissatisfaction or emptiness inside. In time you could discover that this feeling opens out into receptivity and vulnerability.

No 13: This empty unfulfilled feeling that is the major issue in your life right now is dictating your future direction. If you are not already, it may help to be more conscious of what it is that you are missing.

SIX OF CUPS – PLEASURE

Essence: Enjoying, taking pleasure in, keeping things pleasant.

Descriptive Meaning and Symbols

SUN IN SCORPIO

The six orange lotus blossoms pour their emotional energy into the copper-coloured cups that are filled, but not overflowing. This card symbolises the quality of pure pleasure, the right to do something simply because it is enjoyable. It can represent bodily pleasures or emotional pleasures – anything that feels good. Pleasure comes from simply allowing ourselves what we want for no other reason than that we enjoy it. It is a natural right that many of us have lost through years of mental, goal-orientated education where we learned to feel guilty about doing things just for pleasure. We have a right to enjoy ourselves, to simply do what we like. But the fact that the cups are not overflowing shows that this energy does have its limits; pleasure is not a deep emotion. The card can also represent the search for pleasure or need to keep things pleasant that can be a superficial escape from the deeper sides of life.

Variations in the Current Life Reading

When this card appears in:

No. 1 – General Outlook: Your main concern right now is pleasure. This is great if you're having a good time, but check whether you really are or if you could be avoiding feeling deeper.

No. 2 – Communication: You are enjoying relating with people and this is great. But check if there may also be a tendency to keep things pleasant and superficial in an artificial way.

No. 3 – Work: Lucky you if this is your work. It's pure pleasure, so if you're getting paid for it you're doing well. Otherwise it could be that this is holiday time for you.

No. 4 – Inner Self: You are literally enjoying yourself, or maybe it is that you relate to yourself mainly through the energy of pleasure. Beautiful, but be aware that you have more depth in your being than can be experienced through pleasure.

No. 5 – Sexual Energy: You are enjoying your connection with your sexual partner or maybe simply enjoying being around the opposite sex.

No. 6 – Body: You are taking pleasure in your own body and physical energy, which is no doubt making you feel good.

No. 7 – Primary Relationship: You're enjoying being with your intimate connections but are possibly not too interested in going deep. This is not a problem so long as the amiability is not covering an avoidance or fear of intimacy.

No. 8 – New Perspective: How about simply enjoying what's going on or giving yourself the right to do what you like?

No. 9 – Mind: You are thinking about pleasure and probably wanting more of it.

No. 10 – Peak Experience: The best thing you can do in this situation is simply enjoy it. There is no need to get serious, try to understand or work things out. Nothing more is required than simple enjoyment.

No. 11 – Spiritual Message: Existence is encouraging you to give yourself permission to simply enjoy yourself, to do what you want for the pure delight of it. Chances are you've never lived your life with pleasure as the major criterion before. Now is the time to learn how, even though a part of your mind may feel like you are doing something wrong or wasting time.

No. 12 – Meditation: Your meditation is simply to enjoy. This probably means you are not very good at it. Every time you catch yourself feeling miserable or serious, remember growth happens through allowing more pleasure in your life, not by trying to solve problems. You are allowed to enjoy yourself.

No. 13 – Overview: Life is good and you are enjoying the direction it is taking you in. Long may it continue, but when it stops remember that there is a greater depth to be explored beneath the pleasure.

SEVEN OF CUPS – DEBAUCH

Essence: Indulgence, over-indulgence, excessive.

Descriptive Meaning and Symbols

VENUS IN SCORPIO
Too much pleasure becomes over-indulgence, and this is what is symbolised here. The water of emotion has become green and slimy, just as water does when it is not moving. Instead of lotus blossoms, there are tiger lilies drooping with the weight of this thick, unhealthy, poisonous energy. This card symbolises the quality of emotional over-indulgence. It is the state when we are wallowing in negative emotions that almost inevitably have more to do with the past than the present. This is the energy when we are so lost in our own movie and our feelings about it that we have no openness or awareness of the outside reality. It can also represent what we do with our emotional energy to avoid feeling the things we don't want to feel: too much eating, drinking, shopping, sex, drugs etc. All these forms of over-indulgence can be a way of stagnating emotional energy and avoiding the real feeling or energy of the moment. This card represents indulgence in all its different forms, including the times when we need to give ourselves permission to indulge.

Variations in the Current Life Reading

When this card appears in:

No. 1 – General Outlook: Your indulgence is colouring the way you look at life. It is almost impossible to have much clarity with this outlook. It's like trying to look through dirty glasses.

No. 2 – Communication: It could be that you are talking too much, but more likely that you are very emotional and personally indulgent in your way of relating right now.

No. 3 – Work: Either you are a workaholic or you are very emotional around whatever it is you are doing. Just be aware that this is not a very healthy or aware place to be.

No. 4 – Inner Self: There is a lot of emotional energy in your inner being right now that is possibly experienced as self pity and feeling sorry for yourself. Be aware that, if there is no outward expression or clarity in this state, it could stagnate your energy.

No. 5 – Sexual Energy: This could mean that you are using sexual indulgence as a way of escaping from your real feelings, or that your sexual energy is clogged with emotions. Either way, this energy is not flowing cleanly and freely.

No. 6 – Body: Your excesses are affecting your physical energy. It could be too much alcohol, food, drugs or even emoting but, whatever it is, it's causing your energy to stagnate and is having an unhealthy effect on your body.

No. 7 – Primary Relationship: There is a lot of negative feeling around intimate relating. It could be that you're so lost in your emotions that it's difficult for you to know what's really going on. Recognising that much of what you're feeling probably has nothing to do with the other could help to get your head above this emotional swamp.

No. 8 – New Perspective: Has it occurred to you that you could allow yourself to indulge a little more in your emotions, or whatever it is you want to indulge in?

No. 9 – Mind: You are thinking about indulgence; you could be wanting it or you could be regretting it.

No. 10 – Peak Experience: The best thing you can do in this situation is allow yourself to go deeply into your emotions. Don't be reasonable; it is a time to indulge fully in whatever you are feeling.

No. 11 – Spiritual Message: There is a layer of emotions that you need to experience. Transformation can only happen through the feelings, not through the mind, and we all try to repress the things we don't want to feel. Give yourself the space, for as long as you need, to go fully into whatever is there. It doesn't necessarily imply acting out with others; maybe expressing them in the privacy of your own space is enough.

No. 12 – Meditation: Emotional indulgence is your meditation right now. If possible take time each day to cry, beat a pillow, scream and shout – express whatever emotions are there. You can be quite transformed by this meditation.

No. 13 – Overview: Your indulgence has become a major issue in your life. Maybe it is emotions about the future or maybe it's an over-indulgence in something external in your life. Bringing your awareness to focus on what it is about could help you to move through these clouds to find the open sky.

EIGHT OF CUPS – INDOLENCE

Essence: Emotionally drained, depleted, exhausted; laziness or lethargy, non-doing.

Descriptive Meaning and Symbols

SATURN IN PISCES

Two blossoms continue to pour their love, but it is nowhere near enough to fill the shallow cups that are chipped, broken and cracked, so they mainly stand empty. The water no longer appears as sea but as pools in the rotten mud. The brown colour of the water and sky shows the lack of vitality, the heaviness, and the approaching deadness of this emotional state. There is nothing left any more, no movement, no aliveness. We are drained and exhausted with nothing to give, even to ourselves. This state can be a natural outcome of Debauch – from over-indulging, over-giving, over-doing in some way till we literally run out; we have depleted ourselves. In another way it can be seen as the opposite of Debauch: the state of lethargy that comes more from laziness than exhaustion, simply not wanting to move or feel anything. It can also represent the times when laziness or non-doing is something we need to go into.

Variations in the Current Life Reading

When this card appears in:

No. 1 – General Outlook: Getting out of bed in the morning must be difficult for you right now. It could be that you are genuinely exhausted or drained, or it could be that you're just feeling lazy and don't want to do anything.

No. 2 – Communication: You don't have energy for relating right now. It could be that there is stuff that needs saying that you can't be bothered with, or it could be that you are having an antisocial spell.

No. 3 – Work: You have very little energy for your work. Maybe it's because you've burnt yourself out doing too much in the past, or maybe you're just feeling lazy or disinterested.

No. 4 – Inner Self: There is an inner feeling of lethargy or being drained. It could be that you haven't been giving yourself enough care or nourishment but, whatever it is, you should listen more to your inner needs. You are literally not paying attention to yourself.

No. 5 – Sexual Energy: You don't have sexual energy right now, or it could be that you don't have energy for your sexual partner.

No. 6 – Body: Your physical energy is seriously drained and depleted. It's important that you recognise this state and take care of your body in practical ways. You are running on empty.

No. 7 – Primary Relationship: You don't have much energy for intimate relating. It could be that you have over-given beyond your emotional boundaries and now there isn't anything left. Or it could be that you just don't have energy for your current partner or maybe anyone at this time.

No. 8 – New Perspective: Have you thought that maybe you're tired and you need a rest? Or maybe that you just don't want or have to do anything right now?

No. 9 – Mind: You are thinking about being drained, or more likely thinking about wanting to be lazy and not do.

No. 10 – Peak Experience: The best course for you in the current situation is to do nothing. Whatever it is, leave it alone. You've probably done more than enough already.

No. 11 – Spiritual Message: Existence is encouraging you to stop doing and move more into the space of non-pushing that you may relate to as laziness. Chill out, hang out and give yourself a rest. Whether you think you need it physically or not.

No. 12 – Meditation: There are many things in life that we can only get through non-doing. Right now your meditation is to learn how to lie back and do nothing, which is something you're probably not very comfortable with.

No. 13 – Overview: You probably don't have much interest or inclination to go anywhere or do anything right now. This could be because you are feeling too drained or exhausted to bother much, or it could be just a feeling of laziness. Check out for yourself if what you need is a rest to take care of yourself, or a kick to get you moving.

NINE OF CUPS – HAPPINESS

Essence: Expectations, hope; the temporary emotional well-being following the fulfilment of desire.

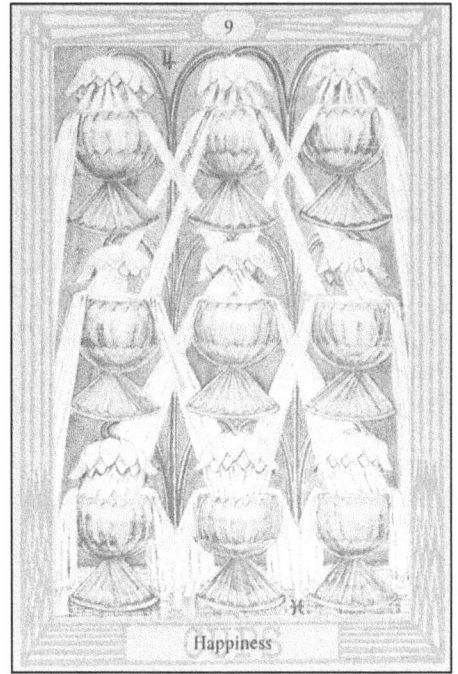

Descriptive Meaning and Symbols

JUPITER IN PISCES

The painting contains nine symmetrically arranged cups, each filled to overflowing by its own delicate lotus blossom. Everything is harmonious and flowing. It symbolises the emotional state where we have everything we could want; we are truly happy. It's the feeling that occurs most often when we have just fulfilled a desire, and with this satisfaction everything in life feels full and perfect. It is a state to be enjoyed but also to be understood. We have all known that moment of perfect happiness that follows the fulfilment of something we hoped for, only to find the elation soon disappears and is replaced by another desire. This is the very nature of desire: it gives us a temporary happiness that is dependent on the external, rather than the joy that comes from connecting with our own inner source of love, represented by Ace of Cups. The card symbolises this transient state of fulfilment and well-being. But most often it represents the state of desiring or expecting something from someone or something outside ourselves to give us this kind of fulfilment – in other words, of having expectations. This can be the state where we are so concerned with what we are expecting or wanting that we can't be open to what is really going on.

Variations in the Current Life Reading

When this card appears in:

No. 1 – General Outlook: It could be that you have just fulfilled some dream. Or it could be that the wanting and expecting of something from the outside is what affects your whole attitude. You will know which it is.

No. 2 – Communication: It could be that your communication is expansive and gushing with the perfection of everything, or it could be that you have a lot of expectations from others.

No. 3 – Work: Maybe something you have wanted in your work situation has happened, bringing great happiness, or maybe you are working towards and expecting that fulfilment.

No. 4 – Inner Self: You could be in a state of well-being with yourself from fulfilling some dream. But it is more likely that you are concerned with your own expectations of how you should be or what life should be giving you to make you happy.

No. 5 – Sexual Energy: Maybe you are feeling fulfilled in your sexual connection with another because they have fulfilled your expectations. It is more likely that you are in the state of hoping for and expecting things in this area of your life.

No. 6 – Body: Maybe you have just got something that your body wanted and there is a feeling of physical well-being as a result. Or maybe the hoping for that is still there, either in the body or the mental patterns that affect the body.

No. 7 – Primary Relationship: It could be that you have just got something you wanted from your relationship and so are feeling very happy. It is more likely that you are preoccupied with your expectations of your partner or yourself in your intimate relating.

No. 8 – New Perspective: Have you considered that you could give yourself what you want to make yourself happy?

No. 9 – Mind: You are thinking about what you expect or want to make you happy.

No. 10 – Peak Experience: If you can't find that feeling of emotional well-being right now, the best thing you can do in the current situation is bring your awareness to your hopes and expectations of getting it from others, with the understanding that these could be getting in the way of you finding it for yourself.

No. 11 – Spiritual Message: Existence is encouraging you to look at what it is you are really wanting or expecting from life or others right now. What would it take to make you feel emotionally fulfilled? Is it realistic or is it stopping you from seeing and receiving what is actually there?

No. 12 – Meditation: Your growth lies in looking at what it is you desire or expect in life to make you feel fulfilled and happy. Probably there is some situation that is forcing you to face these expectations and realise that no one or no thing has any obligation to fulfil them. They are your problem.

No. 13 – Overview: It could be that you are feeling very fulfilled in your life right now. Or it could be that looking at your hopes and expectations is the major issue that controls the direction of your life.

TEN OF CUPS – SATIETY

Essence: Boring, satiated, jaded, enough.

Descriptive Meaning and Symbols

MARS IN PISCES

The ten cups are arranged in the shape of the Cabalistic Tree of Life, the symbol of learning. The enormous lotus is no longer the direct source of the love energy but is distant and indistinct. The cups are full but not as overflowing as in the previous card. The colour red in the background indicates a ripeness or fullness. This card represents the space where the source of the emotional fulfilment is no longer needed. We have had enough and we don't want any more of the same. We are satiated. It is not a judgement on what has been experienced, but simply the feeling of having had all that we want; we have got whatever we needed to get, or learnt whatever we needed to learn and any more would be boring. Or maybe it is already boring and we are feeling over-full. It can also refer to the state of being jaded, or lacking the innocence to see things freshly.

Variations in the Current Life Reading

When this card appears in:

No. 1 – General Outlook: You're a bit bored with your life. It could be caused by the particular situation you are in. Or it could be that you have a slightly jaded attitude to life in general, a kind of 'been there, done that' outlook that takes the excitement out of daily living.

No. 2 – Communication: You are bored with relating right now. It could be boredom with the people around you, or more likely boredom with your way of relating to them.

No. 3 – Work: Your work isn't challenging or stimulating you any more; in fact you have had enough of it.

No. 4 – Inner Self: You are a bit fed up with yourself. Maybe you're tired of your own mind games or maybe you are aware of this boredom inside without knowing what it is about.

No. 5 – Sexual Energy: It could be that there's something in your connection with your sexual partner, or lack of one, that you are bored with. Or maybe it's something in your own way of relating to your partner, or the opposite sex in general, that you have done for long enough.

No. 6 – Body: It could be that there's something with your body or what you are doing (or not doing) with it that you are tired of. Or it could be that your physical energy isn't as alive as it could be and you are feeling dull.

No. 7 – Primary Relationship: Maybe it is a case of over-familiarity, but whatever has been happening between you and the intimate other in your life, you've reached the point where you've almost had enough of it. Basically, you're bored.

No. 8 – New Perspective: Has it occurred to you that maybe you've had enough, that you are bored of whatever it is?

No. 9 – Mind: Your mind is starting to run a 'been here, done that' kind of tape. You are a bit bored with your life, or something specific in it.

No. 10 – Peak Experience: The best thing you can do in the current situation is accept that it has gone as far as it needs; you have learnt what you need to learn or got what you need to get, and trying to push for more would become boring.

No. 11 – Spiritual Message: You have reached a point in your life where there's nothing actually wrong, but it doesn't seem to be exciting or challenging anymore. There is nothing to do about this but allow yourself to feel it. Sometimes boredom can transform into a deeper state of being. Or maybe this is what is needed to push you to change your priorities.

No. 12 – Meditation: Your growth lies in having to experience fully whatever is going on even though you may feel it is enough already. This isn't a card of change but of allowing boredom and seeing where the acceptance of that state takes you.

No. 13 – Overview: The line between satisfied contentment and boredom is very fine. This is the line you're sitting on in your life right, and it's affecting your future direction.

DISKS

DISKS ARE THE SYMBOLS OF EARTH AND REPRESENT THE PHYSICAL AND MATERIAL SIDE OF LIFE

KNIGHT OF DISKS

Essence: Practical confidence; inner strength that comes from being prepared.

Knight of Disks

Descriptive Meaning and Symbols

The Knight of Disks represents the mature, established yang side of earth energy. He is the only knight who isn't in motion. He has already done his warrior preparations of planting and cultivating his crop, and now he relaxes on his strong brown horse with his helmet down, enjoying the sunset. The grain in the field is ripe and he is armed with a thresher for harvesting it, but there is no hurry. He is relaxed and confident knowing he has done all the necessary groundwork. His short sturdy build and dark heavy armour all add to the feeling of grounded earthiness. This card symbolises the place where the work of preparing and building, growing and learning, both inner and outer, has been done. Now we can relax in the confidence that whatever happens, we will be able to deal with it. It is the space of relaxed inner strength that comes from the maturing of inner or outer growth. This is the energy that is at ease in dealing with the world in practical and material ways, and is also confident enough to allow and be with whatever comes up internally without creating tension. In the negative it can refer to the state of being earth bound, heavy or materialistic.

Variations in the Current Life Reading

When this card appears in:

No. 1 – General Outlook: You look on life with a practical and material confidence that comes from feeling you have everything in hand; there's nothing that can happen that you can't deal with.

No. 2 – Communication: You are relaxed and matter-of-fact in your way of relating to others. Maybe you don't say much, but that's because you don't have to prove yourself by trying to be sociable.

No. 3 – Work: You are practical and competent in your work. It may be that you have reached the stage where the preparation has been done and you're able to enjoy the harvest of your labour.

No. 4 – Inner Self: This could be a sense of inner maturity that enables you to accept whatever you experience in yourself without needing to avoid or protect. Or is it that you see yourself in a mainly physical and materialistic way?

No. 5 – Sexual Energy: You are relaxed and confident in the yang side of your sexual energy.

No. 6 – Body: Your body is in excellent shape and you are confident in your physical energy.

No. 7 – Primary Relationship: You are in a space in your intimate relating where you feel comfortable to just be without a lot of emotions or mind stuff going on. Probably you are more into doing things with someone than lots of direct relating.

No. 8 – New Perspective: Has it occurred to you that you could relax a little, knowing that whatever happens now you can handle it?

No. 9 – Mind: You are thinking about practical issues, or maybe about having the confidence to handle them with ease.

No. 10 – Peak Experience: The best thing you can do in the current situation is honour the practical maturity you have already achieved. Relax in the confidence that you have done what you need to do and are competent enough to deal with whatever may happen.

No. 11 – Spiritual Message: Existence is encouraging you to claim the mature yang side of your being. That's the part of you that knows how to deal with life on the inner and outer planes without having to fight or defend. It's time to relax and be confident in yourself and your practical abilities. Any kind of physical exercise that makes you more aware of your body can be helpful in this.

No. 12 – Meditation: Your growth lies in learning to trust and become confident in your ability to take care of whatever happens in a relaxed way. This probably means it is something you're not good at doing. If you find yourself being hesitant or indecisive, try bringing your awareness back to your connection with the earth, feeling your legs and feet, and dealing with the matter at hand in a simple practical way without thinking about it too much. You must be able to do this or you wouldn't have picked this card.

No. 13 – Overview: You are moving ahead in your life in a confident and practical way, knowing you can deal with whatever it may bring.

QUEEN OF DISKS

Essence: Being present, relaxed, receptive earthiness; resting in your own being.

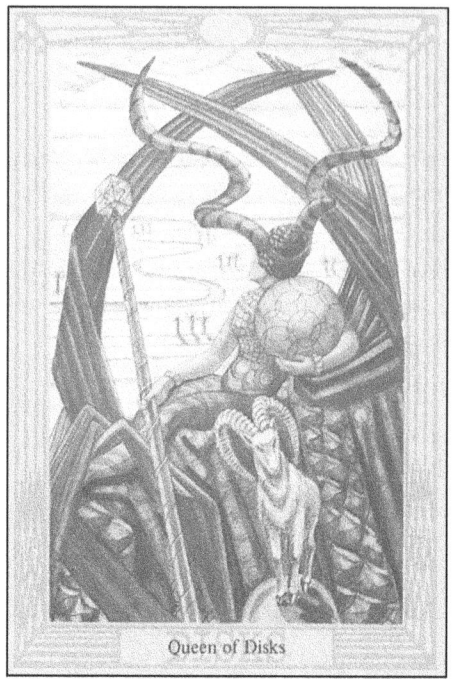
Queen of Disks

Descriptive Meaning and Symbols

The Queen of Disks represents the mature yin quality of earth. She sits on her huge pineapple throne, the symbol of her relaxation into her own fruitfulness. With passive interest, she looks back from her oasis at how the river winds through the desert valley below and starts to make it fertile. She knows there is nothing required from her to make this happen. It carries the same natural trust as the Zen poem: 'When the spring comes, the grass grows by itself.' Her reptilian gown and antler headdress show her connection with the animal world and her own instinctual nature. The globe of the world that she holds in her arm represents her connection to the earth and her comfort at being in the world. Her crystal wand shows the clarity that comes from this relaxed, grounded way of being. The goat represents the grounded practical Capricorn. This card symbolises the quality of relaxed, receptive being that is often achieved only after the long arduous journey of learning to just be oneself. She has travelled far and now is in a space where she can rest in her own maturity and simply be quietly present for whatever is there. In other words, she can just be herself in a relaxed, receptive way regardless of what is going on around. She also knows how to nourish herself and others on a physical level. In the negative she can be dull and mundane.

Variations in the Current Life Reading

When this card appears in:

No. 1 – General Outlook: You have a relaxed, grounded way of being present in whatever life brings, and know how to live by your instincts.

No. 2 – Communication: You are grounded, receptive and present in your way of relating to people. Friends probably enjoy your down-to-earth practicality and feel nourished by your presence, but they don't look to you for intellectual stimulation.

No. 3 – Work: You are practical and present in whatever you are doing. You might not do very much, but you are available for what's needed in a productive way and may bring a quality that is grounding and nourishing to others.

No. 4 – Inner Self: There is a quiet inner quality of feeling relaxed and at home in your own being. You know how to take care of yourself.

No. 5 – Sexual Energy: You are receptive and present in your sexual energy, so probably you're like that with your sexual partner if there is one.

No. 6 – Body: There is a quality of inner nourishment around your body. You know how to listen to your body and take care of your physical needs.

No. 7 – Primary Relationship: You are able to be yourself in a quiet, grounded and receptive way in your intimate relating. Maybe there is a lot of time spent just being together in a comfortable way without having to relate; this earthy quality could be healing to both you and the other.

No. 8 – New Perspective: Has it occurred to you that you could simply be relaxed and present with what is happening and tune into your own instincts.

No. 9 – Mind: You are thinking about being relaxed and grounded in yourself. Or maybe you think you already are.

No. 10 – Peak Experience: The best thing you can do right now is just be present in the current situation as it is. From this simple, grounded, receptive perspective you will have a sense of what needs to happen in a practical way.

No. 11 – Spiritual Message: Existence is encouraging you to develop the quality of relaxed, open being. There is nothing you need to do, nowhere you need to go; as much as possible give yourself time to sit in nature, doing nothing, and be. If there's no time for that in your current lifestyle, maybe you need a long holiday.

No. 12 – Meditation: You need to learn how to be relaxed, grounded and present in yourself without getting lost in what's around or what you think or feel or do. Anything that connects you with your body will be helpful for this, or anything that connects you with nature. Do you like gardening?

No. 13 – Overview: There is a quality of simply being present in your life as it happens. This can have an almost Zen quality of 'chopping wood and carrying water'. It is a simple ordinariness and presence that is guiding your future direction.

PRINCE OF DISKS

Essence: Practical determination to make something happen; goal orientation, future orientation.

Prince of Disks

Descriptive Meaning and Symbols

The Prince of Disks represents a less settled yang or outgoing quality of earth. He sits on a powerful chariot being pulled by a fierce determined bull. The metal chariot represents his staunch resolve to reach his goal, and the bull shows he has the power and strength to get there. His nakedness and well-developed body show his trust in his own power, so that he doesn't need to protect or hide either himself or what he wants. The obstacles he moves through to build or to achieve what he wants are represented by the boulders behind him in the chariot. The sketched tapestry of natural things around him illustrates that he is not really present in the reality as it is because he is so strongly focused on where he is going. This card symbolises the quality of moving determinedly in a particular direction. It is the energy of being concerned with making something happen, or achieving a practical goal, and can also represent the energy of looking into the future for this to happen. In the negative it can illustrate the state of being so much concerned with getting somewhere that we are not in touch with where we are.

Variations in the Current Life Reading

When this card appears in:

No. 1 – General Outlook: You are concerned more with where you're going than where you are. Is it something in particular you are heading towards or is this a general habit?

No. 2 – Communication: You have some goal of how you would like to relate or an agenda of what you would like to happen with others. Maybe this manifests as trying to take the conversation in the direction you want it to go.

No. 3 – Work: You have strong ideas on where you want to go with your work and you are moving practically and probably forcefully in that direction.

No. 4 – Inner Self: You spend a lot of the time by yourself planning where you're going or how you want to be, rather than being where you are.

No. 5 – Sexual Energy: You are focused on having something particular happen with someone of the opposite sex in the future.

No. 6 – Body: There is a certain push in your physical energy that comes from being concerned with where you want to be rather than being relaxed and present in your body where you are. It could be a good space for achieving an exercise routine or diet though.

No. 7 – Primary Relationship: You are concerned with where your relationship is going rather than where it is. Or else you are looking into the future for a relationship to happen rather than being with your own energy in the present.

No. 8 – New Perspective: How about looking where you want to go and what you want to happen in the future?

No. 9 – Mind: You are thinking about the future or the achievement of goals.

No. 10 – Peak Experience: The best thing you can do in the current situation is look at where you are heading and what you want. This is not the time to sit around aimlessly waiting.

No. 11 – Spiritual Message: Existence is encouraging you to look towards what you want in the future and focus your determination on moving in that direction. Maybe you have been drifting or procrastinating for too long and now it is time to start realistically developing your potential and planning where you're going.

No. 12 – Meditation: Your meditation right now is to keep yourself practically focused on where you are heading and maybe check out if this is where you really want to go.

No. 13 – Overview: You are racing ahead in your life right now, fully focused on where you want to go or what you want to happen.

PRINCESS OF DISKS

Essence: Patience, waiting, giving birth to, gestation, postponement.

Princess of Disks

Descriptive Meaning and Symbols

The Princess of Disks represents the establishing or developing yin quality of earth. She is a pregnant young woman who stands covered by a rich fur cape that represents the abundance of her animal nature. Like the Queen, she has antlers on her head but hers are smaller and directed to what is around her rather than upwards to the heavens. The disk in her hand contains the yin/yang sign that represents her inner balance as well as the ultimate creative power of the universe. Her wand, pointing downwards to the earth, is tipped by a crystal to show that she directs the light of her awareness into grounding and rooting in the reality. The accentuated roots on the trees behind her substantiate this theme. For a plant to grow, first it must establish roots. In the same way in pregnancy a seed is planted and needs time to gestate: the child will be born only when it is ready. This card symbolises the energy of waiting for something to happen in its own time. Often it calls for the patience that comes from knowing that things, internal or external, are developing in their own way, and only when the time is right will they happen. In a negative sense, it can signify the state of delaying or postponing something that needs to happen.

Variations in the Current Life Reading

When this card appears in:

No. 1 – General Outlook: Your attitude to life is one of waiting for something to happen. You could check if this is realistic, if the seeds really have been planted and are gestating or if you are avoiding taking necessary steps to move ahead.

No. 2 – Communication: You are available and patient in the way you connect with others. Maybe there's a different way you want to relate, but you feel it's not time yet, which may make you a little timid with others.

No. 3 – Work: This is a time of gestation for you in your work or doing energy. You are waiting for things to establish or develop in their own time and way. Maybe check if this is realistic or if your waiting is a postponement.

No. 4 – Inner Self: There's a feeling of something growing in your inner being. You are patiently allowing this new aspect of who you are to develop in its own way and time.

No. 5 – Sexual Energy: You are in a space of waiting in your sexual energy. Maybe there is something new developing – with your partner if you have one, or with the sexual patterning within yourself if not.

No. 6 – Body: There is a sensation around your physical energy of waiting for something to develop. (You're not pregnant are you?) Maybe something on a physical level is renewing itself or maybe there is a deep conditioning process starting to reveal itself through the energy body. Either way you probably feel quiet and not like pushing yourself physically.

No. 7 – Primary Relationship: Your primary relationship is in a time of gestation. There is probably a feeling of something developing or establishing itself, even if you're not sure what that is. If you don't have an intimate partner right now, you are available and waiting patiently for something to happen in that way.

No. 8 – New Perspective: Has it occurred to you that maybe you've done all you can and now what is needed is to patiently wait and see what develops?

No. 9 – Mind: You are thinking about being patient and waiting for something to develop, which could mean that's not what you've been doing up to now.

No. 10 – Peak Experience: The best thing you can do in the current situation is to wait for things to develop in their own way and time. Be patient, there is nothing to be gained by trying to forge ahead.

No. 11 – Spiritual Message: Existence is teaching you the art of waiting. Not a lethargic laziness, but the pregnant patience of one who trusts that life will give what you need in the right way at the right time. Whenever you feel impatient or want to push ahead, try connecting with nature to see that everything can happen only when the time is right.

No. 12 – Meditation: Your meditation at this time is to learn how to wait patiently, which probably means this is not something that comes easy for you. If you find yourself getting irritated or impetuous, see if it helps to breath deeply, bring your awareness back to your feet and ground yourself in the reality of where you are.

No. 13 – Overview: It is as though you are waiting for life, or something in it, to start moving. There is nothing wrong with this, but check the advice places to see if you need to be a bit more forceful.

ACE OF DISKS

Essence: Pure being, centred; presence, grounded in reality.

Ace of Disks

Descriptive Meaning and Symbols

The single golden disk is surrounded by an intricate wealth of wood, leaf and pinecone designs. It creates a picture of the natural earthiness and richness that comes from the state of being grounded in the space of pure being or self. The winged shape of the design shows the elevated consciousness that is possible in such a state. A tree can only grow as high as it roots go deep, and this is the same for human consciousness. Only when we are rooted in the reality of existence can we start to spread our wings to the sky. When our roots are not firmly planted in the reality of the earth or the situation we live in, we are not connected with what is. The inscriptions in and around the disk are part of the magic symbols Crowley associated with this condition. This card represents the space of pure being or centredness that often comes from being physically centred in the hara or guts. From this space, one is grounded in the reality of existence and consequently often has a certain presence or charisma.

Variations in the Current Life Reading

When this card appears in:

No. 1 – General Outlook: You have a grounded, realistic outlook on life and appear to be centred in the reality as it is.

No. 2 – Communication: Your way of relating is very matter-of-fact and grounded in reality. You have presence when you are with others, whether you speak or not.

No. 3 – Work: You are in a grounded, rooted space in your work. Your ability to stay present with what's happening makes you a powerful force in whatever you do.

No. 4 – Inner Self: There is an inner richness that comes from being deeply connected with your own centre. This is a deep and beautiful space to be in yourself.

No. 5 – Sexual Energy: You are centred in your sexual energy, which makes you capable of being a strong sexual presence. Whatever your reality may be with the opposite sex right now, you are being it.

No. 6 – Body: You are centred in your body and your energy is concentrated around your hara. Whether the sensations are pleasant or otherwise, you are present to the physical dimension.

No. 7 – Primary Relationship: You are present and grounded in the reality of your intimate relationship(s), whatever may be happening. You have a strong presence that doesn't rely on talking or emotions.

No. 8 – New Perspective: How about just being present and experiencing what happens?

No. 9 – Mind: You are thinking that you are grounded in reality, or maybe wanting to be.

No. 10 – Peak Experience: The best thing you can do in the current situation is stay in your own centre and keep contact with what's actually happening. In other words, just be with what is, rather than being concerned with your opinions or feelings about it.

No. 11 – Spiritual Message: Existence is encouraging you to move more into the centre of your being, your hara, and from this space you will see reality around you in a new and deeper way. Maybe it would be good to do physical exercises with the body to help you find this space. Any of the martial arts would work.

No. 12 – Meditation: Becoming centred and grounded in yourself and present in the current reality is your meditation, which probably means you are not very good at it. Developing or remembering your hara can be very good for this, or anything that puts you in contact with your body would help.

No. 13 – Overview: You are grounded in the reality of your life, seeing and being with it as it is. It is irrelevant what you think or feel about it; this 'being' space is deeper than either of those states.

TWO OF DISKS – CHANGE

Essence: Change, transition.

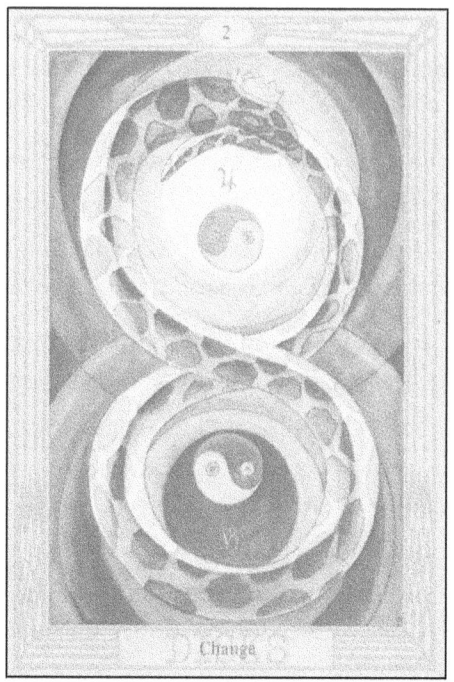

Descriptive Meaning and Symbols

JUPITER IN CAPRICORN

The large snake eating its own tail curls in the shape of a figure eight, or an infinity sign on its side. It signifies the permanent and perpetual state of change; the only constant thing in life is change. The crown on the snake's head indicates the higher consciousness that comes from living rather than resisting this reality. The two disks are yin/yang signs, the Chinese symbol representing the natural movement and balance of male and female energies in the world. They are drawn turning in opposite directions to signify that change can be both internal and external. The tiny coloured triangles inside them are ancient alchemical symbols for the basic elements of fire, earth, water and air to illustrate the elemental nature of change. The card symbolises change in all its dimensions. We often tend to dislike change because it takes us away from what is familiar and disturbs our comfortable and established ways of being. This card reminds us of the necessity of change and that it is a positive force, even though we might not like it at the time.

Variations in the Current Life Reading

When this card appears in:

No. 1 – General Outlook: There is an attitude of change that is affecting the basic way you look at your life. This could be changes that are already happening or changes you want to make.

No. 2 – Communication: There is some kind of change going on in the way you connect with people.

No. 3 – Work: You are going through certain changes in the area of your work. It could be that your work is changing or that you are changing the way you do it.

No. 4 – Inner Self: There is some change going on in your inner being and the way you view yourself.

No. 5 – Sexual Energy: Changes are happening in your sexual energy that could be manifesting in your connection to your sexual partner or simply in the way you relate to the opposite sex in general.

No. 6 – Body: Something is changing in your physical energy. If you are not aware of this, try to bring your consciousness to it because your awareness could facilitate the change if it is positive and stop it if it is negative.

No. 7 – Primary Relationship: You are going through changes in your intimate relating, which may indicate alterations in your way of connecting with your partner or a change in partners.

No. 8 – New Perspective: Has it occurred to you that it's time for a change?

No. 9 – Mind: You are thinking about change – maybe changes that are happening now, or maybe changes that you want to happen.

No. 10 – Peak Experience: The best thing you can do in the current situation is recognise that change is needed and make a conscious effort to allow or make it happen.

No. 11 – Spiritual Message: Existence is telling you that you are entering a major time of change. This could bring up resistance, insecurity and fear of the unknown, but you can trust that it is necessary, timely and positive.

No. 12 – Meditation: Change is your meditation right now, which probably means that you don't like it. It would be helpful for you to retain a constant awareness of the elemental and necessary nature of change to enable you to move through this transition.

No. 13 – Overview: You are going through many changes right now that are having a profound affect on the direction of your life.

THREE OF DISKS – WORKS

Essence: Being creative, doing, making something happen.

Descriptive Meaning and Symbols

MARS IN CAPRICORN
The three red wheels represent the aspects of mind, energy and heart, which must be brought together in the physical realm for any act of doing or work to be creative. When all these parts of the being are harmoniously united in the reality, the disturbance and confusion represented by the background design in the card, gives way to the clear visible form, represented by the crystal. Actions that don't unite body, mind and heart are a partial or uncreative use of the energy, whereas when all these aspects are employed, anything that is done is creative. Creativity isn't necessarily about what we do, but how we do it. We can clean the house or cook a meal in a creative way if we put our hearts in it; and paint a picture or make a pot uncreatively if we do it mechanically. This card represents any kind of creative doing to make things happen, or working creatively with what is. In a negative sense, it can also represent the compulsive doing that comes out of the insecurity to let things be the way they are; the belief that if we don't 'do', it won't work out.

Variations in the Current Life Reading

When this card appears in:

No. 1 – General Outlook: You have a creative outlook on life, which could be very constructive or could mean you don't believe that things will happen if you don't make them happen.

No. 2 – Communication: There is a sense of always having to do something or make something happen when you are with people. In other words you are always 'on'. Maybe there is a genuine joy in creative relating or maybe it is that you don't trust yourself enough to just relax and be with what's really happening.

No. 3 – Work: There is a positive creative energy going into making something happen around your work right now.

No. 4 – Inner Self: It could be that you are bringing your inner awareness to work with certain aspects of your being in a positive, creative way. Or it could be that you relate to yourself through your ability to do and make things happen and that you could be lacking the space to simply relax and be where you are.

No. 5 – Sexual Energy: You are using your sexual energy in a creative way. It could be that you are trying to make something happen or it could be that this basic life force is being channelled into creativity.

No. 6 – Body: There is a creative doing energy in the body, which is great for getting things done and probably means you act in creative ways. But it might sometimes make it difficult for you to just stop and be with what is.

No. 7 – Primary Relationship: You are positive and creative in wanting to make your relationship work and this can be a beautiful thing. But also be aware that you could be lost in a space of doing, rather than simply being present to what is there.

No. 8 – New Perspective: Has it occurred to you that you could do something creative about what's happening; in other words, try to make it work for you?

No. 9 – Mind: You are thinking about doing something, maybe wanting to use your energy in a creative way.

No. 10 – Peak Experience: The best thing you can do right now is use the current situation in the most creative way you can to make it work for you. You can't do this if you are half-hearted or negative about it.

No. 11 – Spiritual Message: Existence is encouraging you to explore using your energy in creative ways. This could involve taking some kind of class or starting a creative hobby but, more importantly, it is an approach to life. Discover the deep satisfaction that comes from putting your body, mind and heart into any situation or activity that you're involved in.

No. 12 – Meditation: Your meditation is to be actively creative – possibly with the ingredients of some particular situation you are in. Be aware when you are negative, unconstructive or lazy and realise that your growth lies in flipping this energy into creative mode.

No. 13 – Overview: You are using whatever is happening in your life in a positive and creative way, probably to head in some particular direction. Don't forget about resting, allowing and trusting, which will balance it.

FOUR OF DISKS – POWER

Essence: Attachment, limitation, containing, creating boundaries.

Descriptive Meaning and Symbols

SUN IN CAPRICORN
The four large square disks are drawn as the corner towers of a fort surrounded by a moat. On top of each tower is an alchemical symbol for the basic elements of earth, fire, water and air. Everything is contained and secure in a closed way, symbolising the power that comes from setting rigid limits, creating boundaries or containing what we have. It gives a certain strength, but that power is dependent on the rigidity of our defences to the outside world. The orange colour of the card connects with the power chakra or energy centre. The whole feeling of the picture is barren and desert-like, representing the price we pay for such holding or containing. The card usually represents the state of being attached, of containing or holding on to something, and the rigidity and defensiveness that comes with that. It can also indicate the setting of necessary limits or boundaries.

Variations in the Current Life Reading

When this card appears in:

No. 1 – General Outlook: Your main concern is of wanting to contain or secure what you think you have.

No. 2 – Communication: You are strong in your way of relating but probably a bit fixed and rigid in maintaining your own opinions or keeping your own territory.

No. 3 – Work: Your attachment to certain things in the area of work is causing you to become rigid or fixed in some ways. If it's not obvious to you, maybe you should check what you are holding on to.

No. 4 – Inner Self: There is a rigidity in your inner being that could come from attachment to something on the outside, or from wanting to create limits or boundaries within yourself.

No. 5 – Sexual Energy: There's a holding in your sexual energy that is probably coming from an attachment to a sexual partner.

No. 6 – Body: There is strength and power in your body that comes from containing your physical energy, but you may be feeling tight or tense as a result.

No. 7 – Primary Relationship: You are going through issues around attachment with your intimate partner right now. Be aware if this makes you feel closed and limited.

No. 8 – New Perspective: Has it occurred to you that you're attached to or limited by something?

No. 9 – Mind: You are thinking about issues of limitation or attachment.

No. 10 – Peak Experience: The best thing you can do in the current situation is experience the limits that you are either creating or needing to create. Sometimes it is necessary to set boundaries.

No. 11 – Spiritual Message: Existence is encouraging you to experience what it means to live your life within limits. These could be boundaries that you have to create, or it could be that you need to become aware of how existing attachments are limiting your life.

No. 12 – Meditation: Dealing with limitation or attachment is your major growth area right now. You probably don't like it, but allowing yourself to go fully into the experience with awareness will be a valuable teaching for you.

No. 13 – Overview: The limits you are creating in your life through your attachment to something is affecting the whole direction that you are moving in right now.

FIVE OF DISKS – WORRY

Essence: Worry, anxiety, brooding, considering.

Descriptive Meaning and Symbols

MERCURY IN TAURUS

The picture shows five disks interlocked like the cogs of an old-styled machine. They are joined by a driving belt in the shape of an inverted pentagram with the tip pointing downwards to show the loss of balance and consequent discomfort and unclarity in this state. The disks are heavy, dark and metallic, blocking out the yellow colour behind the machine to show that the light of consciousness is held back and hidden. In the centre of the disks are the five Tarvas (triangle, square, circle, moon and eclipse), the subtle elements in Hindu thinking that have a vibrational effect on everything in life. Each of the wheels is activated by the movement of the other, showing the nature of this state of being. Once we leave the reality of now and start worrying about what might happen in the future, or regretting things that have happened in the past, the cogs of the mind start to turn more and more. One worrying thought leads to another and another and, if we continue, we end up in a state of anxiety that can completely cut us off from the reality. The card symbolises the state of being concerned, worrying, brooding or anxious. In an advice place it can also represent the need to consider something.

Variations in the Current Life Reading

When this card appears in:

No. 1 – General Outlook: Your worry is colouring your whole attitude to life. There could be a particular reason for this or it could be that you have a habit to worry that is purely an attitude problem.

No. 2 – Communication: Relating with people is something you are worrying about right now. There could be something in particular you are looking at, or it could be a general feeling of anxiety when you are with others.

No. 3 – Work: You are worrying about your work or what you are doing.

No. 4 – Inner Self: There is a lot of inner worry. This could mean that you are worrying about yourself, or it could mean you spend your alone time lost in worries of the future or past. Either way it is probably rather uncomfortable.

No. 5 – Sexual Energy: There is anxiety in the area of your sex energy. Either you are worried about your connection with your sexual partner, or you are concerned about your own sexuality or sexual conditioning.

No. 6 – Body: It could be that you are worried about something that is going on in your body, or that your anxiety is affecting your body. Either way, pay attention to what is happening here.

No. 7 – Primary Relationship: You are brooding about something in your primary relationship – or lack of one. Either way, you may notice that this worrying takes you away from the present and being available to experience what is actually happening.

No. 8 – New Perspective: Has it occurred to you that there's something you need to have a good think about?

No. 9 – Mind: You are thinking about worrying, which means you may be doing it but at least you are aware of it.

No. 10 – Peak Experience: You need to give careful consideration to what is going on in the current situation. This is not something to brush aside; it needs your thoughtful concern.

No. 11 – Spiritual Message: This is a time when existence is encouraging you to take a long hard look at your life. Maybe you have a tendency to take the easy way out and have been drifting along, not really looking at certain things for too long.

No. 12 – Meditation: You need to bring your conscious awareness to the state of worry. It could be that there are things you have been avoiding that you need to consider. But if you are already worrying, make it a meditation to take distance from the thoughts, rather than driving the cogs even faster by getting too involved.

No. 13 – Overview: Your worrying is dominating your life right now. It may be a general state of anxiety or it could be that you are worrying about your future direction.

SIX OF DISKS – SUCCESS

Essence: Behaviour concerned with wanting to succeed, win or be right. Giving yourself the right to be right.

Descriptive Meaning and Symbols

MOON IN TAURUS

The six disks are harmoniously arranged in the shape of a hexagram around the pure light of the sun at the centre of the card. Each disk contains a different planetary symbol to represent the various ingredients needed to succeed or get what we want. The strong dark shapes at the outside of the card are all directed inwards to the light. There is a feeling of strength about the painting that represents the determination involved in the desire to win or succeed. This card can symbolise the state of achieving what we want, or succeeding at what we are doing. But most often it represents a mode of doing or being that is based on wanting to succeed or win, or to be right. This also includes the quality of the 'shoulds' and 'oughts' in life, which are our expressions of the need to do the right thing. In this state we are not doing what we want, we are not listening to our hearts or our truth, but rather we are doing what we have been taught to believe is the right thing to succeed or get us what we want. We are keeping ourselves safe and avoiding the fear of being wrong that would come if we listened to our hearts. This programming is usually deeply buried in the unconscious mind, and it is only when we start to become aware of how often we try to work out what is right that we can start to understand what we are doing and why.

Variations in the Current Life Reading

When this card appears in:

No. 1 – General Outlook: You view your life either from the perspective of winning and losing or of trying to function as you think you should. Whichever, it doesn't give you much room to look at where you are and what you really want.

No. 2 – Communication: You have a tendency to relate with others in what you think is the 'right' or expected mode of behaviour. This could make you either a little righteous or a little timid out of your fear of doing the wrong thing.

No. 3 – Work: You are either succeeding or wanting to succeed in your work. Check if you are becoming too success orientated and paying a price for always having to do the right thing.

No. 4 – Inner Self: You tend to relate to yourself in terms of how you think you should be, in order to get what you want or to succeed. It could be that you are judgemental about yourself.

No. 5 – Sexual Energy: You have lots of ideas about what is right and wrong in your way of relating to the opposite sex. Be aware that they are all based on your learnt beliefs of how you have to be to get what you want.

No. 6 – Body: It could be that your need to succeed and do things right is having an effect on your physical energy. Or it could be that you have ideas about how your body should or shouldn't be.

No. 7 – Primary Relationship: It's possible that your intimate relationship is being treated like a battleground, with you being convinced of your own righteousness. Or it could be that you are so busy trying to do the right thing that you don't really know what you feel.

No. 8 – New Perspective: How about giving yourself permission to recognise that you could be right or that maybe you have succeeded?

No. 9 – Mind: You are thinking about the need to succeed or be right.

No. 10 – Peak Experience: The best thing you can do in the current situation is claim your own right to be right in what you are feeling or doing. You are allowed to succeed at what you are aiming for.

No. 11 – Spiritual Message: Existence is encouraging you to become aware of your own need to succeed, to be right or do the right thing. This usually comes from a layer of conditioned beliefs or morality that exists deep in the unconscious mind and rules the way we behave without us even knowing. Becoming aware of this can be the first step to finding the truth of what you feel.

No. 12 – Meditation: Your major growth lies in giving yourself the right to be right as you are – in putting aside the ideas of how you think you should or shouldn't be, and maybe allowing yourself to succeed in some way.

No. 13 – Overview: There is a focus in your life of making it, succeeding or doing whatever it is you think is right. Knowing that this is having such a strong effect on the direction of your life, check if you are really doing what you want, rather than what you think you should do.

SEVEN OF DISKS – FAILURE

Essence: Fear.

Descriptive Meaning and Symbols

SATURN IN TAURUS

The seven disks are isolated from each other by the thick unnatural-coloured foliage that blocks out any other surroundings. Each disk bears either the Taurus bull or the helmeted figure that represents Saturn. Saturn in Taurus symbolises the limitation and restriction that we experience when we are afraid. This can be the practical limitation of what we are able to do that comes from the fear of failing, or the limitation of our awareness and consciousness that happens when we are ruled by our fear. Fear is isolating; it cuts us off from the reality that is happening around us; it takes us out of our hearts and our trust. Yet fear is a primary emotion; it can not be avoided. The main problem with it is that we try to avoid it or pretend it's not there. We are afraid of our fear. We make up all kinds of reasons for why we do or don't do things, rather than admit the fact that we are afraid. When we accept fear, allowing it to be there, we can move into what it is we are afraid of. Then fear takes on the quality of excitement or adventure. When we avoid it, push it into the unconscious, we become isolated, restricted and limited by it.

Variations in the Current Life Reading

When this card appears in:

No. 1 – General Outlook: You are looking at the world from a fearful and isolated space. Be aware that this is only an attitude and therefore something you can change.

No. 2 – Communication: Your way or relating to others is ruled by fear right now and this makes you feel separate and isolated. You may experience this as fear of expressing, or simply fear of being yourself around others.

No. 3 – Work: Your fear is severely limiting your ability to do what you want to do or be yourself in your work.

No. 4 – Inner Self: There is a fear or anxiety in your inner being that may not make any sense to you and must be very uncomfortable to live with.

No. 5 – Sexual Energy: There is fear in your sexual energy, which may mean you are afraid of sex, or of the opposite sex in general. Or it could mean that you are dealing with a layer of fear in your relating with your sexual partner.

No. 6 – Body: There is fear in your body. You don't have to understand it, but know it is there and that taking space in a secure place to give expression to this energy can avoid it causing physical problems.

No. 7 – Primary Relationship: There is a fear of intimate relating that is keeping you separate from your partner or from having an intimate relationship.

No. 8 – New Perspective: Has it occurred to you that you are afraid and that you need to let yourself feel that fear?

No. 9 – Mind: You are thinking about fear, which may mean you're not letting yourself feel it and therefore move through it.

No. 10 – Peak Experience: The best think you can do in the current situation is allow yourself to feel, accept and go into your fear. Often fear can be the door to something new, and while we avoid it we can't move where we need to go.

No. 11 – Spiritual Message: Existence is encouraging you to own and experience your fear, even if it makes no sense and you have no idea what you are afraid of. Some of your basic life energy is tied up in fear. If you can't move into and through that you can never be fully alive and your life will become more and more limited and small.

No. 12 – Meditation: Fear is your meditation right now. Don't avoid it; keep coming back again and again to that space in your belly and breathing into it. If you can learn the knack of expanding into it rather than contracting from it, the state will start to change.

No. 13 – Overview: Your fear is controlling your life right now. Maybe there is a specific reason for it, or maybe there isn't, but certainly it will be making you feel cut off from where you are in your life and from seeing where you want to go.

EIGHT OF DISKS – PRUDENCE

Essence: Caution, being careful, protecting.

Descriptive Meaning and Symbols

SUN IN VIRGO

The strong tree is firmly rooted in fertile ground. It bears eight perfect blossoms, which symbolise an inner or outer richness that has bloomed quite naturally. Each flower is protected by a large curling leaf that represents the need to protect or be careful with this richness. Things have their own timing and often the newly grown is fragile; we need to be cautious with how we use it, and respect and take care of its delicacy. The strength in the symbol comes from not doing or from pulling back. This card symbolises the quality of using, or needing to use, caution or prudence in whatever we are doing. It is not a time of pushing or haste, but a time of retreat or being careful. It can also represent a caution and protection that is not necessary.

Variations in the Current Life Reading

When this card appears in:

No. 1 – General Outlook: You are cautious in the way you look at the world. This idea that you have to be careful may, or may not, be based on reality.

No. 2 – Communication: You are careful and cautious in how you relate with others. This might have a reason or it may be that you are limiting yourself out of an old habit of protection.

No. 3 – Work: You are moving very prudently and cautiously in the area of your work. It's up to you to check if this is necessary or if you are being over cautious.

No. 4 – Inner Self: You are feeling protective of yourself or of how much you want to look inside yourself. Maybe there is something that you don't want to see or feel.

No. 5 – Sexual Energy: You are protective with your sexual energy or in your connection with the opposite sex. It could be that this is necessary or it could be that you are hiding to avoid exposure and vulnerability.

No. 6 – Body: There is the sensation of needing to protect your body or move cautiously with your energy.

No. 7 – Primary Relationship: You are protective of yourself around your intimate partner, or in allowing intimacy with others. It could be that you need to do this, or it could be that you are being unnecessarily defensive. Check it out for yourself.

No. 8 – New Perspective: Has it occurred to you that you need to move carefully and cautiously right now?

No. 9 – Mind: You are thinking about being careful or cautious.

No. 10 – Peak Experience: There is a need for caution or protectiveness in your current life situation. It's not the time for great decisions or actions that could expose you to risk in any way.

No. 11 – Spiritual Message: Existence is encouraging you to move cautiously and protect yourself in ways you may not be used to doing. Maybe you have a tendency to be impulsive or reckless that is, or will start to have, negative affects in your life. Or maybe something fragile is growing in your inner or outer life and too much haste or exposure will harm it.

No. 12 – Meditation: You're probably feeling impatient or eager to move in some direction, but your meditation is either having to go at the restricted pace that life is imposing, or that you need to impose on yourself. Certainly it's a time to learn what it means to move carefully.

No. 13 – Overview: You are moving ahead in your life in a careful and cautious way. Check the advice cards to see if this is necessary or not.

NINE OF DISKS – GAIN

Essence: Gain, positive, blessings, beneficial, whatever happens is right.

Descriptive Meaning and Symbols

VENUS IN VIRGO

The nine disks are arranged in three groups of three. The circles at the centre of the card represent the unification of wisdom (blue) and creativity (green) with love (pink), which is needed for positive gain in life. When these three aspects of the being come together, anything that happens becomes a positive or gainful experience. It is rumoured that when she painted this card, Frieda Harris, the artist and co-creator of the Crowley Tarot, illustrated the three-way relationship between her, Crowley and his friend Israel Regardie. Each of their faces appears on two of the disks as the symbols of different planets. Even though there were many difficulties in this triangular relationship and it was not how she may have wished it to be, she recognised that by using it creatively and with love, each of them gained and learned from this situation. The card symbolises the state that whatever is going on, whether we like it or not, on some level it is right. It is as it should be, it is a gain. This is so even though we might not automatically see it as such. For instance, you could fall down and break your leg and pick this card for the accident; the message would be that this is exactly what needed to happen. Maybe some kind of rest or slowing down was needed in your life.

Variations in the Current Life Reading

When this card appears in:

No. 1 – General Outlook: You have a very positive outlook on life. Whatever happens you can see the bright side of it.

No. 2 – Communication: Something is happening around your relating that feels right and positive to you. It doesn't necessarily mean it is nice or that you like it, just that you recognise it is beneficial.

No. 3 – Work: Whatever is going on in your work, you recognise it as a positive gain, something that needs to happen.

No. 4 – Inner Self: You are experiencing your inner process as something inevitable and positive, whether you like it or not.

No. 5 – Sexual Energy: Whatever is happening in your relationships with the opposite sex in general, or with your sexual partner, you experience it as beneficial and something that needs to happen.

No. 6 – Body: Even if it feels like something is wrong, whatever is happening in the physical energy is beneficial and needed.

No. 7 – Primary Relationship: Whether there's harmony or conflict in your intimate relationship, you experience it as what needs to happen right now.

No. 8 – New Perspective: Have you considered that what's happening is absolutely what's supposed to be happening?

No. 9 – Mind: You are thinking that things are as they need to be.

No. 10 – Peak Experience: You are getting a strong message to accept that whatever is going on in the current situation, is exactly what should be happening. Don't doubt it just because you may not like it.

No. 11 – Spiritual Message: Existence is encouraging you to relax into the flow of where your life is taking you and accept that everything happens the way it needs to. It is not about an artificial positivity. Rather it is the understanding that using whatever happens in a creative and heartful way turns everything into an opportunity to learn and therefore a blessing.

No. 12 – Meditation: Your meditation is to accept that something in your life, that you probably don't like or don't agree with, is, in fact, exactly what needs to happen.

No. 13 – Overview: You are in a very positive space right now. You are moving ahead in your life with the understanding that whatever is happening is exactly what is needed.

TEN OF DISKS – WEALTH

Essence: Being present and letting things unfold one step at a time; living moment by moment, day by day.

Descriptive Meaning and Symbols

MERCURY IN VIRGO

The ten disks are represented as coins arranged in the shape of the Cabalistic Tree of Life to show that this state of being or doing is connected with the organic whole of life. Behind there is an apparently endless pile of coins but only these ten are highlighted with golden light. They are engraved with a variety of astrological and Hebrew signs. The caduseus (the symbol for healing) at the base of the Tree of Life indicates the healing and richness that comes from being grounded totally in the physical reality of each moment, without getting lost into ideas of what could be happening – in other words, looking at the rest of the pile of coins. This quality of being present comes from a simple trust in the organic wholeness of existence. We can experience this as moving through life one step at a time, relaxing into being totally with what is. It has nothing to do with desire or accumulation, rather it has the feeling of ordinariness and simplicity suggested by the Zen path of 'chopping wood and carrying water'. It is about trusting what is, simply because it is, and letting life unfold in its own time and own way. This quality brings real wealth of all dimensions into life.

Variations in the Current Life Reading

When this card appears in:

No. 1 – General Outlook: You are content to allow your life to unfold one step at a time.

No. 2 – Communication: You are grounded and realistic in your communications, dealing with the matter at hand in a present and simple way.

No. 3 – Work: You are letting whatever is going on in your work unfold step by step in its own way. Trust, rather than ambition, is what rules your working life right now and makes you very present in any project you may be involved in.

No. 4 – Inner Self: There is a simple realistic intunement with your inner being that enables you to stay present, moment by moment, to whatever is going on inside you.

No. 5 – Sexual Energy: You are in trusting contact with your sexual energy and stay present with it moment by moment, either within yourself or in your connection with your sexual partner.

No. 6 – Body: There is a strong sense of being in your body that enables you to be in contact with its messages and trust what it is saying to you.

No. 7 – Primary Relationship: There is a simple quality of being present for whatever is happening in your intimate relating and letting it unfold one step at a time in its own way. You may not know what is going to happen tomorrow, but you are totally present today.

No. 8 – New Perspective: How about just taking things step by step, day by day?

No. 9 – Mind: You are thinking about allowing things to unfold step by step and trusting what is.

No. 10 – Peak Experience: The best thing you can do in the current situation is take it day by day and let it unfold in its own way. Simply be present with what is happening rather than trying to work out your own answers or directions.

No. 11 – Spiritual Message: You are ready to move into a Zen way of being in the world, which is a relaxation into the richness of every moment. This takes a certain trust that will allow existence to be your teacher and take you where you need to go.

No. 12 – Meditation: Maybe you are impatient about something and wanting to make it happen or work out the conclusions. Keep remembering that your growth right now lies in the letting go of control and simply being present with what is happening one step at a time.

No. 13 – Overview: You have simple trust in what's happening that enables you to let your life unfold in its own way, step by step, day by day. This may or may not be out of choice, but you can appreciate that it is what you are doing.

APPENDIX
Summary of Essence

Major Arcana

0. THE FOOL
Issue: Freedom

Freedom, spontaneity, being in the moment, taking space, having the courage to take a risk, scattered.

1. THE MAGUS I
Issue: Doing

Doing or communicating. Activity with intention. Using available elements to make something happen.

2. THE PRIESTESS II
Issue: Sensitivity

Intuition, subtle energy, refined yin energy or power, psychic or telepathic power. Spaced out, over-sensitive.

3. THE EMPRESS III
Issue: Compassion

Compassion, giving space to, mothering, empathy, sympathy, caring.

4. THE EMPEROR IV
Issue: Responsibility

Responsibility, authority, fatherhood.

5. THE HIEROPHANT V
Issue: Understanding

Understanding, wisdom, experiential learning, knowledge.

6. THE LOVERS VI
Issue: Love

Loving in all its dimensions and forms, loving relating.

7. THE CHARIOT VII
Issue: Power

Power in all its dimensions; the ability to make things happen or achieve desires. Control.

8. ADJUSTMENT VIII
Issue: Watching

Watching, witnessing, the state of meditative awareness, taking distance from.

9. THE HERMIT IX
Issue: Aloneness

Aloneness, introspection, going your own way, loneliness.

10. FORTUNE X
Issue: Flowing

Going with the flow, relaxing into life. Karma, fate or destiny.

11. LUST XI
Issue: Energetic Aliveness

Life force, vitality, aliveness, total energy, passion for life, sex.

12. THE HANGED MAN XII
Issue: Suffering

Transformation through difficulty or suffering, uncomfortable processing. Confronting outmoded conditioning patterns.

13. DEATH XIII
Issue: Death

The end of something, death, the gap or void, let go.

14. ART XIV
Issue: Integration

Integration, synthesis, alchemical change, bringing things together. Refining, cooking, digesting.

15. THE DEVIL XV
Issue: Accepting Reality

The basic reality, suchness, accepting what is, dealing with limitation.

16. THE TOWER XVI
Issue: Disintegration

Major transformation, disintegration of the old, things falling apart, chaos, the destroying of old mind patterns to make way for deeper truth.

17. THE STAR XVII
Issue: Trust

Trust in all its dimensions, self-trust, trusting existence.

18. THE MOON XVIII
Issue: The Unknown

The unconscious mind, the unknown or unknowable, the mysterious or hidden.

19. THE SUN XIX
Issue: Wholeness in Relating

Learning to be whole in relationship, relating programmes, the patterns and limitation of contractual relationships.

20. THE AEON XX
Issue: Higher Perspective
New perspectives that come from higher understanding, new beginnings or ways that come from that. Seeing the bigger picture, broader outlook.

21. THE UNIVERSE XXI
Issue: Completion
The organic completion or natural flowering of a situation. Unavoidable consequences. Dissolving into the whole.

Minor Arcana

WANDS

Knight of Wands – Moving in a specific outward direction; focused or dynamic movement.

Queen of Wands – Receiving or inward-directed energy; inner awareness of energy; using available energy for self-awareness.

Prince of Wands – Enthusiastic or keen; intensity or urgency; fresh approach.

Princess of Wands – Flowing with the energy; saying yes to whatever is happening, drifting.

Ace of Wands – Pure, raw or strong energy; creative life force or will.

Two of Wands, Dominion – New direction, dynamic new way.

Three of Wands, Virtue – Integrity, authenticity, natural, ordinary, real.

Four of Wands, Completion – Completing, resolution, finishing.

Five of Wands, Strife – Problem, conflict, difficulty, blocked energy, being stuck.

Six of Wands, Victory – Positive, fine, uncomplicated, no problems, okay.

Seven of Wands, Valour – Courage, being forceful, making an effort.

Eight of Wands, Swiftness – Change of gestalt, new perspective, finding the knack.

Nine of Wands, Strength – Independence, individuality; the strength that comes from standing in your own energy.

Ten of Wands, Oppression – Oppressed or repressed energy; the state of feeling held back or constricted; restraint, depression.

SWORDS

Knight of Swords – Concentration, focused thinking, mental determination, single pointed.

Queen of Swords – Open minded, clarity, objective thinking, the mask cutter.

Prince of Swords – Cutting through limiting ideas or thought forms; critical, impatient.

Princess of Swords – Clearing away the clouds covering practical or realistic thinking; the mood fighter; mental windscreen wiper. Cloudy or nervous mind.

Ace of Swords – Making a decision, pure clarity of mind, flash of insight.

Two of Swords, Peace – Peace of mind, allowing fate, keeping the peace.

Three of Swords, Sorrow – Pain, frustration, anger, negativity.

Four of Swords, Truce – Accepting what is, allowing the reality, isness

Five of Swords, Defeat – Defeat, failure, without hope.

Six of Swords, Science – Objective clarity, analysis, scientific investigation, impersonal thinking.

Seven of Swords, Futility – Futility, pointlessness, waste of time.

Eight of Swords, Interference – Confusion, not knowing, indecision, conflicting ideas.

Nine of Swords, Cruelty – Self-doubt, self-judgement, guilt, mental insecurity, self-examination.

Ten of Swords, Ruin – Let go, the point of giving up, cutting attachment.

CUPS

Knight of Cups – Giving, expressing or sharing feelings; putting your heart into something.

Queen of Cups – Openness of heart, receptivity, vulnerability. Dependence, victim.

Prince of Cups – Emotional desire, wishes, hopes, dreams, fantasy.

Princess of Cups – Emotional freedom, unattached to feelings, friendliness, love with freedom.

Ace of Cups – Pure love energy, self-love, saying yes to yourself and what you feel, trying to prove yourself.

Two of Cups, Love – Being or falling in love; romantic love. The conditioning programmes around emotional need and love.

Three of Cups, Abundance – Playfulness, non-seriousness, light hearted, overflowing abundance, celebration. Superficial, frivolous.

Four of Cups, Luxury – Emotional security issues, keeping things comfortable and safe.

Five of Cups, Disappointment – Disappointed expectations, dissatisfaction, unfulfilled. Yearning of the heart.

Six of Cups, Pleasure – Enjoying, taking pleasure in, keeping things pleasant.

Seven of Cups, Debauch – Indulgence, over-indulgence, excessive.

Eight of Cups, Indolence – Emotionally drained, depleted, exhausted, laziness or lethargy, non-doing.

Nine of Cups, Happiness – Expectations, hope; the temporary emotional well-being following the fulfilment of desire.

Ten of Cups, Satiety – Boring, satiated, jaded, enough.

DISKS

Knight of Disks – Practical confidence; inner strength that comes from being prepared.

Queen of Disks – Being present, relaxed, receptive earthiness; resting in your own being.

Prince of Disks – Practical determination to make something happen; goal orientation, future orientation.

Princess of Disks – Patience, waiting, giving birth to, gestation, postponement.

Ace of Disks – Pure being, centred; presence, grounded in reality.

Two of Disks, Change – Change, transition.

Three of Disks, Works – Being creative, doing, making something happen.

Four of Disks, Power – Attachment, limitation, containing, creating boundaries.

Five of Disks, Worry – Worry, anxiety, brooding, considering.

Six of Disks, Success – Behaviour concerned with wanting to succeed, win or be right. Giving yourself the right to be right.

Seven of Disks, Failure – Fear.

Eight of Disks, Prudence – Caution, being careful, protecting.

Nine of Disks, Gain – Gain, positive, blessings, beneficial, whatever happens is right.

Ten of Disks, Wealth – Being present and letting things unfold one step at a time; living moment by moment, day by day.

Mangala Billson has been an intuitive counselor and psychic reader for almost thirty years. For the last twenty years much of her time has gone into teaching other people how to do the same. She gives workshops in tarot and numerology as well as training people to listen to and develop their intuitive abilities. When she is not traveling around Europe or Asia doing her work, she lives in Pune, India, and watches her garden grow.

For information about Mangala Billson's various workshops contact www.mangalabillson.com or email mangala@gmx.net

www.ingramcontent.com/pod-product-compliance
Lightning Source LLC
LaVergne TN
LVHW061213060426
835507LV00016B/1907